T0261615

The Geography of the Internet

NEW HORIZONS IN REGIONAL SCIENCE

Series Editor: Philip McCann, *Professor of Economic Geography, University of Groningen, The Netherlands and Professor of Economics, University of Waikato, New Zealand*

Regional science analyses important issues surrounding the growth and development of urban and regional systems and is emerging as a major social science discipline. This series provides an invaluable forum for the publication of high quality scholarly work on urban and regional studies, industrial location economics, transport systems, economic geography and networks.

New Horizons in Regional Science aims to publish the best work by economists, geographers, urban and regional planners and other researchers from throughout the world. It is intended to serve a wide readership including academics, students and policymakers.

Titles in the series include:

International Knowledge and Innovation Networks
Knowledge Creation and Innovation in Medium Technology Clusters
Riccardo Cappellin and Rüdiger Wink

Leadership and Institutions in Regional Endogenous Development
Robert Stimson and Roger R. Stough with Maria Salazar

Entrepreneurship and Regional Development
Local Processes and Global Patterns
Edited by Charlie Karlsson, Börje Johansson and Roger R. Stough

Endogenous Regional Development
Perspectives, Measurement and Empirical Investigation
Edited by Robert Stimson, Roger R. Stough and Peter Nijkamp

Media Clusters
Spatial Agglomeration and Content Capabilities
Edited by Charlie Karlsson and Robert G. Picard

Spatial Scenarios in a Global Perspective
Europe and the Latin Arc Countries
Edited by Roberto Camagni and Roberta Capello

Creative Knowledge Cities
Myths, Visions and Realities
Edited by Marina van Geenhuizen and Peter Nijkamp

Societies in Motion
Innovation, Migration and Regional Transformation
Edited by Amnon Frenkel, Peter Nijkamp and Philip McCann

Innovation, Global Change and Territorial Resilience
Edited by Philip Cooke, Mario Davide Parrilli and José Luis Curbelo

The Regional Economics of Knowledge and Talent
Local Advantage in a Global Context
Edited by Charlie Karlsson, Börje Johansson and Roger R. Stough

Entrepreneurship, Social Capital and Governance
Directions for the Sustainable Development and Competitiveness of Regions
Edited by Charlie Karlsson, Börje Johansson and Roger R. Stough

The Geography of the Internet
Cities, Regions and Internet Infrastructure in Europe
Emmanouil Tranos

The Geography of the Internet

Cities, Regions and Internet Infrastructure in Europe

Emmanouil Tranos

Department of Spatial Economics, VU Amsterdam, The Netherlands

NEW HORIZONS IN REGIONAL SCIENCE

Edward Elgar

Cheltenham, UK • Northampton, MA, USA

Published by
Edward Elgar Publishing Limited
The Lypiatts
15 Lansdown Road
Cheltenham
Glos GL50 2JA
UK

Edward Elgar Publishing, Inc.
William Pratt House
9 Dewey Court
Northampton
Massachusetts 01060
USA

A catalogue record for this book
is available from the British Library

Library of Congress Control Number: 2012946686

This book is available electronically in the ElgarOnline.com
Economics Subject Collection, E-ISBN 978 1 78195 337 2

ISBN 978 1 78195 336 5

Typeset by Servis Filmsetting Ltd, Stockport, Cheshire
Printed and bound by MPG Books Group, UK

Contents

Preface

This book represents a long journey started in 2005 towards understanding the spatiality of the Internet. The first step in the journey was when, as a masters student at the Centre for Urban and Regional Development Studies (CURDS), Newcastle University, I was inspired by a lecture given by Andy Gillespie on Internet geography. Because of my prior research experience in transport infrastructure and regional development, I was amazed by the idea that the Internet could be approached as a physical spatial system. But most importantly, I was fascinated by the complex relationship between this technical system and geographical space. Studying the limited, but still exciting relevant literature, not only did I start gaining a better understanding of this "black box", aka the Internet, and its relationship with space, but most importantly, I discovered research gaps, especially in the quantification of the spatiality of the Internet, most of which are discussed in this book. Andy provided guidance on this research and I am grateful for his support and inspiration.

The next big milestone was my collaboration with Peter Nijkamp, to whom I am also grateful. Over the last two years, 2011–12, I have had the privilege of working with him at the Department of Spatial Economics at VU Amsterdam. Working with Peter has been a great opportunity to advance and further expand – both in depth and in scope – my research in digital geographies. Most importantly, this collaboration enabled me to channel my research towards the wider area of spatial economics and regional science.

In total, the present book provides a solid overview of my work in understanding and modeling the spatiality of the Internet infrastructure in Europe. Various papers have been published in peer-reviewed journals and some of them provide the basis of the empirical analysis of this book. More specifically, the analysis of Chapter 5 is based on the paper published in *Environment and Planning A*, 43 (2), pp. 378–92 (Pion Ltd, London, www.envplan.com) entitled "The topology and the emerging urban geographies of the Internet backbone and aviation networks in Europe: a comparative study" (Tranos 2011). In addition, Chapter 7 is based on a paper published in *Spatial Economic Analysis*, 7 (3) 319–37 (www.tandfonline.com) under the title "The causal effect of the Internet infrastructure on the economic development of the European city-regions" (Tranos 2012).

Apart from the influence and the support of Andy Gillespie and Peter Nijkamp, there are more people I would like to acknowledge: Vassilis Tselios and Seraphim Alvanides for guiding my early quantitative journey; ERSA-PREPARE summer school organizers and participants for their constructive comments and tacit knowledge; Thomas de Graaff for his suggestions on the comparison of the Internet backbone with the aviation network; Trey Hood III for providing the STATA code for the Granger causality tests; and also the anonymous reviewers for their suggestions. Of course, responsibilities for errors and omissions are my own. Also, I would like to acknowledge the funders, which financed my research over time: the Greek Scholarship Foundation, Newcastle University and the Complexity-NET Project Complexity in Spatial Dynamics (COSMIC). Finally, I want to acknowledge my family and especially my partner Drew Gertner for her love and support throughout this journey.

Emmanouil Tranos
Amsterdam, June 2012

To the memory of my father,
who taught me to enquire

1. Introduction

"The change from atoms to bits is irrevocable and unstoppable"
(Negroponte 1995, 4)

1.1 AIMS AND RESEARCH QUESTIONS

The main aim of this book is to study the geography of the Internet infrastructure in Europe and highlight not only the strong spatiality of the Internet, but also how it affects and is affected by real-world geography. Using Castells's (1996) "space of flows" as the main theoretical vehicle and drawing upon his seminal work, effort is spent in order to understand and explain the geography and highlight the regional economic impacts of the Internet infrastructure in Europe. The infrastructural element which is under study here is the international backbone network in Europe, aggregated at the level of the city-region. This backbone network consists of the long-haul links, which connect long-distance destinations and are responsible for the global character of the Internet (e.g. Malecki 2004). The resulting outcome is a study of the participation of the European city-regions in this global infrastructural network.

Epistemologically, this book is placed in the emerging field of Internet geography or cybergeography, which is a branch of the field of communications geography focusing on the geographical aspects of the Internet. It feeds the discussion about the relationship between geographic space – the cities and regions – and this supporting layer of the cyberspace identified as the cyberplace (Batty 1997). Using Castells's (1996) framework, this book is concerned with the first and supporting layer of the space of flows.

More specifically, this book aims to answer three research questions (RQ):

RQ1: How is the Internet infrastructure scattered across European city-regions?
RQ2: Which are the geographic and socio-economic factors that shape the distribution of the Internet infrastructure across European city-regions?
RQ3: What are the impacts that the Internet infrastructure can generate on the development of city-regions in Europe?

The first research question is a clear geographic one and aims to explore the geographic pattern of the Internet backbone linkages in Europe. As the Internet backbone is firstly a network, the topology of this network is important. However, because this study has a clear geographic starting point, what is more important is to link the topology of the Internet backbone network (IBN) with the geography of the city-regions. This difficulty is raised by the fact that the Internet and, consequently, its underpinning infrastructural layer were designed to support data communication and therefore its spatiality is mostly a hidden element, which this book aims to explore.

The second research question follows from the results of the first one and intends to explain the geography of the Internet backbone links in Europe. As will be explained later in this book, these long-haul Internet links are mostly privately developed and owned. Consequently, the location decisions behind the installation of this infrastructural layer reflect the perceptions of the telecommunications companies (known as telcos) about the demand for such facilities in order to maximize the returns of their investments (Gillespie and Robins 1989). Based on this, effort is spent in finding these socio-economic and geographic factors that explain the geography of this infrastructure in Europe and consequently the perceptions of telcos for higher demand for their networks.

The third question goes one step further and seeks to examine whether the Internet infrastructure generates economic development impacts at the regional level. As will be discussed in Chapter 3, research has been concerned with the impacts of the expansion of Internet usage in the economy through productivity growth. However, research has not yet focused on the localized economic impacts of the supporting layer of the Internet infrastructure. This book aims to research whether this infrastructure can generate such impacts and also address the issue of the direction of causality between the Internet infrastructure and regional economic development. The latter is a well-known problem in regional science and it will be extensively discussed.

In order to address the above research questions, this study draws upon three different research areas. Firstly, as mentioned above, the basis of this study is the Internet geography research field. It provides the fundamental theoretical and empirical background in order to pursue the above research questions. However, because of the importance of this infrastructural layer in the postmodern economy and society, there is a need to also employ theoretical and methodological tools from other fields to approach the current research questions.

The world city literature is the second theoretical pillar that this study is based on. Telecommunications (just like transportation) is a friction reducing technology because of its ability to reduce the cost of distance (Cohen et al. 2002; Cohen-Blankshtain and Nijkamp 2004). Because of this attribute, the Internet and Internet infrastructure enable global interaction and facilitate global economic activity (Malecki and Wei 2009), supporting the emergence of a world cities network. This theoretical pillar will provide the necessary input in order to understand the importance of this infrastructure from a global (inter)urban perspective.

Last but not least, this book also draws upon regional science and the digital economy as it attempts to map the regional economic impacts of the Internet infrastructure. The digital economy is the main theoretical framework used here in order to explain the link between the new technological paradigm reflected in the expansion of the Internet and economic development through productivity gains. However, as will be highlighted in Chapter 2, this link mostly refers to the scale of the national economies. In order to transfer this argument to the scale of the analysis used in this study, economic geography and regional science literatures and methods are employed.

To approach the above themes, secondary data about the Internet backbone links in Europe and quantitative data analysis methods are utilized. Briefly, the main dataset used in this study contains information about the international intercity Internet backbone links and their capacity, which are present in European cities for the six-year period 2001–06 (TeleGeography 2007). In order to fully exploit the structure of the data, network analysis methods have been utilized. At a first level, the results (global statistics) of the network analysis comment on the topology of the backbone network and effort is spent in introducing a geographic perspective in this exercise. At a second level, the local-level results of the network analysis are translated to attributes for the city-regions which participate in this global network. The geographic and socio-economic factors behind the distributions of these local-level statistics are explained with the use of econometric modeling such as probit regressions and spatial interaction models. Lastly, these city-level attributes, which reflect the Internet infrastructural capital, are used in order to model the impact of the Internet infrastructure on regional economic development. For the latter econometric modeling is employed and, more specifically, panel data analysis and Granger causality tests for panel data.

1.2 RATIONALE FOR THIS STUDY

The main motivation for researching this subject is the growing importance of information and communication technologies (ICTs) in the

economy. ICTs, which include the Internet and its infrastructural networks, are the backbone of the new – digital – economy (Antonelli 2003),
with processes of production, distribution and exchange increasingly
reliant on them. Thus, the Internet is the most essential development as
regards the distribution and exchange of information after the telephone
(Moss and Townsend 2000). Shiller (1999) goes a step further by suggest-
ing that the Internet might be the most rapidly spreading technology in
human history.

From a macro perspective, it is established nowadays that the Internet
and the ICTs affect the economy by improving its productivity (Atkinson
and McKay 2007; Cairncross 2001). Additionally, ICTs and the Internet
along with the aviation network can be said to be the supporting layer of
globalization, as they are responsible for the transportation of the weightless goods and the main actors of the global economy, but also for the
transportation of the ideas which underpin this global process (Taylor
2004; Graham and Marvin 2001; Rimmer 1998; Cieślik and Kaniewska
2004). In such a global economy, a country's importance depends upon
the cities located within it, the importance of which depends in turn upon
the multinational firms located within these cities (McCann and Acs
2011). The function and the global extent of these firms is supported and
enabled by ICTs.

However, ICTs and consequently the Internet are more than just new
technology, despite the rapid pace of their expansion and the wide range
of the impacts they generate. Hence, the wide adoption of these technologies appears to create a new technological paradigm (Perez 1983), which
affects not only production and the economy, but society in general. Upon
this element Castells built his theoretical work about the network society
(Castells 1996).

In terms of geography, ICTs and the Internet are not a homogenous
system equally spread around places (Gorman and Malecki 2000). From
an analytical point of view, despite what average users experience as a
placeless cyberspace, the latter depends on the real world's fixities, which
are found on cyberplace (Kitchin 1998a, 1998b). From a more economic
perspective, neither the outcomes that ICTs and the Internet generate are
homogenous in space. On the contrary, it seems that ICTs can generate
different impacts on different regions. And this differentiation is due not
only to the different level of ICTs' infrastructural capacity, but also to
the different regional capability to exploit benefits from them (Antonelli
2003).

More specifically, the backbone network is one of the most interesting
elements of the Internet infrastructure from the geographical point of
view as it is responsible for the Internet's global reach. From an urban

viewpoint, the structure of the backbone network can potentially provide information about the intensity of the participation of cities in the digital economy. From an analytical perspective, the geography of the backbone networks can provide insights about the determinants of these networks. From a more policy-oriented standpoint, the geography of the backbone links but also (and maybe more importantly) their capacity might have an impact on local economic activities as they can directly affect firms which are highly dependent on global Internet communications (Greenstein 2004). Hence, the Internet's performance between any two places is not dependent on the physical distance between them but mostly on the installed capacity of the backbone connections – known as bandwidth – between them (Gorman and Malecki 2000).

The last argument is fundamental for understanding the importance of the Internet in the frame of the digital economy. However, such argumentation has created misconceptions about the impacts of ICTs and the Internet on spatial structure: early commentators have expressed positions according to which these technologies will result in the "death of cities" (Gilder 1995; Drucker 1998), the "death of distance" (Cairncross 2001), the emergence of "electronic cottages" (Toffler 1980) and in general the "end of geography". All the above rather deterministic approaches foresee the devitalization of centralizing forces and the growing dominance of centrifugal forces, which will eventually result in a decentralized spatial pattern of economic activities. However, as has been proved, the Internet is an urban phenomenon (Rutherford et al. 2004) and consequently the same applies to the IBN, which is characterized as an urban infrastructure (Moss and Townsend 2000).

The above preliminary discussion verifies the importance of ICTs and the Internet from a geography viewpoint. However, in spite of their established importance, it seems that there is still a long way to go in order to further comprehend this new technological paradigm from a geographical point of view. As will be extensively discussed in Chapter 2, ICTs have not been among the leading research subjects among geographers, planners and regional scientists, mainly due to their inherent technical complexity (Bakis 1981; Hepworth 1989; Kellerman 1993). As a result, regardless of the various theoretical geographical approaches concerning ICTs, which emerged even prior to the establishment of a digital economy, it seems that there is a scarcity of empirical studies researching the geography of ICTs. Such a study can shed light on the geographical distributions of ICTs, can explain the factors behind these (centralized) distributions, and also explain the impacts that this new technological paradigm can generate on local economies. The latter, apart from its academic importance, can provide valuable insights to the local and regional development policy agenda.

1.3 STRUCTURE OF THE BOOK

The structure of the book goes as follows: Chapter 2 provides the necessary literature background to reach the research questions. It starts with a brief technical description of the Internet. In spite of the geographical starting point of this study, it is necessary to gain an understanding of the Internet function from a technical point of view. Then, the three main theoretical pillars of this study are critically presented. First, the literature of the emerging field of Internet geography is analyzed. This is the core and the most influential part of the literature for this book. The main subject of this study, the Internet infrastructure, is defined here. Then, the world cities literature is analyzed and the importance of ICTs is highlighted. Thirdly, a theoretical framework is built in order to comprehend potential regional economic impacts of the Internet infrastructure.

Chapter 3 is dedicated in analyzing the data and methods used for this study. As mentioned above, in order to approach the research questions, secondary data about the IBN and quantitative methods have been employed. The rationale of choosing the specific methods is illustrated here as well as the main methodological points. This chapter ends with this book's research framework, where all the research questions, methods, data sources and theoretical pillars are schematically presented together.

The empirical research takes place in the next four chapters (4–7). Chapter 4 presents a descriptive network analysis and it is the chapter where the fundamental analysis of the IBN takes place. The network topology is built and both global and local statistics are calculated. This chapter concludes with some initial results from the exploratory analysis both for the global level of the whole network and for the local level of city-region attributes.

Chapter 5 uses the complex network analysis to perform a structural comparison between the Internet backbone and the aviation network in Europe. As will be highlighted in Chapter 2, the first layer of the space of flows is formed by these two infrastructural networks. The comparison takes place both at the global level of the whole network structure but also – and probably more interesting from a geographic point of view – at the level of city attributes. The latter indicates the different roles that different cities perform in these two networks.

Chapter 6 is dedicated to the explanatory analysis of the IBN. Econometric modeling, such as probit and spatial interaction models, are introduced in order to explain the geographic and socio-economic factors behind the spatial distribution of this infrastructure. The chapter concludes with a set of significant predictors of regional connectedness and installed backbone capacity.

Chapter 7 is the final empirical chapter of this book and focuses on identifying the regional economic impacts that the Internet infrastructure can generate. The analysis explores the direction of causality between the Internet infrastructure and economic development with the use of Granger causality tests.

This book concludes by providing the empirical answers to the research questions stated in this first chapter. Additionally, in this last chapter the further contributions of this research to the relevant literature are highlighted. Drawing on the empirical results some policy recommendations are also stated in order to promote the inclusion of Internet infrastructure in the local and regional policy agenda.

2. The fundamentals of the Internet infrastructure: a cross-discipline review

2.1 INTRODUCTION

This chapter reviews the relevant literature and provides the necessary theoretical framework to further investigate the research questions illustrated in the introductory chapter. The starting point for approaching the Internet infrastructure, even from an economic geography standpoint, is an analysis of its architecture. This provides all the necessary technical knowledge to understand how this complex technical system works. Then, the main core of the relevant literature is grouped in three main pillars: (1) the Internet geography; (2) the world cities literature; and (3) the link between regional economics and the Internet infrastructure. The first element identified as the Internet geography is directly related to all three research questions of this study. As will be further analyzed in the relevant section, this book is part of this emerging research field of the Internet geography. The second pillar provides a wider theoretical framework for this study and for the Internet geography field as it maps and analyses the increased interaction and interdependence among cities, the importance of which is highlighted in the frame of the global economy. Lastly, the third pillar is mostly related to the third research question about the impacts of the Internet infrastructure on regional economic development. The current economic framework and its facilitation by the Internet infrastructure, especially at the level of city-regions, is analyzed.

The structure of this chapter reflects the above three-pillar segmentation. It starts with the technical analysis of the Internet function and it continues with the three theoretical pillars: the Internet geography, the world cities literature and the regional economic developmental impacts of the Internet's infrastructure. The chapter ends with an epilogue which also links the above three-pillar theoretical structure with the empirical research of this study.

2.2 TECHNICAL ANALYSIS OF THE INTERNET

2.2.1 Introduction

This section provides a technical analysis of the Internet in order to facilitate further research on the geography of the Internet infrastructure. Despite the fact that this book is not concerned with the engineering side of the Internet, such knowledge is important to investigate the geography of the Internet infrastructure and the impacts that this might generate. Because of the Internet's strong technical character, any attempt to approach it from a social science point of view would be ineffective without considering its primary technical nature.

Broadly speaking, it could be said that the Internet consists of two layers: a technical layer, and a content layer, with the latter overlaid on the former. The key characteristic of the Internet's technical layer is its network topology as it consists of edges and nodes, which have a specific physical location. In fact, it is not a single network nor one specific system, as many of its users think. The Internet, as the network of networks, consists of several interconnected small, medium-sized and large networks (Gorman and Malecki 2000). Because of this complexity, these networks should be characterized by a specific and predefined hierarchy in order to be functional (Malecki and Gorman 2001).

2.2.2 Internet Service Providers

The Internet's networks can be approached from different perspectives. From the business point of view, the interconnected networks can be identified as being associated with the Internet service providers (ISPs). The latter refers to companies or organizations which maintain one or more interconnected networks and through these provide Internet access. Usually, an ISP in order to achieve the desirable global connectivity (i.e. connectivity with the rest of the Internet's networks and through them with all the interconnected computers) needs to cooperate, interconnect and exchange data with other ISPs. This can happen in various ways, as described in the next section. The distinction among ISPs follows the Internet's rigorous structure. On top of this, the Tier-1 ISPs can be found which are characterized by extensive global networks and which are able to achieve global connectivity without purchasing Internet connectivity from another ISP (that is, exchange data with an upstream provider under a fiscal agreement, known as IP transit). Only a few Tier-1 ISPs exist in the world (TeleGeography 2007) and they are usually part of global telecommunications companies (telcos) which maintain high-capacity backbone networks around the world. Tier-1 ISPs exchange data with each other (known as peering) and sell Internet connectivity (known as IP transit) to lower-ranking ISPs, called Tier-2, which also have their own but less extended networks. On top of their own connectivity, Tier-2 networks also need to purchase Internet access from upstream Tier-1 ISPs in order to gain global connectivity. Tier-3 and Tier-4 ISPs are lower-scale providers, which mainly act at national and local levels (TeleGeography 2007).

2.2.3 Peering and Nodal Locations of the Internet

"Only through peering do two networks interconnect to form what we know as the Internet" (Malecki and Gorman 2001, p. 93).

Peering is an essential process of the Internet function because it integrates different networks by giving them access to each other. The latter takes place in specific nodal locations, such as Internet exchange points (IXPs). An IXP is a facility where different ISPs connect their networks to and place their dedicated routers, and through them interconnect with some or all of the ISPs present in this IXP (Euro-IX 2006).

This part of the Internet's topology was first introduced in 1991 in the United States (US), when a number of commercial backbone carriers founded the Commercial Internet Exchange (CIX) in Santa Clara, California (Kende 2000). Later, in 1995, the National Science Foundation, having as an objective the commercialization of the NSFNET (the ancestor of today's Internet) introduced the four privately managed network access points (NAP) located in San Francisco (operated by PacBell), Chicago (BellCore and Ameritech), Washington, DC (MFS) and Pennsauken, NJ (New York operated by Sprint Link). Similar to CIX, they enabled the ISPs to peer, leading to the emergence of a national commercial Internet (Kende 2000; Grubesic and O'Kelly 2002). Nowadays the term IXP is more commonly used than NAP, especially in Europe.

Apart from the public peering which takes place in IXPs, ISPs also have the option of private peering. Public peering at IXPs seems to be the cheapest choice for ISPs to interchange any volume of data because they are only charged (if any) the IXPs' fees and the logistics costs. In addition, by interconnecting to an IXP which has a national or even a local reach, data-packets with national or local origin and destination can remain at this level, avoiding long data transport only for peering reasons. Such practice results in time and money gains as the unnecessary use of the expensive long-haul links is avoided (Paltridge 2002).

However, public peering is not always the case. Because of the rapidly increased Internet traffic by the end of 1990s, many US IXPs became bottlenecks for Internet data traffic. And this is why some major ISPs started implementing private peering, which refers to bilateral peering agreements between any two ISPs using direct connections, in order to bypass the congested routers of the IXPs (TeleGeography 2007; Kende 2000). Private peering takes place either at IXPs if the two ISPs are already present there, but without using IXPs' routers, or directly at ISPs' points of presence (POPs), which are the nodes where the end-users are connected with the ISPs, and which are further analyzed below.

From the topological point of view, IXPs can be approached as nodes of the Internet, since they represent locations where network edges terminate. However, IXPs are not the only Internet nodes. POPs are also nodal network elements. End users connect to the POPs via the local loop or otherwise the "last mile" (that is the final segment of the Internet physical infrastructure before the end-user premises). The ISPs' routers are located there and through them end-users' connect to the Internet. So, it could be roughly said that POPs are responsible for the end-users' connectivity with the ISPs, while IXPs are responsible for ISPs' universal connectivity. From the hardware point of view, the nodes of the Internet are either routers or switches. IXPs and POPs are equipped with both of them. Their main role is to send the Internet data packets to specific locations, but their difference will be highlighted below in section 2.2.5.

In reality, the distinction between IXPs and POPs is sometimes quite vague, since peering can also take place at the latter under private peering agreements. POPs are usually owned by ISPs since they connect the end-users with the ISP's network. Usually they are located in specific establishments, which are known under various names such as data centers, telecom hotels, data warehouses, collocation, colo centre, server farms and so on, and provide a wide range of services (Evans-Cowley et al. 2002; Townsend 2003). Among others, they include facilities such as collocation, servers hosting, data archives and hardware management in a controlled environment for climate conditions and physical disasters. These facilities are characterized by great Internet connectivity with access to backbone networks and this is why low-ranking ISPs are located there or rent racks to place their routers in order to connect with higher-tier ISPs. Such facilities are usually found in wider metropolitan areas, employing redundant buildings such as warehouses and department stores with high ceilings and high-capacity power supply; they are found in locations which combine access to high-capacity backbone networks and closeness to customers in order for them to have physical access to their equipment. However, usually such facilities can neither afford the cost of nor find buildings with proper specifications in central locations (ibid.). Nowadays, it is also common to find collocation facilities in remote areas which combine access to backbone networks and low-cost electric power. The discussion has also emerged for locating such facilities in areas where renewable energy is available as a low carbon-dioxide emission measure, by exploiting the vast installed bandwidth (for this discussion see Arnaud 2009).

To sum up, ISPs, in order to achieve global connectivity, use different combinations of public and private peering as well as Internet Protocol (IP) transit. The above peering choices are related with factors such as ISPs' customers, business plan and location. From a technical point of view, a plethora of physical facilities support the role of ISPs. All these technical elements form the Internet's physical infrastructure.

2.2.4 The Internet Architecture

From a topological point of view, the Internet's numerous networks are only able to communicate because of the adoption of common protocols. IP is the protocol which determines the Internet's function by enabling data packet transport among the Internet's different sites using switches and the routers which run under the Transmission Control Protocol/ Internet Protocol (TCP/IP) switching technology (Gorman and Malecki 2000). In order for data exchange to take place, all data is fragmented in data packets labeled with their origin and destination address, as well as with the order according to which the data can be rebuilt. Those packets are transported through the different interconnected nodes (UN 2006). Each destination on the Internet (that is, an interconnected computer) has been given a unique IP address in order to be reachable from the rest of the world.

The TCP/IP follows the guidelines of a wider protocol which governs the Internet function. It is known as the Open Systems Interconnection (OSI) model and it was introduced by the International Standards Organization (ISO) in 1984 and updated in 1994 (UN 2006). It is built as a seven-layer system: the lower layers are dedicated to basic technical tasks while the upper, which rely on lower layers' efficient function, are closer to the end-user and include more sophisticated functions. The first layer is called the physical layer and consists of the wires, the fiber, the wireless links and the physical elements in general, which are responsible for data transmission following precisely the directives from the upper layers. The data layer feeds the physical layer with error-free flows, which are transmitted by the lowest layer between two adjacent nodes. The third layer, identified as the network layer, is the first layer where a complete origin–destination route is set up, using the IP addresses. While switches, which function at the data layer, are able to switch data packets only between the adjacent nodes of a complete route, the routers, which function at the network layer, are responsible for setting up and managing the complete routes of the data packets, which usually consists of numerous intermediate nodes. The importance of this layer is that it defines the whole network: if a site is not visible by a router, it is not part of the Internet (Gilder 2000). The next layer is the transport layer, the main protocol of which is the TCP, which certifies that the data packets are received correctly and in the right order. The applications announcement to senders and recipients takes place on this layer (UN 2006). However, the control of the dialog between senders and recipients is a responsibility of the fifth layer, the session layer. The seventh layer is the application layer, where the most common Internet applications such as File Transfer Protocol (FTP) and Hypertext Transfer Protocol (HTTP) function (ibid.). Between the application layer, which is the nearest to the user layer, and the session layer, there is another layer called the presentation layer, which is the interface between these two layers. Gilder (2000, p. 63) describes the OSI model very efficiently using the telephone analogy:

> Pick up the handset and listen for a dial tone (*physical layer*); dial up a number (every digit moves the call another *link* closer to the destination); listen for the ring (signifying a *network* connection and *transport* of signals). Getting someone on the line, you may be said to have completed the first four layers of the OSI stack. Then your hello begins a *session*, the choice of English defines *presentation*, the conversation constitutes the *application* layer. The hangup ends the *session*.

2.2.5   The Physical Layer and its Metrics

The Internet's performance is highly related to its physical layer. There are two main metrics for approaching a computer network's performance: bandwidth and latency. The former simply refers to the "number of bits that can be transmitted over the network in a certain amount of time" (Peterson and Davie 2003, p. 40) while the latter refers to "the time (measured in milliseconds) that it takes to transport and receive data between two nodes on the Internet" (Dodge and Zook 2009). For example, a modern transatlantic circuit can have a bandwidth of 10Gbps, which means that it can transport 10×10^9 bits every second (8 bit = 1 byte = one typed character). The bandwidth is mainly defined by the physical means which transports the data, with fiber optic cables providing today the greatest bandwidth. Latency on the other hand is a more complicated metric, which is measured in time units and refers to round-trip time: the time that a data packet needs in order to reach its destination and return back to its origin. Latency may be affected by (Peterson and Davie 2003): (1) the length of the link and the speed that the data travels in the link; (2) the size of the data packet and the bandwidth of the internet medium;

and (3) processing delay due to switching through various Internet nodes (Obraczka and Silva 2000). Practically, latency is usually appeared when the overall route consists of a high number of hops (Internet terminology for switching through various nodes).

What is also important in order to comprehend the way the Internet functions, and the way its different elements are scattered among and within cities, is to understand the nature of its physical layer. The edges of the Internet are certainly the most expensive and extensive component of an ISP's investment. There are three main media types that facilitate data transmission (Tanenbaum 2003). The oldest one is the "twisted pair", which consists of two insulated copper wires twisted together in order to avoid antenna phenomenon created by two parallel wires. Public Switched Telephone Networks (PSTNs) are still largely based on twisted pair wires. They can achieve several Mbps for a few kilometers. The next category is the coaxial cable, which is also built on copper and it was firstly widely used for television transmission and then for telephone long-haul links. Nowadays, the long-haul links are exclusively based on fiber optic cables. Their main difference is that instead of transmitting electrical pulses, fiber optics transmit light pulses through the fiber, which is generated by a light source (usually LED) placed at one end and recognized by the detector at the other end. The absence of light is recognized as 0, and the light as 1, just like the electricity over copper cables.

Apart from bandwidth, there are a few more differences between fiber optic and copper-based links. First, the low attenuation of the former and consequently the low needs for repeaters, which are used to enhance the signal, make fiber much more suitable for long haul links. In addition, fiber is not affected by external electromagnetic interference, and is less sensitive to environmental conditions. What is interesting is that telcos also prefer fiber because it is much lighter and has lower installation cost than copper wires. Furthermore, it consumes less space in the already narrow and filled ducts. The fiber optic cables, just like the copper wires, are placed in pipes, which are installed either next to pre-existing network infrastructure (motorways, roads, railways and so on) or in pipes that are not used any more, such as sewer networks. By replacing the oversized copper wires with the smaller in volume but higher-capacity fiber, there is a potential gain for carriers. However, fiber's installation and maintenance needs special skills from engineers and it is very sensitive to bending. Moreover, the cost of the optical interface is quite high and it is higher than the equivalent for copper wires (Tannenbaum 2003). Nowadays, the extended interregional links are built on fiber optics, while the last mile is still mostly based on copper wires. However, a growing discussion is taking place nowadays about the implementation of fiber optic technology in the local loop (Fiber To The x, where x represents Home, Building, Premises and Cabinet – FTTH, FTTB, FTTP and FTTC – respectively). For example, the Organization for Economic Co-operation and Development (OECD 2006) states that "fibre to the home is becoming increasingly important for broadband access, particularly in countries with high broadband penetration". Despite these advantages, installation costs are still too high-priced for extensive use of fiber in the local loop, which is related to excavations in heavily populated and urbanized areas with high land costs. It is estimated that this is the most expensive element of a network's roll-out, reaching 80 percent of the total cost (Graham 1999).

2.2.6 A Little Geography

From the geographical point of view, POPs and IXPs are part of the urban Internet hardware. What is also interesting is the location of the rest of the (less visible part of the) Internet's infrastructure analyzed above, such as the IP addresses. However, it is not always easy to identify their physical location. The reason for this is that the Internet is developed not on a geographical basis but rather on a topological basis, as the Internet recognizes the location of its elements only in relation to other Internet components (Dodge and Zook 2009).

All the above seem to be important when the discussion turns to urban geography, because the location of the Internet hardware determines cities' Internet capacity. The number and the capacity of the links a city shares with the rest of the world reflect the city's aggregated capacity to exchange data and digitally interact with other cities. Additionally, the redundancy of Internet links increases the city's digital reliability in case one or more links go down.

However, regardless of the number of links and their capacity, a city could not benefit unless there is a node linking its Metropolitan Area Network (MAN), and through this the local loops and the end-users, with the backbone networks. Otherwise, a city would be bypassed by those networks without gaining access to the rest of the world, just as small towns are bypassed by motorways and high-speed rail, resulting in what is known in the literature as a tunnel effect. So, in order for a city to benefit from the Internet infrastructure, it is not enough to be near to high capacity backbone networks; it also needs to be connected to them with multiple nodes which enable its fast and secure interconnection with those networks. In addition, extended intra-urban hardware, such as MANs, local loops and POPs, is fundamental for end-users to gain global connectivity.

The importance of the intra-city Internet infrastructure is reflected in the fact that nowadays the main Internet bottleneck lies not at the backbone connections nor at the IXPs, but at the last mile, which is still largely not facilitated by fiber optic technology (Pelletiere and Rodrigo 2001; Blum and Goldfarb 2006).

If the above could reflect a city's aggregated Internet capacity, then the geography of IP addresses could indicate something more tangible: the location of the interconnected computers. If the links and the nodes define the Internet infrastructure supply at city level, then the geographical location of IP addresses could indicate origins and destinations of Internet data communications. However, it should be underlined that IP addresses are not related to the Internet's content but rather to its hardware, indicating the location of computers which host the Internet content (a website for example), and not the location where this content is produced (Dodge and Zook 2009). And even this is not very accurate since the only available geographic information for IP locations is the registered postal address and it is very common that this address is different from the actual geographic location of the IP.

To sum up, this section has provided not only a brief technical analysis of the Internet, but also a glimpse of the underlying geography of the Internet's infrastructure. Most of the technical elements presented in this section are graphically represented in Figures 2.1 and 2.2. The above analysis is crucial for supporting the main focus of this study: the geography of the Internet infrastructure.

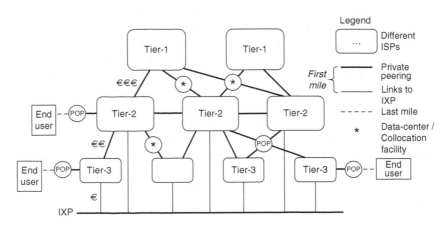

Source: Adapted from AMS-IX (2009).

Figure 2.1   Internet architecture

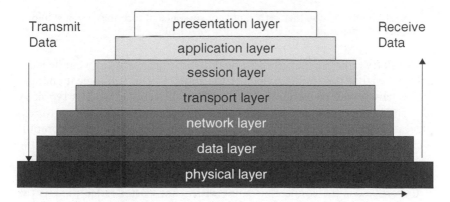

Transmit Data / Receive Data

presentation layer
application layer
session layer
transport layer
network layer
data layer
physical layer

Figure 2.2 OSI reference model

2.3 THE INTERNET GEOGRAPHIES

2.3.1 The Internet Geography – An Epistemological Discussion

The main theoretical pillar of this book is the rather new branch of communications geography identified as cybergeography or Internet geography. The first term, which is the oldest one, is based on the novel term "cyberspace". Indeed, the term was introduced by William Gibson in his novel *Neuromancer* (Gibson 1984, p. 51) in order to describe a virtual conceptual space existing within ICTs (Dodge and Kitchin 2000). The etymology of the word goes back to the ancient Greek word *kyber* which means "to navigate" (ibid.). This term has been much used by Martin Dodge and it was the title of his extensive seminal research project on mapping cyberspace (for a synopsis of his work see Dodge 2008). Nonetheless, the second term, which is more generic, appears more often in the relevant literature (e.g. Townsend 2003; Zook 2006) and is the one adopted here.

Regardless of their etymological differences, both terms focus on the same problem: the geographical representation and analysis of cyberspace, which can be approached as a multi-layer formation that produces new virtual sites (Kitchin 1998b). Dodge and Kitchin (2000, p. 1) illustrate the non-homogenous nature of cyberspace:

> it is a myriad of rapidly expanding cyberspaces, each providing a different form of digital interaction and communication. In general, these spaces can be categorized into those existing within the technologies of the Internet, those within virtual reality, and conventional telecommunications such as the phone and the

fax, although because there is a rapid convergence of technologies new hybrid spaces are emerging.

For Batty (1997), cyberspace is one of the four elements of what he identifies as virtual geography, which is the impact of technological changes and intensive use of technology on traditional geography. His typology of virtual geography consists of: (1) the place/space, which refers to real places; (2) the cspace or computer space, which is the space inside computers; (3) the cyberspace, which is the new emerging space produced by the use of computers; and (4) the cyberplace, which refers to the digital infrastructural layer which underpins cyberspace.

Cyberplace is the connecting point with what Castells identified as the "space of flows". In his work about the network society (Castells 1996), he illustrated the emergence of a new spatial form due to the structural transformation that our society is undergoing because of the extensive use of ICTs. He calls this new spatial form the space of flows and he defines it as the "managerial organization of time-sharing social practices that work through flows" (ibid., p. 442). Such flows are the outcome of the digitally enhanced interaction between remote social actors. In order to better describe this new spatial form, Castells further analyses the space of flows as a three-layer system. The first layer can be parallelized with Batty's cyberplace (Malecki 2002a) and consists of the technical network infrastructure upon which the flows of Castells' network society are transported. This infrastructural layer of communications "defines the new space, very much like railways defined *economic regions* and *national markets* in the industrial economy" (Castells 1996, p. 433). The spatial configuration of the first layer of the space of flows is the focus of this book.

The second layer refers to the hubs and nodes of the space of flows. These are the real places with "well-defined social, cultural, physical, and functional characteristics" (ibid., p. 443) which are interlinked through the first – infrastructural – layer of the space of flows. An example for this layer is the global financial network, which consists of specific places around the world where global financial markets are located. Lastly, the third layer of the space of flows refers to "the dominant managerial elites" and describes the spatial organization of these privileged and leading social groups, which are increasingly located in isolated communities in highly connected places (ibid., p. 433).

While Castells highlighted the importance of the first layer as an underpinning layer of the space of flows, his analysis was mostly focused on the upper layers. The reasons for this can be found in the next section and are summarized here as lack of relevant data and technical complexity.

Despite these difficulties, the main focus of the analysis here is the spatiality of the first layer of the space of flows.

The above two theoretical approaches are the fundamentals of this emerging field of the Internet geography. From an empirical standpoint and based on early research in this field, three key points can be highlighted as the main focal points of this research field (Townsend 2003): (1) the complexity of the internal structure of digital networks; (2) the connection between virtual and physical places; and (3) the use of cybermaps as metaphors for understanding the structure of cyberspace. The diversity of the relevant research questions is inherent to the Internet geography, similarly to more traditional strands of geography. Thus, there is not only one Internet Geography, but instead there are many different Internet geographies (Zook 2006):

- The technical geographies of the Internet, which focus on the spatial aspect of the physical infrastructure of the Internet and were identified before as the first layer of the space of flows or as the cyberplace.
- The human geographies of the Internet, which are further divided into political and cultural geographies and economic geographies of the Internet. The former examine the social nature of the Internet and the impact that the Internet's extensive and diverse usage has on places. Furthermore, the Internet economic geographies are subdivided into urban economic geographies and e-commerce geographies. While the latter refers to the reorganization of the geographies of production and consumption because of electronic commerce, the former focuses on the impact the Internet has on urban development. Most of the empirical studies in this strand of research are mainly based on the study of the physical infrastructure of the Internet, signifying the importance of this layer.
- The visualized geographies of the Internet. This category focuses on visualizing and mapping the topology and even the physical location of the technical, political, cultural and economic layers of the Internet.

In order to bypass the complexity of the above taxonomy and mainly to avoid the confusion of the vague borders between urban economic geographies and the technical geographies of the Internet, these categories will be considered as one here. Such an approach is not new in the field. Indeed, Malecki (2002a, p. 401) in his analysis of cyberplace, recognizes that this element of virtual geography fits well with research questions that economic geography focuses on.

In the same vein, Greenstein (2004) further defines this field as the

economic geography of the Internet infrastructure. Firstly, he defines the
Internet infrastructure as the (ibid., p. 5):

> durable investments in software, communication and computing equipment,
> and related activities associated with operating information technology. This
> common and broad definition of Internet infrastructure encompasses quite a
> lot: capital equipment – such as mainframes, minicomputers, PCs (personal
> computers), LANs (local area networks), WANs (wide area networks), local
> and long-distance telephone equipment, private and quasi-public switching
> equipment, wireless networks for data transmission – and software – both
> packaged and customized. Notice that it also incorporates human capital, a key
> (and often local) input along any value chain for Internet services.

Contrary to the above rather holistic definition, Gorman and Malecki
(2002, p. 391) only consider hardware elements as the Internet infrastructure: "the twisted pair wires to the house, the fiber lines to the central
office, the switch or router, the 28 000 km fiber trunks that connect Japan
to England and all the gear in between" (Stephenson 1996; Gilder 2000).
While the software and the related human capital are of equal importance
for the Internet function, for the needs of this book the Internet infrastructure is directly linked with the Internet's physical layer. Parenthetically, it
could be also said here that the hardware varies more across space than
the software, as will be analyzed below. Indeed, Greenstein used notions
such as economies of density and scale, high sunk cost and infrastructure
upgrade in order to elucidate the geographic properties of the various elements of the infrastructural layer of the Internet, such as the POPs, the
backbone networks, the domain names and the broadband connections.

Because of the strong urban concentration of both the cyberplace and
cyberspace, it is unavoidable for Internet geography not to cross the
borders of the field of urban studies. It is common for such studies in this
field to use tools such as urban hierarchies and urban networks in order
to approach the geography of the Internet infrastructure, as will be illustrated below.

To sum up the above epistemological discussion and to further define
the focus of this book, for the last 15 years we have been able to talk about
this new emerging field of the Internet geography, which is concerned with
the geographic analysis of the different layers of cyberspace and cyberplace. These layers are very diverse as they span from the technical infrastructure, to the users, the content, the social activism and to interpersonal
relations. Therefore there is a need for using very different theoretical and
methodological tools to approach them. Just like traditional geography,
the diversity of the Internet itself and the diversity of the different Internet
geographies require from the research community the use of a variety of

theoretical and methodological tools, tailored to specific research subjects. In this frame, this book is located in this new field of the Internet geography, focuses on the infrastructural layer of the Internet, and uses mostly elements from economic geography and urban studies, as they are illustrated in the following sections of this chapter. Briefly, this book's focus is the urban economic geography of the Internet infrastructure.

2.3.2 An Urban Economic Geography of the Internet Infrastructure – A Generic Approach

There are a few points which need to be highlighted in regards to the Internet infrastructure from the economic geography and urban studies points of view. Firstly, the geography of telecommunications attracts limited interest from geographers. The technical and intangible nature of telecommunications is the main reason why geographers tend to ignore this subject. Indeed, economic and urban geography usually deals with tangible objects, contrary to the elusive nature of telecommunications and specifically the Internet (Bakis 1981; Hepworth 1989; Kellerman 1993). Telecommunication infrastructure, just like other network infrastructures, is fairly invisible when it works properly and only becomes visible when it stops working (Star 1999). In addition, the complex technical structure of telecommunications infrastructure prevents geographers, planners and regional scientists from comprehending the topology, structure and design principles of such networks (Kellerman 1993). Another factor which is also responsible for the lack of interest from spatial scientists is the deficiencies in relevant and accurate data for telecommunications usage and telecommunications infrastructure supply and for the Internet. Secondary data for existing backbone networks is only available nowadays through TeleGeography (2007) and only at an aggregated level. This is the data source used for this book. In addition, demand-side data for Internet communications at a fairly disaggregated level is not available. Despite the fact that ISPs collect such data for managing their networks, this data is not published for competition reasons. Moreover, the privatization of the telecommunications networks which took place across Europe in the late 1990s reduced the data availability because of the heightened competition (Graham and Marvin 1996). The above problematic situation is not new. Batty in the early 1990s declared that there was no interest in the impact of information flows on cities (Batty 1990); Moss in the late 1980s characterized telecommunications infrastructural networks as a mystery to most of the cities (Moss 1987); and Graham and Marvin (1996) admitted that many city planners were not aware of the telecommunications infrastructure supply in their cities. In spite of the above difficulties, the rapid expansion of the Internet in the late 1990s activated geographic research reflexes and led to the emergence of the field of the Internet geography.

Despite from data availability and the field's popularity issues, there is a growing discussion about the implications of the Internet for the broader geography of activities and especially for potential centralization or decentralization impacts on spatial structure. The Internet generates a double-edged effect which simultaneously stimulates both centrifugal and centripetal forces. Using rural and remote areas as an example, the former can be identified as the benefits that people in these areas gain from investments in ICTs such as access to cheaper and better-quality services. For instance, the lack of specialized bookstores in remote areas can be supplemented by access to e-bookstores. Centripetal forces have the same source, but reverse impacts: investments in ICTs in rural areas make local markets more accessible to larger businesses based in core areas (Gorman and Malecki 2000), thereby increasing competition. This may result in diminishing local production because small businesses are unable to compete with larger ones (Richardson and Gillespie 2000). ICTs do not result in the decentralization of economic activity (Richardson and Gillespie 2000), but they generate both centralizing and decentralizing effects, contrary to the early "death of distance" conceptualizations (e.g. Cairncross 2001), which focused only on their decentralizing potential (Malecki and Gorman 2001).

These early assertions about the dominant impact of ICTs on spatial configuration were initially motivated by fears that ICTs would diminish the role of cities. One of the most pessimistic views about the future of cities in the post-Internet era was introduced by the US National Research Council (National Research Council 1998):

> One can anticipate a shift of population away from the metropolitan areas to bucolic agricultural settings (rural Vermont, the California wine country, fishing villages), to resort areas (Aspen, Monterey, Sedona), and to the sunbelt and beachfront. Just as the automobile, superhighways, and trucking helped shift population out of the central city to the suburbs in the 1950's, the computer, the information superhighway, and modems will help shift population from the suburbs to more remote areas.

Although ICTs have managed to remove some of the geographical barriers remote locations face, this evolution has not weakened people's and economic activities' tendency to cluster together in urban areas (Moss and Townsend 2000). Contrary to these early arguments, population and economic activities tend more and more to agglomerate in core metropolitan regions, leading Malecki (2002a, p. 419) to conclude that "world cities are alive and well". Even after the rapid technological changes of the 1990s and the 2000s, cities proved not to be the "leftover baggage from the industrial era" (Gilder 1995; cited in Moss and Townsend 2000, p. 36). And most importantly, the "death of cities" never occurred and the Internet proved to act more as a complement rather than a substitute for face-to-face city-based interactions (Gillespie et al. 2001; Kolko 1999). After all, cities' importance is reflected in the volume of urban population: nowadays more than half of earth's population lives in cities and by 2030 the urban population will reach 60 percent (IHDP 2005).

ICTs, and the Internet infrastructure more specifically, are not an exception in this centripetal tendency as they concentrate in the important nodes of the world urban network (Sassen 1991, 2000a). Indeed, the Internet, and the backbone networks which underpin it, is actually an urban technology (Rutherford et al. 2004) inasmuch as it is located primarily in cities, where demand is concentrated (Gorman and Malecki 2000): "The Internet cannot bypass mega-cities: it depends on the telecommunications [the technical layer of which is concentrated there] and on the *telecommunicators* located in those centres" (Castells 1996, p. 440).

The relation between telecommunications and cities is not unidirectional, though. Not only do cities have the ability to shape the spatial structure of ICTs, but telecommunications also play a role in the urban development process. Maybe the impact of ICTs on spatial configuration is not as strong as of that of previous infrastructural networks such as highways and railways which both reflected and influenced settlements patterns, but the bidirectional relationship is still visible. On the one hand, Moss and Townsend (2000) recognized the reflection of the economic and social realities of the US urban system on the IBN. On the other hand, Graham and Marvin (2001) identified the impact of ICTs on urbanization process due the polarization effect that premium infrastructural networks – including ICTs – generate on urban landscapes by connecting selected places, both within and between cities, while at the same time neglecting the (quality of) connectivity of other less-favored areas.

Apart from the bidirectional relationship between infrastructural networks and urbanization, the above metaphor between ICTs and other non-digital infrastructural networks shifts the focus to the well-established parallel between telecommunications and transportation networks. Even though this parallel is commonly observed in the literature, the effort committed for the study of the Internet and generally ICTs as network infrastructures cannot be compared with the much greater interest in transportation networks (Moss and Townsend 2000).

This parallel takes place at two levels: economy and topology. From the economics point of view, the Internet, just like transportation networks, is an infrastructure as they both serve the production process: the Internet transports the valuable weightless goods of the digital economy in the same way that transportation networks transport industrial goods (O'Kelly and Grubesic 2002; Moss and Townsend 2000). The higher the economic dependency on electronic transactions, the higher the acknowledgement of the Internet as an infrastructure will be. Borland and Hu (2004) highlight this point by arguing that broadband connections are fundamental for the future of the economy, just as road and train networks were during the past two centuries. And they continue by arguing that although Internet is still in its relative infancy, it has managed to transform the way people live and work more rapidly than the previous infrastructural networks.

From a more geographical point of view, transportation and telecommunications networks have strong physical links, since the latter are usually found superimposed on the former. Telecommunication carriers, in order to roll out their intra- and intercity networks, use pre-existing infrastructural networks such as sewer systems and transportation networks (Graham and Marvin 1996). It is common for backbone networks to be embedded alongside motorways and railway lines and for MANs to be installed underneath streets and even inside old sewer pipes.

Another link between transport and telecommunications infrastructure is the commercial partnerships between their operators. Because of the privatization of the infrastructural networks and their splintering character (Graham and Marvin 2001), it is common for older infrastructure network operators (that is, transport or energy) to establish commercial partnerships with telecoms or even to start providing telecommunications services. By such initiatives, the new providers directly benefit from economies of scale arising because of the use of old infrastructural networks and avoiding the high sunk costs related to excavations (ibid.).

Another commonality is the regulatory status (Graham and Marvin 2001). Historically, network infrastructure was developed in a natural monopoly framework because of the market failure in infrastructure provision (Banister and Berechman 2003). This monopolistic framework was accompanied by a regulatory framework in order to prevent customers' overexploitation (Graham and Marvin 1996). Recent technological developments as well as changes in dominant political economy views resulted in more liberal regulatory frameworks. Despite any differences in the liberalization process that the two infrastructural networks underwent, the development and the function of both networks was always and still is related to some kind of regulation.

From an analytical point of view, transport studies have proved vital for understanding and designing the Internet function and routing of IP flows. The most prominent example is the seminal work of Beckmann et al. (1956) on the economics of transportation and the traffic network equilibrium, the relevance of which to communication network analysis was pointed out in Beckman's later work (Beckmann 1967; cited in Boyce et al. 2005). Beckmann et al.'s (1956) novelty lies in the meticulous mathematical solution of the traffic network equilibrium problem in the framework of link cost functions.

Nonetheless, the main meeting point between the Internet and transportation networks from an analytical standpoint is the "Braess paradox" (Boyce et al. 2005). The latter refers to the fact that the outcome of local optimization by individuals (network users) with conflicting interests will not result in a global network optimization (Roughgarden 2005). Put simply, additional extra capacity in a network may result in increased traffic cost for all users (Korilis et al. 1999). Roughgarden (2005) built upon this paradox and also on the concept of "selfish routing", which refers to individually optimized behavior in terms of either commuting flows or IP data flows (Boyce et al. 2005). Having this as a basis, Roughgarden (2005) studied the loss of social welfare due to such uncoordinated network behavior and quantified the highest losses because of selfish routing, a state identified as the price of anarchy.

Both transport and communication networks are friction-reducing technologies as they reduce the cost of distance (Cohen et al. 2002; Cohen-Blankshtain and Nijkamp 2004). Because of this similarity, effort has been spent in research in order to define the relation between them. The literature (Salomon 1986; Banister and Stead 2004; Mokhtarian 1990, 2002) suggests four possible types of interaction between them:

> substitution (reduction, elimination), complementarity (stimulation, generation), modification (change time, mode, destination, and so on with respect to a trip or communication that would have occurred otherwise), and neutrality (no impact of one medium on the other, e.g. as many e-mail messages have no impact on travel and conversely). (Cho and Mokhtarian 2007, p. 5)

Early argumentation was in favor of vast substitution effects on transport because of ICT's expansion. Intensive debates took place in the literature in the 1980s and 1990s (for a detailed review see Graham and Marvin 1996), introducing sometimes rather deterministic argumentations. In reality, such effects were never observed and nowadays it cannot be claimed that the telecommunications infrastructure has a substitution effect on the demand for physical transportation (Black and Nijkamp 2006). On the contrary, complementarities and synergies have been developed between the two infrastructural networks as demand and supply for both of them have considerably increased (Gillespie et al. 2001; Banister and Stead 2004). The extensive use of ICTs and the Internet affected the pattern of transportation of goods and people. While the use of teleconferencing was

Table 2.1   The parallel between the Internet physical infrastructure and road infrastructure

Importance at	The Internet infrastructure		Road infrastructure
Inter-city level	Backbone networks	←→	Motorways
	IXPs / private peering points	←→	Interchanges
Intra-city level	POPs	←→	Access nodes
	MANs / local loops	←→	Intra-city road networks
	IP addresses	←→	Premises

Source: Tranos et al. (2013).

always seen as a substitute for traveling to business meetings, at the same time ICT usage can result in more social contacts and accordingly in more trips in the long term (Geels and Smit 2000).

From the topological point of view, both transport infrastructure and the Internet backbone are rolled out as networks (e.g. Gorman and Malecki 2000; O'Kelly and Grubesic 2002; Wheeler and O'Kelly 1999). Both consist of nodes and edges and both of them can be analyzed using network techniques. Drawing upon previous work (ibid.) Table 2.1 presents this analogy: if backbone links symbolize motorways, IXPs and POPs represent transport nodes (interchanges and access nodes) and MANs and local loops the intra-city roads, then IP addresses stand for the numerous final destinations in the cities – the "Internet real estate" according to Dodge and Shiode (2000).

The Internet backbone network (IBN) is the most interesting part of the infrastructural layer from the geography point of view, because it enables the interconnection of remote places, almost by surpassing the friction of distance. Backbone networks can be regarded as the infrastructural underpinning that enables the Internet to function, seamlessly and apparently placelessly from the end-user viewpoint. According to Malecki (2004, p. 24):

> The backbone networks . . . are the core of the Internet and are essential for all but the most local of interactions. . . . A backbone is a set of paths that local area networks (LANs) connect to for long-distance connection. A backbone employs the highest-speed transmission paths in the network.

One of the basic attributes of the Internet considered above is that it interconnects numerous different and widely dispersed networks. This attribute, which is responsible for its global character, only occurs because of the existence of backbone networks. In reality, backbone networks are extensive interregional networks, built on fiber optic cables, which are interconnected at the main nodes of the Internet, where data peering between them takes place. Batty (1991, p. 142), defines them as "a kind of electronic superhighway which enables networks at the next level of hierarchy down to be interconnected".

Based on the above, it could be suggested that a study on the geography of the IBNs reveals much of the spatiality of the Internet infrastructure and the geography of the first layer of the space of flows. Indeed, the Internet backbone with the global aviation networks are the main elements of Castells' first layer of the space of flows (Taylor 2004).

To sum up, despite the lack of data and the technical complexity of the Internet infrastructure, there is a growing discussion in the literature about the geography of this infrastructural network, as a representation of the first layer of the space of flows. It seems that the early arguments about the end of cities and the death of distance proved to be overly futuristic. On the contrary, the result of the extensive use of ICTs and the Internet more specifically is, to a certain extent, a double-edged effect, with both cities and urban network being affected by but also affecting the spatial structure of the Internet infrastructure. The next section will shed more light on this by reviewing empirical studies about the geography of the Internet infrastructure.

2.3.3 Review of Empirical Studies on the Geography of the Internet Infrastructure

In this section a review of empirical studies about the geography of the Internet infrastructure takes place. Table 2.2 presents published studies in this area from the early days of this emerging field (late 1990s) until recently. It is divided into three sections. The first one contains studies about the Internet edges and mainly the backbone networks. The second section includes the papers which are focused on the nodes of the Internet such as IXPs, the POPs, the collocation facilities and the towers for wireless telecommunications. The studies of the third section focus on the geographical analysis of domain names. The common characteristic of all of these papers reviewed here is that the Internet infrastructure is examined from the geography point of view. In other words, it is not the topology of the Internet infrastructure that is under question, but rather the reflection of this topology on the physical world, and mostly on cities and the urban network.

The first observation from this table is the rather small number of

Table 2.2   Empirical studies on the geography of the IBN

Study	Region	Spatial unit	Indicator	Time
Network edges				
(Wheeler and O'Kelly 1999)	USA	city, backbone networks	tc	1997
(Gorman and Malecki 2000)	USA	city	tc, tb, network distance	1998
(Moss and Townsend 2000)	USA	city	tb	1997–99
(Malecki and Gorman 2001)	USA	city	tc, tb number of hops	1998
(Townsend 2001a)	USA	city	tc, tb, domains	1997, 1999
(Townsend 2001b)	World	city	tb	2000
(Malecki 2002a)	Europe	city	tc, tb, colocation points	2000
	Europe, Asia, Africa, Americas	continent	peering points	2000
	USA	city	tc, tb, b colocation points	1997–2000
(O'Kelly and Grubesic 2002)	US	backbone networks, city	c, tc	1997–2000
(Gorman and Kulkarni 2004)	US	city	tb, tc, c	1997–2000
(Malecki 2004)	US	city	tb, b	1997–2000
(Rutherford et al. 2004)	Europe	city	b, tb, tc	2001
(Schintler et al. 2005)	Europe, US	city	tc	2001, 2003
(Rutherford et al. 2005)	Europe	city	c, tc, tb	2001, 2003
(Choi et al. 2006)	World	city	network centralities	2002
(Devriendt et al. 2008)	Europe	city	intercity links, IXPs	2001, 2006
(Devriendt et al. 2010b)	Europe	city	intercity links, IXPs	2008
(Malecki and Wei 2009)	World	country, city	tc, tb	1979–2005
(Tranos and Gillespie 2009)	Europe	City	connectedness and connectivity	

Table 2.2   (continued)

Study	Region	Spatial unit	Indicator	Time
Network nodes				
(Evans-Cowley et al. 2002)	US	city	conc. of telecom hotels	2001
(Grubesic and O'Kelly 2002)	US	city	conc. of POPs	1997–2000
(Gorman and McIntee 2003)	US	city	conc. of Personal Communication Service Towers (wireless)	
(D'Ignazio and Giovannetti 2007)	World	IXPs	c	2004–05
IP domain				
(Moss and Townsend 1997)	US	city, intra-city	conc. of domains, domain density	1993–97
(Dodge and Shiode 2000)	UK	city	conc. of domains, domain density	1997
(Zook 2000)	US	city, intra-city	conc. of domains, domain density	1998
(Zook 2001)	World	domain names	conc. of domains, domain density	1999

Note: b = bandwidth, c = connectivity (i.e. number of connections), t = total, conc. – concentration.

Source: Tranos and Gillespie (2011).

studies, with the majority of them being published in the early 2000s. The second point that should be highlighted is the geographical focus of the studies. Most of them are concerned with US cities. Such a bias was expected, not only because the Internet itself originated in the US and ARPANET, the today's Internet ancestor, was rolled out among a few American cities, but also because of the US leadership in telecommunications after the Cold War era (Kellerman 2002). Another general comment is that most of these studies are concerned with the edges of the Internet rather than its nodes. As a result, the importance of the nodes is underplayed both from the Internet function, but also from the urban and economic geography point of view.

With respect to the main variables, it seems that the papers which are concerned with the backbone networks are mostly focused on the number of different links terminating in each city and the total bandwidth accumulated at city level. These indicators highlight the city's infrastructural capacity in cyberplace. What these indicators cannot do is to examine the intercity relations. Indicators such as the total number of connections and bandwidth between any two cities reflect the data that these two cities can potentially interchange, and in some way the volume of the virtual interactions that might take place between these two cities.[1]

Additionally, most of the studies use data which usually refers to the late 1990s and early 2000s. Data from this period is unlikely to reflect current conditions in the geography of the backbone networks for two reasons. First, regardless of the high sunk cost of the backbone networks, their upgrade (lighting up the fiber) is easy, and for this reason the spatial distribution of bandwidth capacity can change dramatically. Second, conditions in the telecommunications industry have changed significantly since then. The dotcom bubble of the early 2000 was followed by the telecommunications crash. According to *The Economist* (2002) the latter was some ten times bigger than the better-known dotcom crash. Indeed, one of the reasons for this bust was the unrealistic demand prospects for network capacity which resulted in backbone networks being overbuilt (Kam 2006). All in all, the results of the studies presented here only reflect the reference point conditions and need to be used carefully for other time periods.

A common point for all the papers is the strong urban character of the Internet infrastructure. Because of the private character of this infrastructure, the Internet's physical layer is located where the demand puts it; and the demand for such infrastructure is concentrated in large urban areas (Malecki 2002b; Priemus 2007).

At a wider scale, it could be said that the Internet on the one hand reinforces existing globalization patterns, and on the other results in the emergence of new clusters (Malecki 2002a). The global cities are always in the first tier of the most connected cities, but this tier is no longer a monopoly of the handful of well-established global cities. Both in Europe and the US, the new urban hierarchies resulting from the agglomeration of Internet infrastructure appear to be notably different from the traditional urban geography.

For the case of the US, both old and new geographies coexist. The group of the most connected cities on the US commercial Internet changed very little between 1997 and 2000. New York, Chicago, Washington, DC, San Francisco, Dallas, Atlanta and Los Angeles accumulated the most bandwidth in 2000. Four years earlier, the same seven cities were in the top tier, but in a different order, and with New York being the fourth city (Malecki 2002a; Grubesic and O'Kelly 2002; O'Kelly and Grubesic 2002). Yet, cities which are traditionally significant in transportation networks and information flows such as Washington, DC, Dallas and Atlanta (Wheeler and O'Kelly 1999) accumulated more bandwidth than Los Angeles, one of the most important nodes of the US urban network, and even New York was not for the first three years of the study period served by the highest-capacity links. The above led Townsend (2001a) to conclude that for the case of the US the scatter of the Internet infrastructure is wider than the world cities hypothesis would have predicted.

Indeed, apart from the first-tier cities, the main changes in the urban hierarchy based on the US Internet infrastructure are observed in the lower-tier cities. Portland, Kansas City, St Louis and Salt Lake City became important nodes of the US backbone network either because of their location near existing transportation corridors or because of a strong local information technology economic base – the case of Portland (O'Kelly and Grubesic 2002).

Similar spatial patterns, but slightly more dispersed, have been exhibited for Europe. Apart from the two dominant European world cities, London and Paris, significant bandwidth and backbone links are concentrated in other cities such as Amsterdam, Brussels, Lyons, Milan and four or five German cities, highlighting the more diffused spatial pattern of the European fraction of the IBN when compared to the US one (Rutherford et al. 2004). Also important is the role of some gateway cities, such as Copenhagen, Vienna and Prague, which act as hubs for peripheral regions – Nordic countries and Eastern Europe, respectively (ibid.).

Devriendt et al.'s (2008, p. 25) findings about the European cyberplace are slightly more differentiated. Based on European IXPs data they suggest that "Amsterdam, London, and Frankfurt are far more important in their gateway functions than Paris, Brussels, and Dusseldorf". However, the content-based analysis of the results of web searches showed that Paris, London and Berlin have the most important links, and cities such as Amsterdam, Rome and Frankfurt are secondary.

Regarding the Internet real-estate approach (Dodge and Shiode 2000), which is focused on the geo-location of Internet domain names, all the relevant studies recognize the impact of agglomeration forces on the spatial pattern. Moss and Townsend in their pioneering paper (1997) highlighted the dominance of New York City, and particularly of Manhattan, in US domain names production. In addition, Dodge and Shiode (2000) also identified the concentration of domain names around London. In a wider study, Zook (2001) recognized the US dominance in domain names allocation, despite their global diffusion. According to his research, global cities are still important nodes of Internet content production, but at the same time other cities such as San Francisco, San Diego and Austin in the US, and Zurich, Vancouver and Oslo globally, emerge as major Internet content producers.

A common approach in the above empirical studies is the exploratory analysis of the spatial distribution of the Internet infrastructure. Two studies went a step beyond and used population as the main explanatory variable for the Internet infrastructure (Malecki 2004; O'Kelly and Grubesic 2002), while Tranos and Gillespie (2009) run explanatory statistical models to test the impact of other variables including economic characteristics and spatial structure. All of them recognized the explanatory value of knowledge-related variables in bandwidth accumulation. Variables such as the numbers of Doctorate-granting institutions and patents proved to be better regressors than population in explaining bandwidth distribution. In addition, metropolitan character and market size were also proved to be significant predictors of Internet backbone connectivity.

From a methodological point of view, most of the studies use descriptive statistical analysis and mapping. Nonetheless, a few papers exploit more advanced methods to approach their research questions, such as graph theory, network analysis and rank plots, in order to better explain the network structure; OLS for the explanatory analysis of the infrastructure's spatial distribution; and econometrics for the effect of distance on ISPs' interconnection.

With respect to the nodal infrastructure, only a few studies focused on them. Yet, the spatial pattern of this physical element of the Internet infrastructure is not much differentiated from the edges elements. Grubesic and O'Kelly (2002) concluded that POPs are unevenly spread in the US, and Gorman and McIntee (2003), after investigating the relationship between wireless towers, Internet backbone capacity, collocation facilities and population, highlighted the fact that just as backbone networks, wireless infrastructure follows the diverse localized demand. Evans-Cowley et al. (2002) went a step further and classified the city-planners' responses to this new privately driven infrastructure: some pro-technology cities supported the location of telecom hotels; a second group of cities only addressed this issue after telecom hotels were already located; and thirdly, some cities simply ignored the location of such companies.

To sum up, after more than ten years of empirical research in this emerging field of the urban economic geography of the Internet infrastructure, some first results can be drawn. Based mainly on the research on US cities and secondarily on studies on Europe, it seems that the implementation of this new infrastructural layer results in an urban geography which follows, but at the same time challenges to a certain extent, traditional urban hierarchies.

2.3.4 The Contribution to the Emerging Field of Internet Geography

In short, this book, which is placed in the emerging field of the urban economic geography of the Internet infrastructure, will contribute to this field in the following ways:

- First, by focusing on Europe, it is intended that this study will broaden the knowledge of how European cities are interconnected through the IBN. As mentioned above, some research on Europe has already taken place, but it is dated and rather limited in comparison to the research about US cities. Therefore, there is a need for further exploring the way the European urban network is interconnected through this digital infrastructural layer.
- In addition, this research will not only focus on the infrastructural capital approach and on the way the Internet infrastructure is distributed across European cities, but it will go a step further and include in the analysis a relational approach, in order to identify the different roles that the cities perform in the European part of the first layer of the space of flows.
- Furthermore, based on analytical and conceptual similarities between the IBNs and the transport infrastructure, but also based on the fact that the first layer of the space of flows mostly consists of the Internet backbone and aviation networks, effort is spent to explore how these two different infrastructural layers are deployed across the European cities, and the synergies and the complementarities between them.
- Moreover, this book will also focus on identifying the factors that shape the spatial distribution of the IBN across European cities. Such research is limited, dated and not exhaustive.
- Apart from the above direct contributions to the emerging field of the urban economic geography of the Internet infrastructure, this study will also contribute to the field of the world cities research and to regional development studies. The interurban relational nature of the IBN and its identification as the main component of the first layer of the space of flows facilitate the global city process and the

world city network. Moreover, the infrastructural character of the IBN, in addition to its tendency to accumulate in specific nodes of the urban network, might result in spatially differentiated developmental results. The above literatures are examined in the following two sections.

● In order to approach the above, this book will use a wide range of quantitative methods and will attempt to go a step further than the descriptive approach of most of the existing studies in this field.

2.4   WORLD CITIES

2.4.1   Introduction

The second theoretical pillar of this study is the world city literature. Different terms have been used in order to describe this contemporary phenomenon which is related to the growing interaction and interdependence among a selected set of cities, the importance of which emerges not only within the border of their national economy, but also in the frame of the globalized economy. Among others, Friedmann (1986) referred to the world city hypothesis, Sassen (1991) recognized global cities, Castells (1996) highlighted the global city process and Taylor (2004) analyzed the world city network. Peter Hall, starting in the 1960s, approached world cities as entities which perform multiple roles (Hall 1966; see also Hall 1998): they are national and international centers of political power, centers of trade, banking, insurance and related financial services, centers of advanced professional activity of all kind, centers of knowledge and technology, information gathering and diffusion, centers of consumption, centers of arts, culture and entertainment, and of the ancillary activities that cater for them.

2.4.2   World City Hypothesis

However, it was not until the mid-1980s that the discussion about cities with global reach was materialized to something more concrete; and this was the world city hypothesis of the "spatial organization of the new international division of labour" suggested by John Friedmann (1986, p. 69). As he admitted, this hypothesis was not a robust theory linking urbanization with global economy, but rather a starting point for research (ibid.). Some ten years after his path-breaking work, Friedmann (1995, p. 22) returned with a revised version of his hypothesis, approaching cities as "spatially organized socio-economic systems". According to this work, the world city hypothesis can be summarized in the following five points (ibid., p. 22):

- "World cities articulate regional, national, and international economies into a global economy." The main role that these cities perform is to act as the key nodes of the global economic system. Over the last 30 years, the discrete role that world cities carry out has increased because of the economic transformation that took place during this period: as Amin and Thrift (1992) claim, between the 1970s and 1980s the universal economic system shifted from an international to a global economy. The intensity of the global economic interactions and their importance for the global economic system and the globally (inter)linked national (subglobal) systems resulted in empowering the world cities.
- "A space of global capital accumulation exists, but it is smaller than the world as a whole." Despite the growing interaction of world cities because of economic globalization, not every corner of the world is included, at least with the same intensity, in this planetary economic system. As Sassen (1991) highlights, the degree of globalization goes hand in hand with the increase in the concentration of central functions in a few locations, known as global cities.
- "World cities are large urbanized spaces of intensive economic and social interaction." Undoubtedly, world cities are extensive metropolitan areas, acting as large pools of labor power with high densities of economic and social activities.
- "World cities can be arranged hierarchically, roughly in accord with the economic power they command." This hierarchical structure of world cities is one the main points of Friedmann's hypothesis. Based on this, he created a taxonomy of world cities distinguishing them as primary and secondary, in core and semi-periphery countries (Friedmann 1986). Almost a decade later, he revised this taxonomy on the basis of global financial, multinational, national and subnational/regional spatial articulations (Friedmann 1995), most likely influenced by Sassen's global city approach, the main element of which is the financial power of the global cities (Sassen 1991). Such hierarchical relations can be read as relations of power and competition, for instance in attracting foreign direct investments (FDI), or headquarters of important multinational firms. Interestingly enough, this hierarchy is not characterized by longitudinal stability (Friedmann 1995) as the complexity of the globalized economy and the equally complex urban dynamics continuously affects it. The main exemption to this is probably the highest tier of

cities, which consists of New York, London and Tokyo. These cities are identified as global cities by Sassen (1991), and through the short history of the world city research their dominance remained mainly unchallenged.

● "The controlling world city strata constitute a social class that has been called the international capitalist class." The main characteristic of this class is its cosmopolitan view of the world, extensive usage of the English language and its consumerist ideology (Friedmann 1995, p. 23).

Following Taylor's (2004) comments on Friedmann's work, two points need to be highlighted. First, the world cities hypothesis gave the necessary push to include world cities-related research questions in the urban research agenda. It was the first time that such a theoretical framework had been introduced, even in the form of a hypothesis. From the geography point of view, Friedmann's main contribution was the establishment of a global perspective in understanding world cities, surpassing state boundaries and the already existing and extensive literature about national urban systems (ibid.). It should be noted here that despite the importance of hierarchical relations in the world cities hypothesis, the criteria and the methodology behind this ranking are not explicitly specified, especially in the revised version (Friedmann 1995).

2.4.3 Global Cities

Despite the novelty of Friedmann's ideas, the main growth of the world city studies was initiated by Saskia Sassen's work on global cities (Sassen 1991). Her starting point was the opposed forces of spatial dispersal and global interaction. Building upon previous studies on world cities, which identified them as international centers of trade and banking, she identified four new functions and roles for global cities: (1) hosting the decision centers of the world economy; (2) concentration of the financial and specialized producer service sector, which can be approached as the successor of manufacturing as the leading economic sector; (3) hosting and enhancing innovation activities and global production in leading economic sectors; and (4) consumption centers of the leading sectors products. Simply put, "the things that a global city makes are services and financial goods" (Sassen 1991, p. 4). All the above resulted in control and power concentration in specific cities, the leading league of which consists of New York, London and Tokyo.

Sassen did not extend her research outside the leading league of global cities and consequently does not provide empirical results for a wider set of world cities. As Taylor (2004) highlights, she is not much concerned with the relations between world cities – no matter that this is slightly changed in the revised version of her study (Sassen 2004) – and she instead performs a comparative study of the three global cities. Interestingly enough she does not adopt the most common term of "world cities", but she chooses to use the term "global city" to differentiate her leading league of cities from similar past studies such as the world cities hypothesis.

Although both world city and global city concepts were introduced to explain the same phenomenon – the transnational urban interdependencies – differences exist between them. Derudder (2006) sheds light on the ambiguity observed in empirical studies trying to measure the "world-ness" or "global-ness" of different cities. The distinctive characteristic between these two concepts is the main function of cities: while global cities' main engine is hosting advanced producer services, world cities gain power by hosting multinational corporations. Based on this distinction, global city functions are usually found in central business districts (CBDs) or equivalent business-intensive areas in edge urban locations, while world city functions can be found in wider metropolitan regions (Derudder 2006).

From the Internet geography point of view, the most valuable input of Sassen's study is the appreciation of ICTs' role in supporting global cities. ICTs are essential in the two main processes which aid the spatial concentration of control and ownership: both the spatial dispersion of economic activity and the reorganization of the financial industry are strongly based on ICTs. Such infrastructure enables the long-distance management of production and instant financial transactions, overcoming the barrier of physical distance. In addition, Sassen (1991) highlights the agglomerative character of ICTs as well as their economic impact: the high entry cost for providing extensive ICT infrastructure is an agglomerative factor itself, since not all cities can afford such an investment; yet, she continues, the established provision of high-quality ICTs equates to "an almost absolute advantage" for a city (ibid., p. 19).

2.4.4 Global City Process

The global urban interdependencies were also the focus of Castells's study, but from a different more relational perspective (1996, p. 417):

> the global city is not a place but a process. A process by which centers of production and consumption of advanced services, and their ancillary local societies, are connected in a global network, while simultaneously downplaying the linkages with their hinterlands, on the basis of informational flows.

Indeed, Castells adopted a more dynamic approach for the world city phenomenon compared to the rather static view of Sassen. While he identified that the outcome of this process is the concentration of economic activities in some selected global nodes, he also recognized the geographically diffused character of the global city phenomenon. Simply put, the global city process cannot be limited only to "a few urban cores of the hierarchy" (ibid., p. 411). On the contrary, such a network architecture can be identified even at much lower scales: regional and local centers, or more specifically, parts of these centers' socio-economic systems, are intensively linked with the global economy.

Castells identified the global economy as one of the three elements of what he calls the "new economy". This is a world-scale economic system, which appeared in the last quarter of the twentieth century and is "informational, global and networked" (ibid., p. 77). The informational character of the new economy is analyzed in section 2.5.2, but it can be briefly mentioned here that the new economy is informational and not just information based, just as the industrial economy was something more than just an economic system based on manufacturing. Indeed, the emergence of the industrial economy was accompanied by the emergence of a broader social culture, the industrial culture.

The second element of Castells's view of the current economic system is scale. He recognized scale not as world, nor as universal, but rather as global. Having elaborated on that, he defined the global economy as an economic system which has the ability to work as an entity on a planetary scale. This global economy comes as an evolution of the world economy, which has existed at least since the sixteenth century (that is, the Mediterranean world economy as described by Braudel 1984; see also Wallerstein 2004), and which only refers to capital accumulation throughout the world (Castells 1996). Conversely, the global economy refers to the global integration of the actors of capital accumulation.

The integration element leads us to the third characteristic of Castells's approach to the new economy: its network character. The new economy is networked because productivity and competition are influenced and at the same time occur in global networks of business interactions (ibid.). Such networks are global but not universal, meaning that they are spread around the world, but they do not include every settlement on earth. On the contrary, they are very selective on which nodes of the world cities network they include.

To summarize, Castells defined the new economy in accordance with the world city phenomenon and he strongly linked these two notions. Regardless of the universal impacts it generates, the new economy is mostly apparent in places which experience the global city process. This process, though, which is typified by a global scale and a network topology, is mainly based on the recent advances in telecommunications and computing. As Castells states, "without new information technology global capitalism would have been a much limited reality" (1996, p. 19). Throughout his work, Castells highlighted the importance of ICTs in supporting the global city process and the new economy. Their importance is highlighted by their distinctive role in the first layer of the space of flows.

2.4.5 World City Network

Following Castells's work, Peter Taylor (2004) developed his perspective of the world city phenomenon, which is summarized in the term "world city network". His main point was the relational thinking about cities. Indeed, his book starts with the statement that he is not concerned with the relations within the city or even with its hinterland; on the contrary he is focused on relations between cities, their "dependencies and interdependencies" (ibid., p. 1). In this frame, he is focused on how cities, through the networks they form, work together as economic entities. He suggests that:

> concepts such as space of flows and cities as networked entities are transferable across different historical specificities. Thus, what [he is] basically taking from the above [different approaches of the world city phenomenon] is the necessity to think of cities relationally, as the product of networking activities (ibid., p. 27).

Taylor not only understood the emergence of a network logic in the world city phenomenon, but he moved one step further by empirically testing his model. He created a three-level interlocking world city network. Usually, networks are two-level entities: they consist of links and nodes. Taylor, instead of directly using cities as the nodal level of his network, created a third subnodal level, in order to include in his analysis the agents which "taken together, are primarily responsible for shaping the world city network"; these are service firms, city governments, service sector institutions and nation-states (ibid., p. 58). From these four, he recognized service firms and, more specifically, Sassen's advanced producer services as the main agent for the world city formation. His latest version of the world city network (Taylor et al. 2010) is based on relational data[2] from about 175 multinational firms, which can be identified as advanced producer services. Using the intra-firm connections, he created a roster of 525 cities.

Apart from the theoretical value of Taylor's research in highlighting the relational nature of the world cities, his main contribution is the empirical testing of the world city phenomenon. It is the first such extensive empirical intercity study in the field of world city research. From such an analysis, a wide range of conclusions can be drawn. Firstly, in spite of the network topology of the world city system, there is still a core–periphery geography: "while command power remains resolutely in core-located cities, the creation of a worldwide network of cities diffuses another sort of power. This network power is found in non-core cities that have been integral and essential to the servicing of global capital" (2004, p. 199).

Secondly, Taylor recognized the impact that globalization has on cities' independence from the state economy. Network structures enabled world cities to function outside state borders and create their own hinter-worlds. In analogy to hinterlands, the above term describes the links of a given world city with other world cities in the framework of the world city network and the globalized economy (Taylor 2001). Operating on such networks and mainly interacting with other world cities makes the classic national urban hierarchy goal of spatial integration within national borders appear as an oversimplification (Taylor 2004).

Despite the popularity of Taylor's approach, some criticism has developed over the years, mostly against the use of firm-level data. More specifically, questions have emerged such as why the internal properties of firms (the third subnodal level according to Taylor's network concept) reflect the structural attributes of an interurban network (Nordlun 2004). Simply put, according to Taylor's approach, the fundamental element of a city-to-city link is the co-location of the same advanced producer service firm in any two cities. However, this might reflect better firm structural attributes rather than interurban relations.

2.4.6　World Cities, World City-Regions and Some Scalar Issues

Despite the above rigorous analysis of the world city network, what has not been yet incorporated in the discussion about globalization and the city network is the notion of scale: it is well accepted that London is a global city, but how is the global city of London defined in geographical terms?

Such a debate is much wider than the current discussion about world and global city and is inherent in the field of urban studies and planning. Different terms have been introduced in order to approach different urban agglomerations and their adjacent areas, such as conurbation (Geddes 1915), megalopolis (Gottmann 1961), mega-city region (Hall and Pain 2006), functional urban areas (FUA) (Cheshire 1990; Cheshire et al. 1986; ESPON 2005a), and American metropolitan statistical area (MSA) (Hall 2009). It is beyond the scope of this study to further facilitate this ongoing discussion. However, there is a need to adopt a definition for the spatial unit upon which this book focuses. As such, the use of the "city-region" is preferred, a notion which was introduced almost 60 years ago (Dickinson 1947). Despite the wide range of different approaches for this term (see Rodríguez-Pose 2008) and the related ambiguity, the notion of city-region has been increasingly used lately (Parr 2005).

The first reason for adopting this concept in this book is its strong urban and metropolitan character. Based on Rodríguez-Pose's (2008) meta-analysis of the use of this concept, the main criteria for defining a city-region is the existence of a highly urbanized metropolitan area. Indeed, Ache (2000) highlighted that from a spatial perspective a city-region is very similar to a conurbation or to a metropolitan area. Others also included in the discussion the core urban areas' hinterlands (Scott 2001), or the surrounding territory of the core urban areas (Parr 2005). However, the main determinant for a city region is the existence of a highly urbanized core. Charles et al. (1999, p. 1) consider the above and define the city-region as "a functionally inter-related geographical area comprising a central, or core, city with a hinterland of smaller urban centers and rural areas, which are socially and economically interdependent". The urban nature of the city-region notion supports its choice as the preferable unit of analysis which matches the urban character of the Internet and the Internet infrastructure as analyzed in section 2.3.

Additionally, the concept of the city-region is linked with the notion of a regional economy. The scale of the city-region (above the local level) and the regional character of this concept incorporate some degree of functionality, which signifies the existence of an integrated regional economy in the city-region. This is why, according to Davoudi (2003), the city-region concept is in accordance with the notion of the metropolitan economy, and Scott and Storper (2003, p. 581) identify city-regions as the "locomotives of the national economy". This element is also very helpful for the third research question of this book as it enables the use of the city-region concept as the study unit for analyzing the regional economic impacts of the Internet infrastructure.

Furthermore, the city-region concept appears to be related to the world city literature. Indeed, when Kunzmann (1998) refers to the world city phenomenon, he prefers the "world city-region" term in order to incorporate a more functional approach to the nodes of the global urban network. Similarly, Scott (1998) introduces the notion of the "global city-region". The above approaches are consistent with Friedmann's (1995) thesis about the contemporary role of cities in the world economy, according to which cities are the organizing nodes of world capitalism and the articulations of regional, national and global commodity flows (Brenner 1998b).

On the contrary, this functional approach of the world city-regions seems to incorporate the space of flows concept. Maybe from a world-scale perspective cities can be seen as nodes of a planetary economic system; in reality, though, cities are not homogenous spatial entities but rather heterogeneous and non-continuous territorial formations with an internal network structure.

From another perspective, Brenner (1998b, p. 3) adds to the above discussion that global cities are related both to the "globalization of capital" but also to the "regionalization/localization of state territorial organization". However, he recognizes that large urbanized regions rather than territorial economies of state are the basic units of global capitalism. In a similar vein, Harvey (1982) links globalization with capitalism and more specifically with capital's tendency to remove spatial barriers to its circulation and to accelerate its turnover time, resulting at the same time in the formation of fixed and immobile spatial configurations known as capital's "spatial fix".

The above are highly related to the focus of this book on the Internet infrastructure. Harvey's spatial fix incorporates the use of investments in infrastructural capital such as transportation and telecommunications networks as tools for territorial organization. Such networks, and particularly telecommunications networks, are multiscalar developments in a world city framework: they both influence and are influenced by "national territorial cohesion, urban regional cohesion, and local territorial cohesion on parallel" (Rutherford 2004, p. 55). They are "glocal" networks as they can interlink localities at different scales: the CBD with the new developments at the edge of the city, and both of these local sites with another world city thousands of miles away. Brenner (1998a) identified these networks as "glocal scalar fixes", because instead of homogenizing space at the national level as infrastructural networks used to do, they result in increasing capital's uneven geographic distribution.

To summarize, the conceptualization of the city-region facilitates the present study as it addresses the urban orientation, the world city perspective, the regional economic importance and the glocal scalar issues related with the Internet infrastructure. In addition, the above discussion can further support the following section, where the world city literature is examined from the telecommunications perspective.

2.4.7   World Cities and Telecommunications

The previous sections identified the main contributors in the transnational urban networks research. Nonetheless, apart from these generic approaches, more specialized studies have also taken place, focusing on specific aspects of the globalization process and the urban function. The interest here lies in studies which bring together telecommunications and the different world city conceptualizations.

Such a case is Kellerman's (1993) work on telecommunications and geography, where he adopts a "transactional city" approach (Corey 1982; Gottmann 1983) for explaining the global system of cities. In a nutshell, "transactional city specializes in the generation, processing, management and transmission of information, knowledge and decisions, rather than in the production of tangible goods" (Kellerman 1993, p. 98). According to his concept, telecommunications is the main means for the realization of these transactions. And here is the importance of Kellerman's research: although all the above urban researchers included the importance of telecommunications in their analysis of the world city phenomenon, Kellerman uses telecommunications as one of his structural elements for shaping the global urban hierarchy.

Based on the above argumentation, he produced a rather descriptive four-tier global urban hierarchy, which is presented below, emphasizing the telecommunications-related attributes of each tier. The first tier refers to domestic cities. Among other characteristics such as strong manufacturing and/or tourism sectors, these cities utilize telecommunications limitedly, at least regarding the international and business control aspects. The second tier consists of world cities. This term indicates that a significant part of these cities' economies is internationalized. In regards to telecommunications, world cities offer sophisticated services and act as national hubs. Regional hubs are identified as the third tier of Kellerman's global hierarchy. As far as telecommunications infrastructure is concerned, such cities provide services not only for their own country but for neighboring countries as well. At the top of the hierarchy, the global hubs are found. Kellerman (1993) follows Sassen's approach regarding the global role of the leading league of New York, London and Tokyo, and he identifies these cities as the top of his conceptual pyramid. Although his global urban hierarchy cannot be characterized as relational – at least following Taylor's thesis (2004) – but chiefly as hierarchical, in this top tier of cities the relational element is present. These three cities because of their unique roles and functions are tightly linked together and this tightness is reflected in the telecommunications infrastructure as well.

To sum up, despite the fact that Kellerman is not usually included in the rather narrow group of researchers of the world city phenomenon, his global urban hierarchy research has a twofold added value for this book. Firstly, the role of telecommunications in defining global urban hierarchy appears to be more central in comparison to other studies including Taylor's (2004) work, where the infrastructural element is not considered as a structural and relational element of the world city network. Just like Castells (1996), who highlighted the underpinning role of telecommunications – digital – infrastructure and its relational character, Kellerman (1993, 2002) successfully incorporated such attributes in a global urban hierarchy study. Secondly, Kellerman extended his global hierarchy to cities of local importance. This also agrees with Castells's approach to the extent of the global city process and fits well with the needs of this book: because of the smaller and more detailed scale of this study (mainly European instead of global) more cities of lower ranking can be included in the analysis of the world city phenomenon.

2.4.8 The Link with and the Contribution to the World Cities Field

After analyzing the different conceptualizations of the world and global city phenomenon, this section emphasizes on how this phenomenon is related to the research questions of this study, and the contribution of this book to the global urban network research field. First of all, it should be noted that this research does not attempt to present a new global urban hierarchy based exclusively on the urban distribution of the Internet infrastructure. The complexity of cities and the complexity of the relational character of what is identified here as world and global cities prevent such a unilateral approach. However, all the above theorists of the urban phenomenon of the global cities agree on one point:

> Transport and communication have played a critical role in shaping the evolving world city system. In turn, world cities have been instrumental in shaping global, regional, and local transport and communication networks. (Keeling 1995, p. 128)

Indeed, both telecommunications and transportation have facilitated the world city phenomenon by decreasing and even extinguishing communications costs, enhancing the interaction of the globally spread actors of capital accumulation and supporting their integration. Both the Internet and more specifically the IBN as well as the aviation network carry a significant part of this interaction (Taylor 2004), facilitating not only global urban interdependencies but also globalization itself (Graham and Marvin 2001). Information is distributed around the world settlements through what is known as the information highways (Gore 1993). In the same way, people are being brought together via the aviation network in order to interact and acquire complex knowledge (Rimmer 1998). These processes enable Smith and Timberlake (2002, p. 139) to recognize world cities as the "spatial articulations of the global flows that constitute the world economy", and Rimmer (1998, p. 439) to identify them "as junctions in flows of goods, information and people rather than as fixed locations for the production of goods and services". However, these flows are not transported in the abstract space, but rather on this specific infrastructural layer, identified by Castells as the first layer of the space of flows, which is (unequally) spread around cities in a global network topology. This infrastructural layer is the necessary means for the circulation of flows and, further, for the emergence of the world and global cities phenomenon.

On the other hand, the infrastructural layer is also structurally affected by the shape of the world city network. Because of the private character of telecommunications and aviation industries, the spatial distribution of their infrastructural networks is mostly shaped by the spatially differentiated demand for such services. Taking into consideration that the demand for communications – electronic or air transportation – is maximized among the world cities and their hinterworlds, it is economically rational for carriers to focus on and invest in locating their networks among such locations. This demand, which is reflected in the fiber-filled corridors, enables Graham and Marvin (1996, p. 3) to announce cities as the "power houses of communications".

Drawing upon the different theoretical conceptualization of the transnational urban network, Castells's (1996) "process-based" rather than "place-based" approach (the global city is a process rather than a place; see section 2.4.4) is the most influential for this study. In addition, the relational understanding provided by Castells and empirically implemented by Taylor (e.g. 2004) is also fundamental for this book. In terms of the adopted terminology, the "global city" term will be mostly avoided in order to highlight the inclusion of lower-ranking cities in this book. Nonetheless, the importance of the digital infrastructure in the formation and maintenance of the global urban network is one of the main highlights of this book, following conceptions introduced by Castells, Kellerman and Sassen, as discussed in the previous sections. In a nutshell, following Derudder's (2006) typology, one of the aims of this book is to analyze transnational urban networks from an infrastructure standpoint.

To sum up, there is a twofold contribution of this book to the field of world cities research. Firstly, despite the fact that this research will not propose a new global urban hierarchy, it will shed light on this "symbiotic" relation between communications infrastructure and world city formation (Keeling 1995). In more detail, this study's main contribution to the field of world city research is the geographical analysis of one of the main facilitators of this global urban phenomenon, the Internet infrastructure. In addition, a topological and geographical comparison with the other essential facilitator of the global city process, the aviation network, will also be made in order to investigate the degree of synergy between the two infrastructural networks in facilitating the global city process (Choi et al. 2006).

Additionally, this study also attempts to bridge the gap between the theoretical sophistication in the work of Sassen (2000b), Friedmann (1986, 1995) and Castells (1996) and the lack of empirical evidence to back up their claims concerning an emerging network of flows. The above is illustrated by Taylor (1999, p. 1904) as an "evidential crisis" in the burgeoning field of world cities research. In particular, Taylor highlights the surprisingly limited use of relational data in the key studies in the field, given that it is precisely relations between cities that constitute the key to understanding the new world city networks that analysts contend are emerging. Although this study is not based on relational data for the actual flows between the cities, it exploits relational data for the supporting infrastructural layer of this interaction.

2.5   THE INTERNET INFRASTRUCTURE AND REGIONAL DEVELOPMENT

2.5.1   Introduction

The last section of this literature review chapter explores the link between the Internet infrastructure and regional economic development, which is the third pillar of this book. Firstly, the general economic framework, under which the Internet appears to be a valuable means for economic growth, is analyzed. Secondly, the role of the Internet in the production process is highlighted. Thirdly, based on the above as well as on relevant theoretical approaches for regional economic development, a conceptual research framework for the economic development impacts of the Internet infrastructure at regional level is suggested. Lastly, empirical studies concerned with the direction of causality between ICTs and (regional) economic development are reviewed.

2.5.2   General Economic Framework

The massive technological improvements which took place in the post-industrial era, apart from having wider social impacts, resulted in structural changes in the economy. Soft factors such as information, knowledge and technology became fundamental factors in the production process and in the related policy agenda. Nevertheless, there is not a single conceptual framework which encompasses all these changes in the postmodern economy (Cohen et al. 2000). Among others, the most widely used concepts describing this post-industrial economy are the "information economy", the "knowledge economy" and the "digital economy".[3] The rest of this section is spent in critically analyzing these approaches.

The concept of the information economy is the oldest one. In 1977, Porat (1977, p.204; cited in Hepworth 1989, p.7) recognized that:

> [We] are entering another phase of economic history. We are just on the edge of becoming an information economy. The information technologies – computers and telecommunications – are the engines of this transformation. And we are now seeing the growth of new information industries, products, services and occupations, which presage new work styles and lifestyles based on intensive use of information processing and communication technologies.

Hepworth (ibid.), building on Porat's definition, further explained the information economy as a "new phase of economic development", the main characteristic of which is the dominance of information in goods and services production and in growth in general. The further enlargement of the information economy will result in wider transformation of economic products, activities and actors, which will not only affect the information-intensive sectors, but will also lead to the emergence of a wider techno-economic change (Miles and Matthews 1992). In addition, Castells (1996) identified the new economy as informational rather than information based, as analyzed in the previous section. From an economic standpoint, although information is the main input for productivity growth and competitiveness, the effect of the information economy is wider than such a production–input change. This is why the informational economy is not just the product of the technological improvement in the fields of computing and telecommunications, but instead is the result of the change of the techno-economic paradigm, a term which is traced back to Perez (1983). The latter refers to the "combination of interrelated product and process, technical, organizational and managerial innovations, embodying a quantum jump in potential productivity for all or most of the economy and opening up an unusually wide range of investment and profit opportunities" (Freeman and Perez 1988, pp, 47–8).

From a historical perspective, this new techno-economic paradigm, which is materialized by the information economy, can be also approached using Nikolai Kondratieff's "economic waves" (1926).[4] He identified long phases of development – almost half a century long – based on the shift of technological paradigms. Starting from the industrial revolution and early mechanization Kondratieff (wave), he continued with the steam power and railway and the electrical and heavy engineering Kondratieff. After his death, the Fordist mass production wave was introduced and according to Freeman (1987) we are currently experiencing the fifth Kondratieff of information and communication.

Kellerman (2002), in his attempt to further explain the information economy, identified its structural elements:

- Infrastructure: the technical layer of the information economy, where the ICTs are located.
- Information: all kinds of information – personal, business, educational and so on – the delivery of which to customers (users) is based on the infrastructural layer.
- Media: they are responsible for the consumption of the various types of information (TV, radio, the Internet and so on).
- Operators: which refers to companies which deal with the operation of business for all the above layers (that is, production and servicing of the infrastructure, information and the media).
- Users: the customers who make use of the infrastructure, information and media. Users can be both households and businesses.

The above five elements of the information economy are combined together and form the three economic functions as are illustrated in Figure 2.3a. All elements of the information economy are merged in Figure 2.3b to facilitate the needs of the final user-customer.

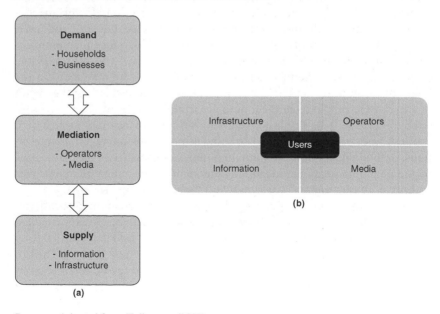

Source: Adapted from Kellerman (2002).

Figure 2.3   Major elements of the information economy

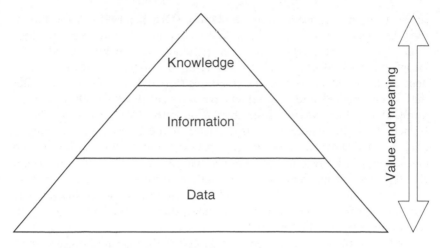

Source: Adapted from Burton-Jones (1999)

Figure 2.4 Data, information and knowledge

The second concept analyzed here is the knowledge economy. Knowledge is directly linked to information because "knowledge is more than information as information is more than simply data" (Malecki and Moriset 2008, p. 29). The relation between these notions is hierarchical, as one step higher in the hierarchy reveals a higher level of sophistication, codification and consequently value. The relation between data, information and knowledge is illustrated in Figure 2.4. Nijkamp and Johnkhoff (2001, p. 2) identified knowledge as the "accumulated stock of information based on synergies" contrary to these "structured flows of data", which form information. The adding, restructuring, editing and other operative changes of information result in the formation of knowledge (ibid.). Leydesdorff (2006, 17) further explains the notion of knowledge and distinguishes it from information:

> Knowledge enables us to codify the *meaning* of information. Information can be more or less meaningful given a perspective. However, meaning is provided from a system's perspective and with hindsight. Providing meaning to an uncertainty . . . can be considered as a first codification. Knowledge enables us to discard some meanings and retain some others in a second layer of codifications. In other words, knowledge can be considered *as a meaning which makes a difference*. Knowledge itself can also be codified, and codified knowledge can, for example, be commercialized.

This last point is the key characteristic of the knowledge economy: knowledge, as a commercialized entity, has become one of the factors of

production, in advance of capital and labor (Drucker 1998). According to
the OECD's (1996, p. 7) definition, knowledge-based economies are economies "which are directly based on the production, distribution and use of
knowledge and information". However, the economy was always dependent on knowledge, even in ancient times (Quah 1998). Despite the fact
that steam engines and clay tablets are physical products, they embody
knowledge, which was used for their production (Maignan et al. 2003).
Nonetheless, the distinctive characteristic of the knowledge economy is
that knowledge became a stand-alone product (Quah 1998). Additionally,
investments in knowledge and knowledge products can have horizontal
effects, affecting all the production factors and even transforming them
to new products and services. "And since these knowledge investments
are characterized by increasing . . . returns, they are the key to long-term
economic growth" (Stevens 1998).

But how is the knowledge economy linked to the information economy?
Maignan et al. (2003, p. 4) differentiate the above notions as follows:

"Knowledge represents the capacities or capabilities of an individual or a social
group . . . associated with meaning and understanding, as well as the abilities to
organize, interpret and assess information" (Cohendet and Steinmueller 2000),
while information is "knowledge reduced to messages that can be transmitted
to decision agent" (Dasgupta and David 1994).

The notion of knowledge is tied with the notion of learning. The latter,
as a collective ability of a society or a locale, appears to be central in the
development process (Pike et al. 2006; Lundvall 1992). Additionally,
advances in ICTs – identified as the infrastructural layer in Kellerman's
model of the information economy – resulted in the acceleration of the
codification of this fraction of knowledge which is able to be codified.[5]
This rapid change in the knowledge codification process resulted in the
transformation of knowledge into a market commodity: "large chunks of
knowledge can be codified and transmitted over computer and communication networks" (Stevens 1998, p. 90). Due to this function, technological
improvements are integral elements of the knowledge economy and technology can also be approached as applied, routinized and transferable
knowledge (Landes 1998).

The third and most recent theoretical attempt to describe the current
economy is summarized under the term "digital economy". The latter
is usually related to economic transactions taking place in the Internet
(Atkinson and McKay 2007). However this is only part of what the
digital economy really is. Atkinson and Mckay (ibid., p. 7) define it as
follows:

The digital economy represents the pervasive use of IT (hardware, software, applications and telecommunications) in all aspects of the economy, including internal operations of organizations (business, government and non-profit); transactions between organizations; and transactions between individuals, acting both as consumers and citizens, and organizations. Just as 100 years ago the development of cheap, hardened steel enabled a host of tools to be made that drove economic growth, today information technology enables the creation of a host of tools to create, manipulate, organize, transmit, store and act on information in digital form in new ways and through new organizational forms. (Cohen et al. 2001)

The key point of this concept is the pervasive character of ICTs in all sectors of the economy. The information economy concept is roughly linked with specific sectors of the economy. Porat (1977; cited in Hepworth 1989, p. 15) identified the informational worker and he developed a register with 422 information occupations based on the US Census of Population workforce classification. Additionally, concepts such as "quaternary employment", which refers to services "closely related to the production, processing and distribution of information" (Gottmann 1983, p. 66) and the "informational sector" were introduced to frame the information economy (Hepworth 1989). Moreover, the concept of the knowledge economy is more widely defined: no explicit knowledge sector was identified and the definition of knowledge-based occupations was also extended out of the service sector (Neef 1998).

However, such a sector-based approach does not apply to the digital economy. Indeed, the concept of the digital economy is by definition horizontal and refers to the impacts that the economy in total can enjoy – mostly through productivity gains   because of the extensive use of ICTs in all aspects of the economy (Atkinson and McKay 2007). Simply put, computers, telecommunications and their combined function, known as "infocommunications", support downstream industries in all sectors of the economy (Malecki and Moriset 2008). This process results in productivity effects, which according to Atkinson and McKay (2007) can be distinguished in capital deepening and total factor productivity gains. While the former refers to the fact that increased capital results in increased labor productivity, the latter refers to productivity increases when the same amount of capital is used more efficiently. In addition, the OECD (2003) suggests a third path for the expansion of the productivity gains: the productivity acceleration in the ICT-producing sector and the expansion of the ICT-producing sector in the economy. In a nutshell, such productivity gains can significantly affect economic growth.

However, much discussion has taken place in the relevant literature with regards to the productivity gains due to the use of ICTs. This debate is known as the "Solow productivity paradox" because of his quote: "You can see the computer age everywhere but in the productivity statistics" (cited in Triplett 1998, p. 1). Regardless of the commonly accepted view that the use of ICTs will result in productivity gains, productivity indicators remained stable until the mid-1990s. Cairncross (2001) provides three explanations for this paradox. Firstly, there was a waste of resources, especially in the first stages of the diffusion of computer usage. Many office workers did not have the knowledge to use this new device in a productive and efficient way. Secondly, economies usually do not immediately take advantage of new technologies. A couple of generations are needed for the economies to learn how to utilize new technologies proficiently. And thirdly, productivity itself is difficult to measure, especially in the service industry, where the impacts of ICTs are likely to be greatest.

It was not until the end of the 1990s that the first evidence of productivity growth appeared. Two-thirds of the productivity growth in the USA between the first and the second half of the 1990s was due to the investment in or the production of computers (Cairncross 2001). In Europe, where the ICT sector is smaller, more than half of productivity growth emerged because of ICTs. Productivity growth between 1995 and 2000 was around 1.4 percent and over 0.7 percent was due to ICTs. These productivity gains were widely explained by the production of high-value goods based on ICTs and the adoption of ICTs in the production procedure (EC 2004).

To sum up, a common characteristic of the above analyzed concepts is their extent, as they are not limited only to the Internet-based new economy (Malecki and Moriset 2008). As explained above, the challenges and changes that the post-industrial economic system underwent and is still experiencing are wider than this. Additionally, despite the different starting points, there are overlaps between the three different concepts discussed above, since they approach the same phenomenon from different perspectives: the new techno-economic paradigm of the post-industrial economy. While the first two approaches mostly focus on the soft factors of this paradigm (information, knowledge and the learning process), the digital economy framework mostly emphasizes the hard factors (ICTs). However, all three theoretical concepts agree on the central role of the ICTs in this new paradigm. This led Antonelli (2003, p. 197) to characterize advanced telecommunications services as the backbone of the new economy; this is the focus of the next section.

2.5.3   The Infrastructural Character of the Internet

This section attempts to illustrate the economic function of ICTs in general and the Internet more specifically. Effort is spent to identify and analyze these economic characteristics of the Internet which enable it to affect the production process.

The starting point for such an attempt is the notion of general purpose technologies (GPTs). The latter is part of the wider notion of "drastic innovations", a term which can be traced back to Bresnahan and Trajtenberg (1995). It refers to innovations that create discontinuities as they result in radical changes in the used technological means, which even lead to the replacement of old technologies (Helpman 1998). This approach identifies GPT as those technologies which have the:

> potential for pervasive use in a wide range of sectors . . . As a GPT evolves and advances it spreads throughout the economy, bringing about and fostering generalized productivity gains. Most GPT play the role of "enabling technologies", opening up new opportunities rather than offering complete, final solutions. For example . . . micro-electronics . . . industries . . . benefit from the surging power of silicon by wrapping around the integrated circuits their own technical advances. (Bresnahan and Trajtenberg 1995, p. 84)

Lipsey et al. (2005) further analyzed the concept of GPT and they identified the following key characteristics:

- Firstly, GPTs are generic products, processes or organizational forms that regardless of their evolution are widely recognized as such. For instance, major technological advances have been applied to the first PC, but it is still recognized as a PC.
- Secondly, GPTs can be both exogenous and endogenous production factors. The electronic computer for example was developed in universities and private firms labs with military funding in order to meet the World War II needs for a machine able to break the enemy's codes and conduct complicated ballistics calculations. So, the early electronic computer was exogenous to the economic system because it lacked economic applications, but endogenous to the military one.
- Additionally, GPT are not usually technology-radical, but use-radical. This means that the expansion of a GPT is gradual over time, but once it reaches the GPT threshold it expands radically and generates impacts on its users.
- The next characteristic is the scope for improvement, as for a technology to become a GPT an evolution process over time is unavoidable.
- A GPT is characterized by the variety of different applications that this technology can have. This is different from just being widely used because the latter does not necessarily include variety in usages.

For instance, the electric bulb is widely used across the economy, but its only use is to produce light.

- GPTs are valuable from the economy point of view because they create spillovers. The complex technological interrelations of a developed economy spread the effect of a GPT beyond the initial users.

- Lastly, many non-GPTs might have some of the above characteristics, and even to a greater extent than a GPT, without being a GPT.

Based on the above detailed approach of Lipsey et al. (2005) and in accordance with Harris (1998), Malecki (2002a) and Atkinson and McKay (2007), there is little doubt that the Internet is a GPT: it is a generic technology, which was gradually developed, but once it reached a specific threshold – privatization in this case – was radically expanded across the economy with a huge variety of different applications, creating spillovers which enabled the emergence of the digital economy. From the economy point of view, such spillovers represent productivity increases in downstream sectors (Helpman 1998; Malecki 2002a) which result in economic growth and development. In simple words, even the least sophisticated aspects of the Internet are essential to the production process. For example, albeit that e-mail technology is more than 20 years old[6] it is still the most broadly used information technology and its significance to the production procedure is beyond doubt (Batty 1997).

However, in order for a GPT to start having such impacts on the economy, investment in infrastructure is needed. To put this simply, electricity required huge investments in production and distribution systems in order for society to benefit from this GPT (Lipsey et al. 2005). In the same way, in order for consumers (users) to take advantage of the Internet, a global-scale infrastructural basis was developed, identified here as the Internet infrastructure.

Before analyzing the Internet infrastructure further, infrastructure as a generic notion is discussed. Infrastructure or otherwise infrastructural capital is identified by neo-classical economics as part of the overall capital stock and is characterized by a blend of publicness and capitalness (Biehl 1991). While the former is linked with non-rivalness and non-excludability – the two goods' properties that cause market failure (Musgrave and Musgrave 1984; Biehl 1991), the latter highlights the significance of infrastructure as a factor of production, admeasured in the capital.[7] Traditionally, infrastructure is mostly related to transport infrastructure. Banister and Berechman (2003, p.35) defined infrastructure as: the "durable capital of the city, region and the country and its location is fixed". Jochimsen (1966; cited in Biehl 1991) suggested a broader definition and also included all types of public services and institutional infrastructure. Hirschman (1958, p. 83) introduced the notion of "social overhead capital", which is defined as:

> comprising those basic services without which primary, secondary, and tertiary productive activities cannot function. In its wider sense, it includes all public services from law and order through education and public health to transportation, communications, and power and water drainage systems. The hard core of the concept can probably be related to transportation and power.

In addition, Kay (1993) attached five characteristics to infrastructure:

- It is usually developed in a network structure and can be approached as a delivery system. In order to achieve this there is a need for considerable interactions among the different infrastructural networks.
- Infrastructure results in the reduction of the production cost for a wide range of products, the production and distribution of which utilizes infrastructural networks.
- It is very common for infrastructural networks to have characteristics of natural monopolies, as infrastructure provision under market economy rules and open competition is costly.
- The necessary capital for infrastructure development is larger than the running cost.
- Infrastructure provision is linked with high sunk cost as most of the cost has been occurred before the provision of any kind of services based on the infrastructure.

Reviewing the above approaches carefully, it seems that the Internet infrastructure fits well with all the above points but one, the publicness. Although this characteristic is not as strong as it used to be after the extensive implementation of public–private joint projects for infrastructure provision, infrastructure still has elements of natural monopoly. For example, transportation networks are developed today as joint projects privately (co-)funded, but there are still monopolistic elements as these networks will be the only ones providing this service in this specific area. However, this is not the case with the Internet. Despite the different regulatory frameworks that affect the Internet function (IP addressing, access to the local loop and so on) most of its hardware is privately developed with local loops being the main exemption. Final users and intermediates (ISPs) have the ability to choose between different hardware owned by different providers, indicating that the market economy has not failed to the same extent as with transport infrastructure in providing the Internet infrastructure.

But what exactly is the Internet infrastructure? In section 2.3.1 two approaches were described: while Gorman and Malecki (2002), Stephenson (1996) and Gilder (2000) strictly link the Internet infrastructure with the Internet's physical layer, Greenstein (2004) also includes in his definition soft elements such as software and human capital. In order to better define the Internet infrastructure, we will again use the OSI, presented previously in section 2.2.5. As mentioned there, while the lower part of the OSI model is related with the physical infrastructure or hardware, the upper part can be identified as the soft infrastructure. Indeed, as mentioned in section 2.2.5, the routing of the IP data packets takes place in the third layer of the OSI model. Additionally, this is the layer where the complete origin–destination paths are formed – contrary to the one-hop links which take place on the second layer. Switches, backbone networks and routers are part of the physical layer of the OSI (layer 1), but function at level 2 (switches) and 3 (backbone and routers) (Gilder 2000). In brief, the Internet physical infrastructure consists of the physical layer of the OSI model plus the two higher layers, which shape the network structure of the Internet.

The remaining four layers of the OSI model contain only soft elements and they form the "infratechnologies" of the Internet infrastructure. This term refers to these technology elements usually identified as industrial standards which include research tools (measurement and test methods), scientific and engineering data, and the technical basis for both physical and functional interface standards such as factory automation and communications (Tassey 1992, 2008). Interestingly enough, these technologies have a quasi-public character, but they are not provided by the state and are usually used freely in order to support the industry. Yet, the four higher layers of the OSI model support the Internet function not by supplying the physical links, but by standardizing the Internet function.

The above physical and non-physical infrastructural elements, which can be alternatively identified as the hardware and the software of the Internet, constitute the Internet infrastructure (Table 2.3). From the geography point of view, what is interesting is the study of the physical layer of the Internet infrastructure, because its distribution is spatially differentiated contrary to the infratechnologies and similarly to more conventional forms of infrastructure such as transport infrastructure. From the regional development point of view, it is interesting to examine whether this spatially differentiated distribution of the infrastructure of the digital economy can result in localized developmental impacts. The next sections provide the theoretical background for such a research investigation.

Table 2.3   The infrastructural approach of the OSI model

OSI	
7. Application 6. Presentation 5. Session 4. Transport	Soft infrastructure / infratechnologies
3. Network 2. Data link 1. Physical	Physical infrastructure

2.5.4   Regional Development and the Internet Infrastructure

This section does not intend to provide an extensive review of the numerous regional development theories, but rather to highlight the way some of the main regional economic development theoretical approaches feature technology and infrastructure. This review will be the supporting theoretical fabric for the empirical investigation for the impacts of the Internet infrastructure on regional economic development, which is presented in Chapter 7.

The starting point for such a review is the neo-classical growth model introduced by Solow (1956). The basic characteristic of this model is the free-market approach, according to which the convergence of regional disparities will happen despite any policy interventions; the latter will only accelerate or decelerate the convergence process (Pike et al. 2006). The main methodological tool is the aggregated production function, which identifies three sources of output growth: capital stock, labor force and technology. The underlying assumptions of unobstructed interregional factor mobility and perfect knowledge about factor prices in all regions explain long-term convergence: capital and labor will migrate towards those regions where their marginal returns are higher (Armstrong and Taylor 2000). For example, a region with high capital stock, because of the assumption of constant returns to scale, will experience an outflow of capital towards regions with lower capital stock, where the capital will be facilitated by higher marginal output. The same adjustment mechanism applies also to the labor force.

In regards to technology, it appears to be disembodied with capital and labor (Pike et al. 2006). This is the reason why the neo-classical model is also known as the model of exogenous growth (Aghion and Howitt 1998). Despite the fact that knowledge in the form of technology was included in the model as one of the three inputs for production, this factor was approached as exogenous and residual:

> Solow discovered that the contributions (the inputs) from the production factors labor and capital to the production process could explain less than 50 per cent of economic growth. The rest *had to be* explained by technology. (Lambooy 2002, p. 1022, emphasis added)

Apart from the above critique on the exogenous character of technology, the neo-classical model was also criticized for the unrealistic assumption about constant returns to scale, an attribute which was not part of the non-equilibrium approaches. Myrdal (1957) introduced the notion of cumulative causation according to which growth is a circular and cumulative process. Increasing returns to scale and agglomeration are strong explanatory factors for the development level and far more realistic assumptions. Infrastructure provision is included in the cumulative process since it tends to agglomerate in the already developed regions, enhancing regional inequalities and polarization in space. Later, other researchers also built upon Mydral's work such as Kaldor (1970) and Dixon and Thirlwall (1975). The latter introduced the homonymic model according to which regional output growth is affected by two factors: growth in the capital–labor ratio and the rate of technological change (Pike et al. 2006).

In regards to the impact of technology on the growth process, the most important progress was the endogenous growth theory, firstly introduced by Romer (1986, 1990). Recognizing the value of technological progress in growth process, the main idea of this approach is the endogenous character of technological change, which is treated as a positive externality (Button 2000). Such models also accept the assumptions for increasing returns to scale and cumulative causation, but they follow a more sophisticated path than Mydral and Kaldor, by accepting the formalities of the neo-classical model such as the production function and the general equilibrium framework. According to this theory, technological knowledge will increase over time with a rate of change shaped by: (1) the volume of the workforce in the knowledge-producing sectors; and (2) by the existing stock of knowledge (Armstrong and Taylor 2000).

Finally, one of the latest advances in the field of economic geography, the "new economic geography" (NEG) introduced by Krugman (1991a, 1991b), is also linked with the infrastructural layer of the digital economy. NEG, or according to others "new geographical economics" (Martin 1999), "might best be described as a 'genre': a style of economic analysis which tries to explain the spatial structure of the economy using certain technical tricks to produce models in which there are increasing returns and markets are characterized by imperfect competition" (Krugman 1998, p. 10). The focal question of NEG is to explain the formation of agglomerations in space (Fujita and Krugman 2004). The central argument behind the NEG is that its main features, which are increasing returns to scale and imperfect competition, are more important factors for trade and spatial specialization than perfect competition and comparative advantage, which are basic elements of neo-classic economics. Most importantly, NEG, following the Marshallian external economies, recognizes spatial structure as a result of the simultaneous act of centripetal and centrifugal forces (Krugman 1998). But what is the role of ICTs in the balance between these opposing forces? According to Maignan et al. (2003) the establishment of the digital economy results in dramatic transport and communications costs reduction, which can lead in a change of the current equilibrium of centrifugal and centripetal forces and can affect the existing spatial structure and economic landscape.

In more detail, it is proposed that ICTs can affect the existing spatial structure by reducing the (Venables 2001; Maignan et al. 2003):

- search and matching cost for trading partners;
- shipping cost of weightless products, which can be codified and digitized;
- control and management costs;
- cost of time in transit due to shipping and communications with distant locations;
- cost of personal interaction[8] and knowledge spillovers;
- commuting cost and transportation cost within the agglomeration (teleworking, teleshopping);
- cost of products replication;
- relocation cost.

However, as mentioned in section 2.4.2, the above cost reductions will not lead to a new spatial equilibrium, in which geography and distance, agglomeration and increasing returns to scale, and the distinction between core and peripheral regions do not matter. The above described transaction cost reductions could lead to further concentration of economic activities in the well-known dominant urban agglomerations, which can be characterized as complex, knowledge-intensive and in need of face-to-face communications. On the other hand, due to the transaction cost reductions, activities which are more footloose and less dependent on (the handshake component of the) face-to-face communications might migrate to peripheral locations and create new clusters, specialized in activities such as back-office services (Venables 2001).

In a nutshell, all the above theoretical approaches agree on the importance of infrastructure and technology for regional economic development. What they do not explain is how exactly the infrastructure of the digital economy can affect development at the regional level. The next section deals with this complex issue.

2.5.5 Conceptual Framework for the Research on the Regional Development Impacts of the Internet Infrastructure

Based on the above analysis the following points can be drawn. Firstly, in the frame of the digital economy and at a national scale, the Internet affects the economy through productivity increase, because of its attribute as GPT and through the required Internet infrastructure. Secondly, at a regional level, all the reviewed theories – despite the different standpoints – agree on the positive impact that infrastructure and technology can generate on the development level. And mostly drawing upon the core of the endogenous growth theory, it seems that technology is a growth driver even at the local level.

The emerging question is whether the physical layer of the infrastructure of the digital economy, the allocation of which is spatially differentiated, can affect economic development at the regional level. It would be easier to comprehend such a question if the discussion was about transportation networks (see for instance Biehl 1991) instead of Internet infrastructure, because of the more tangible nature of transportation networks. Indeed, while transportation infrastructure reduces transaction costs on trade in goods, telecommunications infrastructure lowers transaction costs of trading ideas (Cieślik and Kaniewska 2004). And from the technical point of view, in spite of what the average Internet user experiences, the Internet is not a unique system evenly scattered across the globe, regardless of core or periphery (Gorman and Malecki 2000). And despite being a fairly young large technical system (LTS), at least for commercial usage, users consider it as a black box, something which is usually related to other older urban infrastructure networks such as water and sewerage (Graham and Marvin 2001). In reality, geographic location affects Internet connectivity and the speed at which data can be transmitted and received. The latter is the result of the uneven spatial allocation of the Internet's physical infrastructure (routers, switches, IXP, POP, cables, fiber optic links) across space (Malecki and Moriset 2008). However, the above differences in the quality of Internet connectivity are mostly visible not to end-users, but to large corporations. For instance, the DSL population coverage reached almost 90 percent in Europe in 2006 – a type of Internet connection which is considered as broadband. Such a connection will hardly dissatisfy any average home-user.

However a transnational corporation (TNC), in order to locate a branch in a city, will need a different type of physical infrastructure (you cannot squeeze 500 employees into a domestic usage DSL connection). For the accommodation of such users, a city needs to be served by the highest rank of the Internet's physical infrastructure: not only backbone networks need to have a node in the city-region, but additionally the city-region needs to benefit by direct end-to-end links with the main world cities where the TNCs are agglomerated, providing secure, fast and low-latency connections. Moriset (2003), using Lyons as a case study and after performing a survey with 92 multimedia firms, identified among other factors the value of the installed Internet infrastructure for the firms' location decisions. Cushman and Wakefield (2008) identified a city's quality of telecommunications as the fourth most essential factor for locating a business in Europe, one place higher than the transport links. Graham (2004, p. 10) highlighted the above locational logic by saying that the focus of real estate has changed from "location, location, location" to "location, bandwidth, location" (Malecki and Moriset 2008). And even at a lower spatial level, office buildings need to combine the physical qualities of high ceilings, high power and back-up electricity supplies with nodal positions on fiber networks (Graham 2004). In general, it seems that ICTs not only stimulate the development of urban networks, but they also strengthen the urban economy (Lambooy et al. 2000; Louter 2001; van Oort et al. 2003, cited in Priemus 2007).

Going back to the above question, the answer is yes: there is a rationale in investigating the localized economic impacts of the physical infrastructure of the Internet, because the concentration of this infrastructure in specific locations may affect the economic development of these areas as it will provide better access to the backbone of the digital economy. The concentration of infrastructure such as IBNs and IXPs in a city-region can affect the competitiveness at micro and territorial level: through efficiency and effectiveness effects, Internet infrastructure can result in cost reduction and revenue increase for corporations; and through connectivity effects and the endowment of location factors it can impact the accessibility and the attractiveness of territories (Camagni and Capello 2005). Put simply, Internet infrastructure can both result in attracting new firms (Cornford and Gillespie 1993) in a city-region which can exploit such infrastructure (financial firms, back-office activities, creative industries), and increase the productivity of the existing firms. Additionally, such infrastructure might also result in higher-quality digital services for end-users.

On the other hand, it needs to be highlighted here that the reverse relation might also exist on space: instead of the Internet infrastructure affecting regional economic development, the regional economic development level might also be a pull factor for the distribution of Internet infrastructure. This causality problem is common in regional science and especially in the discussion about the relation between infrastructure and regional economic development. For instance, Banister and Berechman (2003) found mixed empirical evidence: while some researchers conclude that increases in productivity may result in increases of infrastructural capital, others argue the opposite direction in this causal relation. Interestingly enough both causal relations might also co-exist simultaneously. The next section presents evidence from the literature on this issue.

Parenthetically, it should be mentioned here that usually, infrastructure deployment is related to short-term increase in employment due to the necessary large-scale civil engineering works (Banister and Berechman 2003). This is also the case for the Internet networks. Indicatively, Liebenau et al. (2009) suggested that 50 percent of broadband networks deployment cost is due to labor cost. However, this is not the case of the international Internet backbone links because the main excavation and civil engineering costs are allocated for intra-urban networks. Backbone links are developed across existing infrastructural corridors (motorways and railways) or as submarine cables, and consequently the excavation costs as well as the short-term employment impacts are minor and not included in the analysis here (Rutherford et al. 2004).

Schematically, the above discussion is illustrated in Figure 2.5, which forms the conceptual research framework for the regional economic development impacts of the Internet infrastructure. The empirical research based on this framework is covered in Chapter 7.

2.5.6   A Review of Empirical Studies on the Causal Relationship between ICTs and Economic Development

Indeed, the direction of causality between infrastructure provision and economic development was always a complicated problem in regional science. Despite the rather limited interest of geographers, urban planners and regional scientists in telecommunications for reasons highlighted in section 2.3.2, there is a disproportional interest in studying the direction of causality between technology, telecommunications and ICTs. The main motivation for such research is the policy implications of a causal relationship. In more detail, if causality runs from ICTs to economic development, then investments in ICTs can be used as a policy tool for economic activity stimulation. On the contrary, a unidirectional causal relation with causality running from economic development to ICTs will vitiate the efficiency of such policies. On the other hand, a bidirectional causal relationship

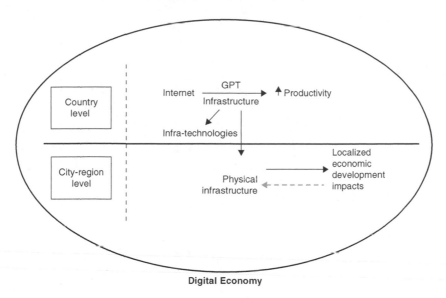

Figure 2.5   Conceptual research framework for the regional economic impacts of the Internet infrastructure

will result in a cyclical phenomenon: policies for ICTs' stimulation will also result in economic development, which in turn will result in further stimulation of ICT demand and supply. However, the lack of a significant causal relationship between ICTs and economic development prevents policymakers from using one of them as a stimulating tool for the increase of the other (Wolde-Rufael 2007).

Early work by Hardy (1980) identified the role of the telephone on economic development using panel data for 60 countries. He concluded that the telephone contributes to economic development, but he did not analyze further the causal relation between these two elements. The main barrier in analyzing the direction of causality between ICTs and economic development is the methodological difficulties. This issue is discussed in detail in section 3.3.3, but it can be briefly mentioned here that simple regression analysis cannot identify the direction of causality between the two geographical phenomena. For such an analysis more advanced econometric methods are necessary, such as the Granger causality test (see section 3.3.3). Despite the complexity of the methods and the rather limited number of scholars in this research area, Table 2.4 reviews a number of studies which have dealt with this problem.

Most of the studies presented here focus on national economic development. However, two papers are concerned with regional economic

Table 2.4 Causality studies on ICTs and economic growth based on Granger causality tests

Reference	Geographic/time extent	Direction of causality
Cronin et al. (1991)	USA; 1958–88	Telecom investment ←→GDP
Cronin et al. (1993a)	USA; 1958–90	Telecom investment → aggregate and sectoral productivity growth
Cronin et al. (1993b)	Pennsylvania, USA; 1965–1991	Telecom investment ←→ employment
Dutta (2001)	15 developing and 15 industrialized countries; 1960–93	Teledensity → per capita GDP Telephones → GDP
Chakraborty and Nandi (2003)	12 Asian countries; 1975–2000	Degree of privatization: High: teledensity ←→ GDP Low: teledensity → GDP
Cieslik and Kaniewsk (2004)	Regional panel data, Poland; 1989–98	Teledensity → retail sales per worker
Shinjo and Zhang (2004)	Japan: 38 industries USA: 31 industries	Japan: productivity growth → ICTs investment USA: ICTs investment ←→ productivity growth
Yoo and Kwak (2004)	Korea; 1965–98	Information technology investment ←→ GDP
Beil et al. (2005)	USA; 1947–96	GDP → Telecommunications investments
Chu et al. (2005)	New Zeland, 1987–2003	ICTs → GDP
Wolde-Rufael (2007)	USA; 1947–96	GDP ←→ Telecommunications investments
Shiu and Lam (2008)	Regional panel data, China; 1978–2004	GDP → Teledensity/penetration rate High income/teledensity/penetration: Teledensity/penetration → GDP

Source: Adapted from Shiu and Lam (2008, p. 707).

development and ICTs. Additionally, none of the above studies is concerned with the Internet infrastructure. On the contrary, most of them use as proxy for ICTs the provision of more traditional indicators such as fixed telephone lines per 100 habitants. The above observations illustrate the importance of the current study in identifying the regional economic development impacts of Internet infrastructure, as such research questions are still emerging in the literature.

Nonetheless, the most important finding of the table is the opposing results of the different studies. Almost half of them concluded a bidirectional relationship between the different measures of ICTs and economic development. Slightly less, but still a significant number, of studies found a unidirectional relationship with ICTs causing economic development. Interestingly enough, only a few studies came up with a reverse causal relationship where ICTs are pulled by economic development. This wide range of results on the causal relationship between ICTs and economic development signifies the need for further exploring this research area in regards to the Internet infrastructure.

2.6   EPILOGUE

This chapter's main objective is to critically present and analyze the relevant literature in order to create the theoretical framework for approaching the research questions of this book. First of all, a brief technical description of the Internet was provided. Such technical knowledge is vital for this research: despite the geographic orientation of this study's research questions, there is a need for the reader to become familiar with the technical nature of the Internet.

Then, the three main theoretical pillars of this study were explored. Firstly, the new and emerging field of the Internet geography was introduced. Secondly, the world city literature was analyzed. This research field is highly related to the research subject as the Internet infrastructure facilitates the global city process. Thirdly, the infrastructural character of the Internet as well as a conceptual framework for analyzing the regional economic development impacts of the Internet infrastructure was introduced.

The above three theoretical pillars support and are directly linked with the empirical aspects of this research (Table 2.5). While the Internet geography pillar is linked with all of the four empirical chapters, the world cities literature is mostly linked with the comparison between the Internet backbone and the aviation network (Chapter 5) and with the descriptive network analysis of the IBN (Chapter 4); the explanatory analysis of the socio-economic factors that shape the Internet backbone distribution in

Table 2.5　　*Links between theoretical pillars and research elements of this book*

Theoretical pillars	Chapter 4 Descriptive (network) analysis	Chapter 5 Comparison with aviation network	Chapter 6 Explanatory analysis of the (unequal) distribution of the Internet	Chapter 7 Internet infrastructure and regional economic development: a causality analysis
Internet geography	++	+	++	+
World cities	++	++		
Internet infrastructure and regional development			+	++

Europe (Chapter 6) is directly linked to the Internet geography field, but also to the third pillar of this book; and finally the last empirical chapter (Chapter 7), where the regional economic impacts of the Internet infrastructure are evaluated, mostly draws upon the Internet infrastructure and regional economic development, but also upon the Internet geography as well. Before moving on to these research chapters, the main methodological issues are discussed in Chapter 3.

3. Methodology and research framework

3.1 INTRODUCTION

The aim of this chapter is to describe and justify the utilization of specific methods and data sources used in this book in order to address the research questions defined in Chapter 1. Firstly, the lack of data in the field of the Internet geography is addressed as well as the research choices made in order to overcome this problem. Additionally, in section 3.2 the other data sources used in this study are discussed. Section 3.3 describes the quantitative methods used for approaching the research questions. While section 3.3.2 focuses on the methods which deal with the network topology of the research subject, section 3.3.3 describes and justifies the utilization of statistical and econometrical modeling. Lastly, section 3.4 summarizes this chapter and presents the research framework of this study, which is the fundamental for the empirical analysis which takes place in the following four chapters.

3.2 DATA

As identified in Chapter 2, there are two main difficulties in approaching the physical layer of the Internet infrastructure: firstly, the invisible character of the infrastructural network; and secondly, the lack of data due to confidentiality reasons. Various approaches have been introduced in the literature in order to overcome the latter and analyze the physical layer of the Internet infrastructure and, more specifically, the main core of this infrastructure, the Internet backbone networks (IBNs). In the early stages of the field of Internet geography, researchers combined the few free sources available at this time and they constructed databases for the US intercity Internet backbone links. The main sources were the *Boardwatch Magazine* and its Boardwatch Directory of Internet Service Providers and also the Cooperative Association for Internet Data Analysis (CAIDA 2009; for example see Moss and Townsend 2000; Malecki 2002a; Gorman and Malecki 2002). However, the former ceased publication in the early

2000s and the latter stopped updating the relevant research project called Mapnet (CAIDA 2009).

Apart from these freely available data sources, two other data sources for the physical infrastructure of the Internet were used over the (short) history of the emerging field of the Internet geography, and both of them were private consultants: TeleGeography (2007) and KMI Research Group (2001). The former has provided telecommunications analyses and specialized datasets over the last 30 years (TeleGeography 2011). It has been used in various papers and it can be said that it is the usual data source when the discussion turns to data about IBNs (Devriendt et al. 2008; Evans-Cowley et al. 2002; Gorman and Kulkarni 2004; Gorman and Malecki 2002; Malecki 2002a, 2004; Prufer and Jahn 2007; Townsend 2003). The second consultant provided similar data and has been used as a source for ESPON (2005b), Rutherford et al. (2004, 2005) and Tranos and Gillespie (2009). However, KMI Research Group no longer exists as a firm.

Thus, nowadays the only available source for secondary data in regards to the IBNs is TeleGeography. Among others, TeleGeography provides data for international intercity backbone links, which function at level 3 of the Open Systems Interconnection (OSI) model. This data refers to the Internet bandwidth (capacity), but not to the Internet traffic (capacity usage) and represents point-to-point rather than end-to-end relationships. As analyzed in section 2.2 of Chapter 2, Internet data may travel between any two points anywhere on the network, but the Internet bandwidth shows only the routes available for each individual hop between those points. As TeleGeography highlights (2007, p. 1), "end-to-end traffic data are based on an aggregate of individual usage, while point-to-point bandwidth indicators aggregate IP [Internet Protocol] capacity logically provisioned over a physical network". Briefly, it can be said that the TeleGeography dataset has the following advantages: (1) it is more recent – up to 2006; (2) it includes data for network capacity; (3) it includes extra-European links; and (4) it is a longitudinal dataset containing observations over time.

As expected, the network capacity and usage are not unrelated. By assuming that the market economy works efficiently, supply meets demand and consumers (users in this case) act rationally, then from the supply side carriers would install enough bandwidth to meet the demand for this infrastructure, and from the demand side users would pay to use as much bandwidth as they would really need. Therefore, all the installed bandwidth would be used and as long as the data exchange reflects the interaction between two cities, then the installed bandwidth would indicate the interaction between these two cities.[9] But in fact, most installed bandwidth is unused. For example, in 2004 only 3 percent of the total bandwidth capacity in Frankfurt was lit and by the end of 2006 only 14 percent of the total capacity of major submarine cables was being used (Roberts 2006). Before rejecting the previous argumentation as a market failure, the special characteristics of this infrastructure should be considered. The main cost in IBN investment is digging trenches in order to install ducts, rather than laying fiber once the ducts are installed. In other words, unlike the case of transport infrastructure, the main cost is the network's first installation and not its expansion in terms of extra fiber cables (placed in existing ducts) and bandwidth. Therefore, the volume of the lit and the unlit or in other words "dark" fiber, as well as the ISPs' philosophy of "build it and they will come" (Youtie 2000), indicate the expectations about current and future demand for intercity links.

In order to obtain the above data, TeleGeography integrated three research methods:

> confidential surveys, informal discussions, and follow-up interviews were conducted with network engineering and planning staff of major backbones. [Additionally] standard and slightly modified network discovery tools were deployed from a large number of locations to gather an extensive data set on network topology, which was then parsed for identifiable characteristics, including geographic location. Finally, additional public and private information sources were consulted to verify and add to the data already in place. (ibid.)

Based on the above, on its long history, but also on the fact that nowadays TeleGeography is the only provider of secondary data on the Internet infrastructure, the main data used for this book is a dataset produced by TeleGeography on the international intercity Internet backbone links for the period 2001–06. It should be highlighted here that an individual researcher would not be able to build such a dataset on her own, mostly because of lack of trust on behalf of the carriers. As mentioned above, the main reason for the lack of data in this field is the confidentiality of such data. Therefore, the strategic advantage of TeleGeography is that it managed to overcome this difficulty over the years and can now accumulate and provide such data. It should be noted here that TeleGeography's data is aggregated, so the least amount of detail possible is revealed for individual carriers. This specification is not a problem for the needs of this study as the focus here is not the individual Internet backbone providers, but instead their aggregated capacity, in order to examine the urban economic geography of these networks.

While a more detailed description of the dataset takes place in Chapter 4 with the first analysis of the data, the aim here is to provide a brief description of the data and mostly justify its value added in approaching the research questions of this study. Initially, the data was provided in the form of a table with the international intercity links and the total capacity of these links for the years 2001–2006. The first step was to link the European cities with NUTS 3[10] regions. In the cases where more than one city of a NUTS 3 region was connected with at least one IBN, these cities were summarized in a way that no NUTS 3 region has more than one representation in the database. This database cleaning process under-lies the assumption that a NUTS 3 region is the nearest statistical unit to the notion of city-region described in section 2.4.6, and it means that all the Internet backbone nodes in this region facilitate the same urban area. The choice of NUTS 3 instead of NUTS 2 was made as the former has a stronger urban character since the latter includes a more extended area. Two processes took place after this. The first one was to build a network topology based on the above links over the period 2001–2006.[11] This process included intensive data manipulation in order to bridge the tabular form of the initial data with the needs of a network topology. The latter is the medium to apply network analysis. A basic description of the main theoretical elements of network analysis and complex network analysis is presented in section 3.3.2.

The second process was to build a database linking the results of the network analysis, which refer to the nodes of the network (city-regions) with socio-economic indicators, using again the NUTS 3 regions as the spatial unit. The main sources for such socio-economic variables were Eurostat (2011) and ESPON (2011). Such a database is fundamental for the explanatory analysis presented in Chapter 6 and the analysis of the regional economic impacts of the Internet infrastructure, which takes place in Chapter 7. However, in order to exploit to full capacity the exist-ing data and, more importantly, to obtain as robust results as possible, instead of creating a simple cross-sectional database, a panel dataset was built. A brief methodological description of this takes place in section 3.3.3.

Additionally, two other datasets are used in this study. The first repre-sents aviation flows and it is used in Chapter 5, where a topological com-parison of the Internet backbone and the aviation network in Europe is made, following the argument presented in Chapter 2 that Internet infra-structure and aviation comprise the first layer of the space of flows. The aviation data comes from the International Civil Aviation Organization (ICAO), which is a specialized agency of the United Nations (UN) setting "standards and regulations necessary for aviation safety, security, effic-iency and regularity, as well as for aviation environmental protection" (ICAO 2008). This dataset also refers to the capacity of international intercity links, but the main measure here is annual intercity passenger flows. The aviation data was initially provided by ICAO in a semi-tabular form (html web pages). So, the first step was to create actual tables with bilateral links, and then based on this and in a way similar to the TeleGeography data, the network topology of the international intercity aviation links of the European cities was built. Effort was spent to keep the two different networks as compatible as possible in order to facilitate the topological comparison.

3.3   METHODOLOGICAL ISSUES

3.3.1   General

Although the focus of this book is not to introduce methodological advancements, the complexity of the research questions and the diversity of the datasets to be analyzed led to an innovative mix of dissimilar quantitative methods. All the empirical analysis of this book is based on merging network analyses and econometric modeling. The first addresses the network topology of the Internet backbone and that is based on concepts and methods from complex network analysis. The outcome of this analysis bridges topological with geographic space as it provides the basis for the econometric modeling which is used to explain the spatial distribution and the regional economic impacts that this infrastructure might generate. The software package UCINET (Borgatti et al. 2002) was employed for complex network analysis, while the statistical and econometric analysis was based on STATA. The rest of this section is dedicated to further analyzing these two methodological blocks.

3.3.2   Complex Network Analysis: A Brief Review

Because of their complex network topology, Internet backbone and aviation networks can be approached using concepts from complex network analysis. Their complex network nature is well established in the literature (Gorman and Kulkarni 2004; Faloutsos et al. 1999; Schintler et al. 2005; Gastner and Newman 2005; Guimera et al. 2005; Amaral et al. 2000). Complex network analysis focuses on large-scale networks with topologies complicated enough not to be easy to understand at a glance (Fosco 2004). More specifically, when the discussion turns to complex networks, what is important is not the behavior of the single actor, but the information of "who is connected to whom" (Latora et al. 2003, p. 2). The main elements of networks are the nodes (known also as vertices) and the links (edges). Networks were always part of graph theory, whose origins can be traced back to the eighteenth century and to Leonhard Euler's work on small graphs with high degrees of regularity. Thus, initially graph theory was focused on graphs in which all the network nodes have the same degree, or in other words all vertices are connected with the same number of other vertices. Later, twentieth-century graph theory was influenced by advances in mathematics and statistics and became more algorithmic (Albert and Barabási 2002; Bonarich 2007). Network analysis went a step further with the introduction of random networks (RN) by two Hungarian mathematicians, Paul Erdös and Alfréd Rényi, which refer to large-scale networks with no obvious structure (Erdös and Rényi 1959). The distribution of vertices degree follows a Poisson distribution, which means that the majority of the vertices on the network have the same number of links and they are found near to the average degree $<k>$; vertices that deviate from this are rare (Reggiani and Vinciguerra 2007; Albert and Barabási 2002; Fosco 2004). RN received a lot of attention for decades after their introduction. The main motivation for further evolving the network analysis, though, was the question of whether this model can represent the real-world networks such as the Internet or the cell (Albert and Barabási 2002).

In the following decades, complex networks played a more important role in different fields, from social science to biology. Albert and Barabási (2002) indicate four different reasons for this: first, the digitization of data in many different fields and the abundance of large databases enabled scientists to approach different real-world systems from the network analysis perspective; second, advances in computer science and in computing power enabled scientists to handle very large databases, which represent real-world systems; third, the looseness between different disciplinary boundaries gave network analysts the opportunity to use real-world network databases from many different fields; and finally (and maybe because of all the above) reductionist approaches lost ground in favor of holistic research approaches, which try to understand the system as a whole.

The second milestone in the evolution of complex network theories is the "small world effect" and the Watts and Strogatz (1998) "small world networks" (SW), no matter that in order to move from the former to the latter 30 years have passed. The small world effect refers to the well-known study of Milgram (1967), according to which there is an average distance[12] of six degrees (known as six degrees of separation) between most potential pairs of people in the United States. In other worlds, the small world effect is a characteristic of numerous networks and identifies the short average distance among network vertices, enabling the actors of a network to reach all the rest within a few steps (Reggiani and Vinciguerra 2007). It has been found that most real-world networks such as the Internet, the actors in Hollywood, the chemicals in a cell and so on are characterized by short average distances. However, the small world effect is a structural characteristic rather than an organizing principle and even RN networks are characterized by short average distances (Albert and Barabási 2002). Watts and Strogatz (1998) developed this attribute further by introducing the SW model. The basic feature of this model is the coexistence of short average distance with high clustering coefficient. The latter, as we will see later, is a measure of a node's cliquishness (Latora and Marchiori 2001). In fact, SW networks are located between regular and random networks; they are highly clustered like regular lattices, but they also have small distances like random networks (Latora and Marchiori 2002). In addition, their degree distribution is quite similar with the RN networks with a peak value $<k>$ which decays exponentially for large k (Albert and Barabási 2002). So, a SW network can be approached as a set of clusters of nodes, which are highly connected at a local level, but in which there are also some links which span the entire network, linking the furthest clusters. In other words, an actor in such a network can benefit from the high local connectivity but can also be easily transferred to a remote cluster using the intra-cluster links, and then take advantage of the high local connectivity in this domain (Batty 2001).

A common characteristic of the RN and SW models is that the probability of finding a highly connected vertex decreases exponentially. This means that the highly connected vertices, which are known as hubs, are practically absent in RN and SW models. And here lies the third milestone of the complex network theory; the introduction of the scale-free (SF) networks, which are characterized by the existence of a few highly connected hubs and a vast majority of less connected vertices (Barabási and Albert 1999). The term "scale-free" refers to the fact that their vertex degree distribution follows a power law distribution regardless the observation scale (Reggiani and Vinciguerra 2007). Such networks are being formed according to two mechanisms: growth and preferential attachment (Albert and Barabási 2002). The former refers to an attribute which is common in many real-world networks, that is, the expansion of networks over time by adding new vertices and edges. The second mechanism refers to the fact that this growth is not equally dispersed across vertices. Highly connected vertices are more likely to be preferred by the new vertices. Because of preferential attachment, a vertex that acquires more connections than another one will increase its connectivity at a higher rate; thus, an initial difference in the connectivity between two vertices will increase further as the network grows, indicating a "rich get richer" phenomenon. The probability Π that a new vertex will be connected to a vertex i depends on the degree k_i of the vertex i:

$$\prod(k_i) = \frac{k_i}{\sum_j k_j} \text{ (Barabási and Albert 1999)} \qquad (3.1)$$

The above mechanisms resulted in networks with vertex degree distribution which are governed by power law. So, the probability $P(k)$ that a vertex has a degree k, or in other words interacts with k other vertices, decays with a power law:

$$P(k) \approx k^{-\gamma}, with 2 < \gamma < 3 \text{ (Barabási and Albert 1999)} \qquad (3.2)$$

In order to replicate the power-law distribution present in many real-world networks, the above two mechanisms should be present simultaneously (Albert and Barabási 2002). It should be highlighted here that initially the SF model included only the above mechanisms for networks evolving. The importance of this model in the multidisciplinary field of complex networks is indicated by the numerous studies published later on SF networks. As a result, more realistic approaches regarding networks evolution were introduced. According to them, a network can be changed by any combination among the following four events: addition or removal of a vertex and addition or removal of an edge. Nevertheless, in real-life networks the above happen simultaneously resulting in a phenomenon identified as "rewiring" (for an extensive review see Albert and Barabási 2002).

Table 3.1 summarizes the basic characteristic of the above three network models. If we were to compare them, it could be said that both RN and SW have short average distances, but RN cannot be included in SW because they lack the high clustering coefficient (Reggiani and Vinciguerra 2007). In addition, SF networks share the short average distance and the high cluster coefficient of SW ones, but the SW are not characterized by scale-free distribution (Gorman and Kulkarni 2004). Or, in other words, all scale-free networks are believed to display small world properties while all small world networks are not necessarily scale-free (Sen et al. 2003). Amaral et al. (2000), further analyzing the above, suggested that because of SF networks' small world properties, SF networks are also part of SW. And they continue by distinguishing SW in three subcategories: (1) SF networks with a power law degree distribution; (2) "broad-scale" networks, which can be recognized as truncated SF networks, which have a power law regime in their degree distribution followed by a sharp cut-off, such as an exponential or a Gaussian tail decay; (3) single-scale networks with an exponential or Gaussian degree distribution.

Another important element of the above network models is their tolerance against faults and attacks. According to relevant studies (Albert

Table 3.1   Overview of main complex network characteristics

	Physical measures		Statistical measures	
	Average shortest path	Clustering Coefficient	Vertex degree distribution	Exponent
RN	Short	Low	Poisson	
SW	Short (scales as $L \sim lnL$)	High	Similar to RN, decaying exponentially for large set of vertices	
SF	Very short (scales as $L \sim lnlnN$)	High, but it decreases with the increasing of the network size N	Power law	$2 < \gamma < 3$

Source: Adapted from Reggiani and Vinciguerra (2007).

et al. 2000; Albert and Barabási 2002; Crucitti et al. 2004; Li et al. 2005; Audestad 2007), SF networks are characterized by high tolerance in randomly connected nodes failure. On the contrary, such networks are vulnerable in attacks to specific vertices. More specifically, Albert et al. (2000) showed that the average short distance of a SF network, which is a proxy of the network's efficiency, remains the same even if a randomly selected 5 percent of vertices fail. This happens because of SF networks' severe inhomogeneous connectivity distribution, which occur because of the power law degree distribution. In plain English, because only a few of the nodes in a SF network enjoy high connectivity and the rest are less connected, there is a small probability that among the nodes that fail, which presumably are randomly chosen, some of the highly connected ones are included. This is not the case for random networks. Because of their homogeneity, which is reflected in the fact that most of the vertices have similar degree, random nodes' failures have significant effects on networks' efficiency. On the other hand, when a SF network is under attack, which presumably will target its mostly connected nodes, it is more vulnerable than homogenous random networks because of its heterogeneity. If 5 percent of its most connected vertices are removed, the SF network's average short path is doubled. However, RN networks have the same behavior both when randomly selected nodes are down and when the network is under attack because of their homogeneity (Albert et al. 2000).

Usually, the empirical verification of a SF network is limited by studying its vertex degree distribution and assuming that because it follows a power law the rest of SF networks attributes are present. However, Li et al. (2005) proved that there is a great variety of networks whose vertex degree distributions follow the same power law, but they are characterized by different quantitative and qualitative attributes. In order to better define the SF character, Li et al. (2005) introduced the *s* metric:

$$s(g) = \sum\nolimits_{(i,j) \in \varepsilon} d_i d_j \qquad (3.3)$$

where d_i and d_j are the degrees of any nodes *i* and *j* respectively, which are connected by a link and ε is the array of all the links present in the graph *s*. In order to compare the *s* metric of different networks, the indicator is normalized by the s_{max} value, as described in Li et al. (2005). This indicator measures the hub structure of the network and the higher the value of the *s* indicator is, the more common it is for highly connected nodes to be connected with similar highly connected ones. So, in order to confirm the robust yet fragile structure of the SF networks it is not enough to identify the existence of some highly connected nodes and a vast majority of less connected ones, as it is reflected by the power law degree distribution. The importance of the highly connected nodes in holding the network together is identified by the interconnection of the highly connected nodes together. For instance, if a high-degree vertex, which is only connected with low-degree vertices, is removed from the network then the worst-case scenario is that some of the low-degree nodes, which enjoyed connectivity only through the removed hub, will be disconnected. On the contrary, if a highly connected node, which is connected with a similar degree vertex, is removed from the network, the results might be more severe and affect the efficiency of the whole graph because of the higher structural importance of such a node. Accordingly, the power law vertex degree distribution cannot prove on its own the existence of highly connected hubs, which play the role of the Achilles heel for SF networks. On the contrary, such nodes appear in a network with a power law vertex degree distribution, only when this network is characterized by high *s* value.

To sum up, Albert and Barabási (2002) suggested three key elements of complex networks: the small average distances and the high cluster coefficient, which are related to the small world phenomenon, as well as the vertices degree distribution. In addition, the *s* metric is equally important in order to identify the importance of hubs. The above are empirically studied in Chapters 4 and 5 for the Internet backbone and aviation networks.

3.3.3 Statistical and Econometric Techniques

The second block of methodologies employed in this book is based on modeling exercises using econometric techniques. This analysis is directly linked with the topological analysis of the network space, as the main focus of the modeling exercises is the derivatives of the network analysis which are allocated at the city-region level.

There are two main themes for the analysis of which such methodologies were adopted: (1) the explanatory analysis of the spatial distribution of the IBNs across European city-regions which is presented in Chapter 6; and (2) the analysis of the impacts that the Internet infrastructure, as it is reflected in the IBNs, can generate on the economic development of the city-regions in Europe which is presented in Chapter 7. In order to approach the above, specific econometric techniques have been adopted.

According to Wooldridge (2003, p. 1) "econometrics is based upon the development of statistical methods for estimating economic relationships, testing economic theories and evaluating and implementing government and business policy". In other words, econometrics is the social science which combines tools from economic theory, mathematics and statistics in order analyze economic phenomena (Goldberger 1964). Common to the econometric analysis of Chapters 6 and 7 is the utilization of panel data. The latter refers to those datasets which apart from having a cross-section dimension also include time as a second dimension of the dataset. In simple words, while a cross-section dataset only includes data for the different cross-section units – city-regions in our case – for a number of variables, a panel dataset also includes different observations for the same variables and for these cross-section units over time (Wooldridge 2003). In the case of this book, the panel data specification is chosen contrary to a cross-sectional approach as it enables us to assess the impacts of the Internet infrastructure over time. As was described in Chapter 2 in the discussion about the productivity paradox, it might take time for the impacts of a specific technology to become visible. The panel data specification provides the necessary framework to assess the impact of the infrastructural capital installed in year *t-n* on the economic development level of year *t* across a set of city-regions. What is more, panel data also enables the researcher to control for omitted variable bias and therefore panel data is a better methodological choice in explaining the spatial distribution and analyzing the impact of the Internet infrastructure on the economic development of city-regions. In order to do so, panel data regression models are developed in Chapters 6 and 7. These models are directly linked with the network analysis which takes place in Chapters

4 and 5 as the main variables for these models are the different centrality measures arising from this analysis.

Firstly, the explanatory analysis of the spatial distribution of the IBNs is based on a combination of multivariate panel models. The first one is a probit model which predicts the probability that a city-region is connected with at least one IBN. Based on the relevant literature, a set of explanatory variables is constructed to test a range of hypotheses explaining regional connectedness. The dependent variable in this model is a binary variable including all the NUTS 3 regions and indicating whether a region is connected or not with an IBN. This variable has been constructed based on the results of network analysis presented in Chapter 4.

The second model utilized in Chapter 6 is a simple spatial interaction model (SIM), which test the impact of physical distance on the installed capacity between any two connected city-regions. The underlying hypothesis is that the tyranny of distance is valid in the cyber place (CP) as well, and the capacity of the Internet infrastructure installed between places is negatively affected by distance, following the Newtonian argumentation. Both of these models are estimated using panel data regressions. The model specifications as well as more details econometric discussion can be found in Chapter 6.

The dependent variable for these models is always the economic development level, and in addition a number of control socio-economic variables are also included in the models.

Secondly, in Chapter 7, the analysis focuses on exploring the direction of causality between the Internet infrastructure and regional economic development. As was illustrated in Figure 2.4, the link between infrastructure provision and regional economic development usually goes hand in hand with a causality problem. In other words, it is not always clear which the direction of causality is, and whether the infrastructural capital is the cause or the result of economic development. The panel data specification contributes in addressing this phenomenon, something which is not possible with simple cross-section data. More specifically, recent developments in panel data analysis enable the application of the Granger causality test (Granger 1969), which was initially introduced for time-series,[13] on panel data (Hoffmann et al. 2005).

Such a test enables the researcher to investigate the direction of causality between two variables. Briefly, the Granger test is based on a model where the dependent variable y is regressed against k lagged values of y and k lagged values of x. Based on such a model the null hypothesis can be tested according to which x does not cause y. If the test proved to be significant then the null hypothesis can be rejected and then it could be concluded that x causes y (Hood III et al. 2008). This latter means that y

is better predicted if all the information (both the lagged values of y and x) is included in the model than when the lagged values of x are excluded (Hurlin and Venet 2003). In order to evaluate both potential directions of causality, the above model is used twice, interchanging the dependent with the independent variable in order to evaluate the impact of Internet centrality on economic development, but also the impact of economic development on the centrality of the city-regions. The value of using panel data for the Granger causality test instead of time series is twofold, in addition to the omitted variable bias described above (Shiu and Lam 2008): not only does panel data provide more degrees of freedom than conventional time series, but it also takes account of the heterogeneity among the cross-section units. The latter is very important for a study in the field of geography because the direction of causality can be differentiated across the cross-section units. Put simply, the Internet backbone centrality might have a significant impact on economic development in some city-regions while in others it might not or even, for some cases, the Internet backbone centrality might instead be the result of economic development.

In general, the Granger causality test appears to be the most widely used method for empirically assessing causal relationships in the field of regional science, but also in econometrics (Erdil and Yetkiner 2009; Bronzini and Piselli 2009; Hoffmann et al. 2005; Chamberlain 1982; Florens and Mouchart 1982; Hood III et al. 2008). Even more specifically, it has been widely used in defining the causality between telecommunications and (regional) economic development (see Table 2.4 in Chapter 2). It is preferred by econometricians as an empirical method which can be easily implemented at least for time-series, where commercial econometric packages include specific ready-made routines (Hoover 2001). However, the implementation of the Granger causality test for panel data is a rather more complicated process as no commercial econometric package to date includes such a routine.

3.4 RESEARCH FRAMEWORK

The aim of the last section of this chapter is to review the above discussion about the methods and the data used in order to answer the research question stated in Chapter 1. In order to address the three research questions of this study two diverse blocks of quantitative methods (complex network analysis on the one hand and econometric modeling on the other) and four main data sources (TeleGeography 2007; ICAO 2008; Eurostat 2011; ESPON 2011) are utilized in the following four chapters. This research

Table 3.2　Research framework

Research question	RQ1	RQ2	RQ3
Methods	complex network analysis	Probit models; spatial interaction models; panel data regressions	Granger causality test for panel data
Data sources	TeleGeography (2007) ICAO (2008)	TeleGeography (2007), Eurostat (2011), ESPON (2011)	TeleGeography (2007), Eurostat (2011), ESPON (2011)
Theoretical pillars (from Chapter 2)	IG, WC	IG, WC	IIRD, IG, WC
Chapters	4, 5	6	7

RQ1: How is the Internet infrastructure allocated across the European city-regions?
RQ2: Which are the geographic and socio-economic factors that shape the distribution of the Internet infrastructure across the European city-regions?
RQ3: What are the impacts that the Internet infrastructure can generate on the economic development of the city-regions in Europe?

Note: IG: Internet geography; WC: World cities; IIRD: Internet infrastructure and regional development.

process is supported by the three theoretical pillars of this study as discussed in Chapter 2. The above elements are summarized in Table 3.2, which presents the research framework of this book.

4. The network nature of the Internet infrastructure

4.1 INTRODUCTION

The main objective of this chapter is to analyze the Internet backbone networks (IBNs) and understand how European cities are interconnected through this infrastructure. More specifically, in this chapter the initial exploration and mapping of the international Internet backbone links, which enable Internet protocol (IP) communication between European cities, takes place. In addition, network analysis measures will reveal the different roles different European cities perform in the Internet function, at least from the physical infrastructure point of view. Although the outcome of this chapter's analysis is important on its own, it will also facilitate the empirical analysis of the following chapters.

This chapter starts with a short description of the data used here. As the overall data presentation took place in section 3.2, a brief but more detailed and targeted for the needs of this chapter description is presented here. Then, basic descriptive statistics and mapping of the Internet backbone links take place. Afterwards, network analysis methods are applied in order to better analyze the role of the European cities in the IBN and to take a first glance at the geography of the Internet infrastructure. Different centralization and centrality measures are applied in order to explore the cities' role as nodes of such networks. The synopsis of the above indicators is made using cluster analysis, resulting in a taxonomy of European cities regarding their role in the network. Then, complex network theory is used in order to explore whether the IBN fits with the well-known theoretical network models. This chapter ends with some first conclusions.

4.2 DATA DESCRIPTION

The Internet backbone dataset utilized for the needs of this book refers to all international backbone connections present in European cities for each year of the period 2001–06. It represents Internet links, which follow the IP and they are characterized by capacity counted in Megabits per second (Mbps). In reality, the links included in the database are aggregations of the different fiber links installed and managed by different internet backbone providers for each pair of cities. For example, the 58 fiber optic circuits that connected London with Paris in 2006 were managed by 35 Internet backbone providers but they are represented in the database by a unique link, the capacity of which is equal to the sum of all the different backbone links (TeleGeography 2007). Comparing the above network with the overall global network, it becomes apparent that intra-country connections and non-European connections are missing from the available dataset. For example, connections between London and Manchester and Tokyo and New York are missing, while connections between London and New York and London and Paris are present in the dataset. This limitation is due to data unavailability. In terms of geography, the absence of non-European international links prevents us from discussing the importance of cities outside Europe because we are only aware of a fraction of their total connectivity (that is, their connectivity with Europe and not with the rest of the world). In addition, the absence of domestic connections prevents us from looking into the cities which only have domestic roles and direct the analyses on cities with international importance in the IBN. However, because of the structure of this network, cities which are important at an international level are also important at the domestic level because they act as hubs for the whole country, enabling the rest of a country's cities to obtain universal Internet connectivity through them.

In order to further analyze the data, a sub-network of the backbone connections including only the intra-European links for the six years was subtracted from the initial one. For example, links such as London–New York were removed, leaving networks with only intra-European links. The reason behind such an extraction is to focus on cities' importance at the European level, without taking into consideration their non-European connections. However, it should be highlighted that the interpretation of such a subtracted network is not always straightforward. For instance, it is well known that because of the dominance of the US in the development of the Internet, a significant part of the intra-European Internet traffic was routed through the US (Townsend 2003). By extracting the links that connect Europe with the US, the infrastructure which facilitated such transatlantic Internet packet flows is missed, diminishing the importance of the US cities in global (and even in European) Internet function and also overestimating the importance and the autonomy of European cities. However, taking the above scalar limitations into consideration, we can study the European part of the above global infrastructural network and the way it interconnects the European cities. And by adding the extra-

European links in the analysis when needs be, the big, universal picture of this infrastructural network can be approached.

Another point is whether the network is weighted or not. For the case of the IBN, the edges are valued with the actual bandwidth of the link (or the summation of the bandwidth of all the different fiber optic links between two cities). However, it is very common in network analysis to use binary edges instead of weighted ones. The reason for this is to simplify the network and to highlight its structural characteristics. In this case, the value 1 depicts an active link, while a value 0 indicates the absence of a connection between two nodes in an adjacency table. For the needs of this study, both network versions have been developed and are used when appropriate.

4.3   DESCRIPTIVE STATISTICAL ANALYSIS

The above process resulted in two different extractions of the same network (for all the cities and for only the European ones) and in two different versions of them (binary and weighted) for each year of the period 2001–06. Figures 4.1 and 4.2 present the Internet backbone links among European cities for 2001 and 2006 respectively. The links are classified based on how many standard deviations above the mean of all the links the capacity is. In 2001, the links with the highest capacity (bandwidth greater than 2.5 standard deviations above the mean) connected London with Paris, Brussels and Amsterdam, Frankfurt with Paris and Amsterdam, and Amsterdam with Brussels. It is not coincidental that these links, which are the peaks or otherwise the outliers of the backbone links distribution in Europe, are concentrated in Europe's pentagon.[14] The only backbone link, whose capacity was more than 1.5 standard deviations greater than the mean and was outside of Europe's core, was the link between Stockholm and Copenhagen. Light grey color depicts the links which are between 0.5 and 1.5 standard deviations above the average. Again, most of them are found in Europe's pentagon but also in the two corridors connecting the Scandinavian countries with Western Europe. This class's links towards Central and Eastern Europe are rare and only a few of them terminate in Vienna, Budapest and Prague. Interesting is the vast amount of low backbone links that crosses Central Europe and most of Germany, and terminate in Eastern Europe and, mainly, Vienna. Regarding Europe's western edge, Madrid is the main gateway city, since it is the only city in the area which has at least one link of higher than the average capacity.

In 2006, the spatial allocation of the intra-European backbone links is

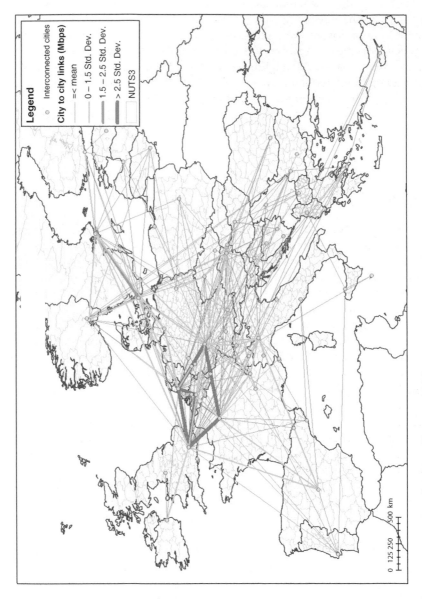

Legend

○ Interconnected cities

City to city links (Mbps)

— =< mean
— 0 – 1.5 Std. Dev.
— 1.5 – 2.5 Std. Dev.
— > 2.5 Std. Dev.

☐ NUTS3

0 125 250   500 km

Figure 4.1   International IBN in Europe, 2001

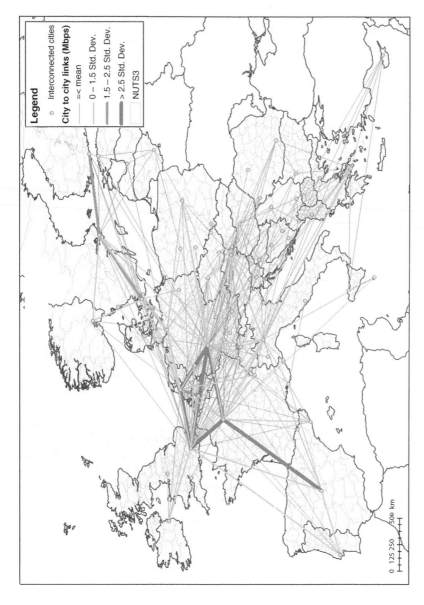

Figure 4.2 International IBN in Europe, 2006

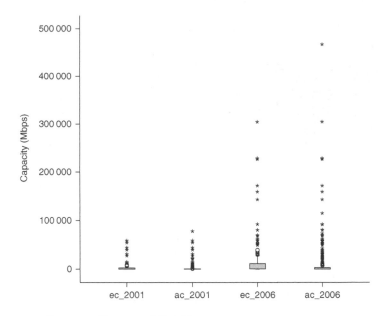

Note: ec = European cities, ac = all the cities.

Figure 4.3 *Box-plots for backbone links*

rather changed. The outlier backbone links are still focused in the pentagon connecting London with Paris, Amsterdam and Frankfurt, Paris with Madrid, and Amsterdam with Frankfurt. The capacity of these links is higher than 2.5 standard deviations above the mean. Comparing with the 2001 allocation, the main change is the upgrade of the link between Madrid and Paris as well as the absence of Brussels in the cities which are served by the highest-capacity backbone links. In addition, the link between Stockholm and Helsinki was also upgraded. However, the main differentiation with 2001 is the expansion towards the east. More specifically, more backbone links with capacity between 0.5 and 1.5 standard deviations above the mean terminate in Central, Eastern and South-Eastern European cities. Vienna, Bratislava and Prague seem to be better connected with the pan-European IBN. In addition, even more remote links such as these between Frankfurt and Warsaw as well as Milan and Athens are characterized by capacities greater than the average. Furthermore, Madrid's monopoly in high-capacity backbone links in the Iberian Peninsula does not exist any more since both Lisbon's and Barcelona's backbone links are above Europe's average in 2006.

In order to wrap up the above discussion, Figure 4.3 presents the box-

Table 4.1   *Descriptive statistics for the capacity of backbone links in Mbps*

Extent	Year	Minimum	Maximum	Mean	Std. deviation	Coefficient of variation
Intra-	2001	0.128	58 641	2589	7808	3.016
European	2002	2.000	65 041	3433	8667	2.525
links	2003	2.000	96 870	4850	12 575	2.593
	2004	2.000	153 529	7223	19 156	2.652
	2005	2.000	240 952	10 724	27 568	2.571
	2006	2.000	305 169	14 150	36 565	2.584
All links	2001	0.064	77 768	1609	6813	4.234
	2002	0.190	95 665	2318	8218	3.545
	2003	0.256	165 760	3558	12 969	3.645
	2004	0.260	241 391	5423	19 496	3.595
	2005	0.256	398 149	7495	28 281	3.773
	2006	1.500	467 671	9347	34 453	3.686

plots for both versions of the Internet backbone networks in 2001 and 2006 and for both geographical extents, and Table 4.1 presents some basic descriptive statistics. The shrink boxes and the dispread extreme values in the box-plots indicate the nature of the dataset: there is a significant number of backbone links the capacity of which is far away from the median capacity.[15] These links play a structural role in the Internet function, but also indicate the volume of the potential interaction of the cities they interconnect. Additionally, the box-plots reveal that the frequencies of lower capacity are much greater than the frequencies of links with great capacity, indicating a highly skewed distribution.

Moving into a more detailed level of analysis, descriptive statistics of the Internet backbone links are discussed here. According to Table 4.1, the maximum capacity has been continuously increased over the six-year time period, resulting in a five-fold increase. The same applies to the average capacity. This increase has a twofold explanation. Firstly, this is because of the overall technology change and the newly introduced bandwidth-demanding Internet applications, which is evenly spread around places. Secondly, it is due to the localized capacity demand change. This is the interesting part from the geography point of view since spatial heterogeneity emerges. This is demonstrated by the minimum capacity, which has only slightly increased during the six-year period. Even in 2005 there were still extra-European links with capacity less than 1 Mbps. In order to eliminate the (geographically even) technology change and bring forward

Table 4.2   Basic network statistics

	Vertices	Change (%)	Edges	Change (%)	Density	Change (%)
IBNs						
2001 all	184		417		0.025	
2002 all	168	−8.7	373	−10.6	0.027	8.0
2003 all	173	3.0	399	7.0	0.027	0.0
2004 all	169	−2.3	399	0.0	0.028	3.7
2005 all	181	7.1	438	9.8	0.027	−3.6
2006 all	194	7.2	476	8.7	0.025	−7.4
% point change		5.4		14.1		0.0
2001 E.c.	69		196		0.084	
2002 E.c.	71	2.9	194	−1.0	0.078	−7.1
2003 E.c.	76	7.0	211	8.8	0.074	−5.1
2004 E.c.	73	−3.9	218	3.3	0.083	12.2
2005 E.c.	72	−1.4	215	−1.4	0.084	1.2
2006 E.c.	76	5.6	225	4.7	0.079	−6.0
% point change		10.1		14.8		−6.0

Note: all = network including all the links terminating to European cities, E.c. = network including only the links between European cities.

the localized capacity change, the capacity classes in the maps presented here are based on standard deviations above the mean. However, because of the technology change and the overall bandwidth increase, standard deviation between the two different time points cannot be compared in order to draw conclusions for capacity dispersion. In order to overcome this, the coefficient of variation is introduced and presented in Table 4.1. The coefficient of variation is a normalized version of the standard deviation and is defined as the ratio of the standard deviation to the mean (Rogerson 2006). Based on this statistic it could be said that the capacity of the intra-European international backbone network is more dispersed through time, resulting in more cities being served by relative higher capacity links.

Furthermore, Table 4.2 presents the basic network statistics of the different versions of the IBNs. These include the number of vertices, the number of edges and the network density. The latter refers to the number of edges present in a network, expressed as a fraction of the number of all the possible edges. This indicator is also known as γ in graph theory and for the case of the non-planar networks is defined as (Taaffe et al. 1996, p. 254):

$$\gamma = \frac{E}{\frac{1}{2}V(V-1)} \tag{4.1}$$

where E is the number of edges and V the number of vertices.

The size of the network for all the cities is bigger than the intra-European one in terms of the number of vertices by a factor of 2.3–2.7 for the six-year period. However, in terms of the number of edges the factor varies from 1.8 to 2.1, indicating a denser intra-European network. Indeed, according to γ the intra-European network is denser than the overall one by a factor of 2.7–3.4 in 2001–06. This difference in density is not surprising, since the overall network lacks a (significant) proportion of the global links; that is the non-European links (such as New York to Tokyo according to the previous example).

In more detail, the change of the main network characteristics over time is also of interest here. Regarding the overall network, an important decrease of 8.7 percent in the number of vertices and 10.6 percent in the number of edges took place in 2001–02, reflecting the dotcom crash of 2000 which was followed by the telecoms crash (Kam 2006). Nonetheless, these changes led to an 8 percent denser network. This decrease, though, only concerns the overall backbone network, because the number of intra-European nodes was increased by almost 2.9 percent at the same time. During the next year, the global backbone network was increased both in terms of interconnected vertices and edges among them, but its density remained steady. The unstable character of the backbone network is reflected by a decrease of 2.3 percent in the number of vertices in 2003–04. During the same period the number of edges remained the same and as a result density was increased by 3.7 percent. After this, and for the next two-year periods 2004–05 and 2005–06, a stable increase of 7.1–7.2 percent and 9.8–8.7 percent took place in the number of vertices and edges respectively. However, the increase in the number of edges was not big enough to prevent a decrease in the network's density. The last periods' network expansion might signal a new era of a (stable) increase in the Internet infrastructure development.

Regarding the intra-European network, the downturn periods do not exactly fit with those for the overall network. The intra-European networks kept increasing until 2003, faced a decrease in 2003–04 and 2004–05 and grew again in 2005–06. Interestingly enough, the decrease in the number of intra-European nodes of 2003–04 was accompanied by an increase in the number of edges, resulting in a 12.2 percent density increase. Similar to the overall network, the increase of 2005–06 in the number of vertices and edges resulted in a less dense network.

All in all, the intra-European network grew more and faster than the overall network during the period 2001–2006. The overall increase in the number of intra-European vertices and edges was 10.1 percent and 14.8 percent, respectively, while the same figures for the overall network were 5.4 percent and 14.1 percent. These differences in increase rates resulted in an overall global network, the intra-European nodes of which increased from 37.5 percent in 2001 to 39.2 percent in 2006. Despite how small such differences seem to be, they reflect a growing participation of the European cities in this global infrastructural network.

4.4   NETWORK CENTRALIZATION MEASURES

The next two sections are dedicated to two fundamental types of network measures: centrality and centralization. These measures provide insights on how centralized the overall network is (centralization), but mainly on how central each node is (centrality). The above can be approached in a way equivalent to global and local statistics. These measures can be distinguished on the basis of the edges' weights. Thus, centrality measures can be vastly differentiated when the network is weighted. In this section various central-ity and centralization indicators are presented for both the weighted and the binary IBN for its global extent, but also for its European extraction.

Table 4.3 presents the centralization indicators for the six-year time period. The upper part of the table refers to the global extent of the network and the lower to the intra-European connections. Four differ-ent centralization indicators are presented here: degree, betweenness and eigenvector for the binary (b) and the weighted (w) network. The common characteristic of the above is that they compare the centralization of the current network with the centralization of the most centralized network, which is a star topology network (Figure 4.4). In such a network all the nodes are only connected with the central node (the star) and all the above centralization measures are equal to 1 or (100 percent). On the contrary, for a circular network centralization indicators are equal to 0.

The degree centralization, which is the simplest measure, is based on the degree centrality which is the sum of all the edges starting or ending to this node. In Figure 4.4, node A of the star-like network has a degree central-ity equal to 4, while the degree centrality for the rest of the nodes is equal to 1. The degree centralization is the "variation in the degrees of vertices divided by the maximum degree variation which is possible in a network

Table 4.3   Centralization measures

	Degree (b) (%)	Betweenness (b) (%)	Eigenvector (b) (%)	Eigenvector (w) (%)
2001 all	43.4	46.4	54.5	83.6
2002 all	43.4	48.1	55.3	87.4
2003 all	47.3	50.7	57.4	89.8
2004 all	49.0	46.9	59.1	91.3
2005 all	50.1	46.1	59.5	93.3
2006 all	50.3	45.6	60.1	89.4
% point change	16.1	−1.7	10.2	7.0
2001 E.c.	33.8	21.2	43.4	76.0
2002 E.c.	34.6	24.9	46.7	81.0
2003 E.c.	36.2	24.8	45.5	79.8
2004 E.c.	45.7	27.1	49.6	85.6
2005 E.c.	39.2	20.8	47.2	86.4
2006 E.c.	41.2	29.4	47.2	84.1
% point change	21.9	38.7	8.9	10.6

Note: all = network including all the links terminating to European cities; E.c. = network including only the links between European cities.

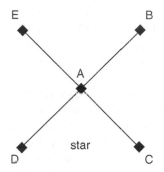

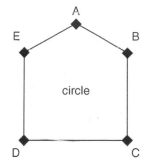

Figure 4.4   Star and circular networks

of the same size" (Nooy et al. 2005, p. 126). According to Table 4.3, the IBN seems to be quite centralized, since in 2006 its degree centralization reached 50 percent (that is, half of the degree centralization of maximal centralized network). However, the intra-European subtraction is less centralized. This is not surprising because of the nature of the data. As mentioned before, the overall network does not include the links among extra-European cities. This results in a more centralized network with a significant number of cities (cities not in Europe) being only connected with European ones. Consequently, the intra-European subnetwork is more realistic. However, even this network enjoys around 40 percent of the maximum centralization, indicating the structural importance of its main hubs. What is also interesting here is the change of centralization over time. The centrality of both networks grew over time, but when only the intra-European links are included in the analysis, the centrality of the IBN grew faster. In simple terms, it could be said that degree centralization is a measure of infrastructural supply because it is based on the actual count of backbone links at city level. All in all, IBN is moderate centralized and over time the importance of the Internet backbone hubs in Europe grew faster than their importance at the global scale.

The second measure presented here is the betweenness centralization, which is based on the homonymic measure of centrality. The latter defines the centrality of a node as an indication of being between other nodes. Freeman (1978–79, p. 224) identified betweenness centrality as an "index of the potential of a point for control communication". This notion of centrality fits better with the technical structure of the Internet and the structure of the Internet data packet transport system, which is based on packet switching. Some nodes are central because they are in-between numerous origins and destinations and the Internet function is based on the efficiency of these hubs to transport data packets. Before defining further the notion of betweenness centrality, the notion of geodesics should be explained first. "A geodesic path is the shortest path, in terms of number of edges traversed, between a specified pair of vertices" (Newman 2008, p. 5). Of course, the geodesic paths between any two vertices might not be unique. Based on the above, the betweenness centrality of a vertex is defined as the "proportion of all geodesics between pairs of other vertices that include this vertex" (Nooy et al. 2005, p. 131). In the case of the star network the central node has betweenness centrality equal to 6 because six geodesics pass by it (D–E, E–B, B–C, C–D, E–C and D–B) while the other nodes have betweenness centrality equal to 1. Just like the degree centralization, the betweenness centralization is defined as the "variation in the betweenness centrality of the vertices divided by the maximum variation in between centrality scores possible in a network of a same size" (ibid.).

According to betweenness centralization, the IBN seems to be less centralized in comparison to degree centralization measures. This is not coincidental because this measure better reflects the Internet's function since the Internet was initially designed as a decentralized network (Baran 1964). The centralization of the overall network has slightly decreased during the six-year period, contrary to the intra-European one, the centralization of which increased almost 39 percent. Although the IBN appeared to be less centralized, it is moving fast towards a more centralized structure in functional terms, at least according to its European subset. In simple terms, the IBN appears less centralized than the infrastructural capital, which is indicated by the degree centralization, and the role of the hub cities in the IP data packets movements is increasing over time in Europe.

Contrary to the above indicators, eigenvector centrality does not consider all the connections being equal: the connections of a node to more central vertices are more important than the connections to less central ones. It is important to have a large number of connections, but a node with fewer but more important connections is more central than a node with more but less important connections (Newman 2008). Eigenvector centrality considers not only direct links, but also the indirect ones and focuses more on the global structure of the network rather than the on the local ones, which are the main focus of the degree centrality (Bonarich 2007; Hanneman and Riddle 2005). The above considerations are important for the analysis of the IBN, the function of which is based on the indirect connections, as they are represented by peering agreements. Eigenvector centrality is widely used, with the most well-known application being Google's web pages rank (Newman 2008). The eigenvector centrality calculation is based on factor analysis, which identifies new factors based on the distances among the vertices. The Eigenvalue is the location of each node regarding the new factors produced and the collection of such values is called the eigenvector. The first factor resulted from factor analysis reflects the global aspects of the distances among vertices while the second and the remaining factors reflect local structures (Hanneman and Riddle 2005). The eigenvector centralization is defined as the variation in the vertices' eigenvector centrality divided by the maximum eigenvector centrality variation which is possible in a network of the same size (Borgatti et al. 2002).

The IBN is becoming more centralized over time according to eigenvector measures, both for its global extent but also for its European subnetwork. For 2006 and for the former case, the centralization score reached 60 percent, which is the highest among all the different measures. At the same time, the intra-European IBN centralization was 47 percent which is again the highest value. The differences between the degree and eigenvector centralization indicate that the network is more centralized when the indirect links are taken into consideration. Furthermore, the small decrease in centralization in 2005, which is also present in the other centralization measures as well, echoes the decrease in the number of intra-European vertices and edges in the same year, as was illustrated in Table 4.2. Over time, eigenvector centralization increases almost equally for both subsets. In overall, the European hub cities appear to have more central roles in the

IBN, which is also increasing over time, when not only the infrastructural supply but also the indirect links are taken into consideration.

The above three centralization indicators refer only to the binary network, without taking into consideration the actual weights of the connections. For the case of the IBN the weights of the links represent the bandwidth of the line connecting the two cities. Considering how important the bandwidth is in order to better understand the structure of the Internet infrastructure, it is worth including the links' weights in the calculation of the network's centralization. Borgatti et al. (2002) introduce eigenvector centralization and centrality using weighted network edges. The results are presented in Table 4.3. When the bandwidth is included in the analysis, then the network seems to be much more centralized. Especially for the intra-European network, eigenvector centralization is more than double the degree centralization and it is very close to the centralization value for the whole network with the global extent. Over time, centralization increases, indicating again an increase in the importance of the European hub cities. In short, when the diffusion of the technology is taken into consideration – that is, the roll-out of high-capacity fiber links for long-haul backbone Internet connections – then the network is more centralized, better resembling a star-like topology.

To sum up, it could be said that degree centralization provides a measure of how centralized is the distribution of the Internet infrastructure at the city level. The other two centralization measures are more related with the function and the technical nature of the network: betweenness centralization provides a view on how vertices act like hubs; and eigenvector comments on centralization based on indirect connections, also taking into consideration the weights of the links. All in all, the European subtraction of global IBN is moderately centralized when only the infrastructural supply is taken into consideration. When indirect links are also considered, the network appears to be more centralized. But the main difference emerges when bandwidth is included in the analysis; in this case the highly centralized character of the network is revealed. Lastly, according to almost all measures, the importance of the hub cities increases, revealing the strength of centripetal forces in the formation of cyberplace.

4.5   CITIES' CENTRALITY INDICATORS

4.5.1   Degree Centrality

In this section, the focus turns to local statistics reflected in different centrality indicators at the city level. Table 4.4 presents the degree centrality

Table 4.4   *Binary degree centrality, 2001–06*

	2001 E.c.		a.c.		% Eur. links	2006 E.c.		a.c.		% Eur. links	Change 2001–06 for E.c. (%)	Change 2001–06 for a.c. (%)
Frankfurt	85.7	*3*	44.6	*3*	*64.9*	100.0	*1*	70.3	*2*	*50.7*	16.7	57.7
London	100.0	*1*	100.0	*1*	*33.7*	91.7	*2*	100.0	*1*	*32.7*	−8.3	0.0
Vienna	60.7	*5*	24.1	*5*	*85.0*	66.7	*3*	27.7	*5*	*85.7*	9.8	15.0
Amsterdam	85.7	*3*	39.8	*4*	*72.7*	61.1	*4*	31.7	*4*	*68.8*	−28.7	−20.3
Paris	89.3	*2*	66.3	*2*	*45.5*	58.3	*5*	48.5	*3*	*42.9*	−34.7	−26.8
Milan	53.6	*6*	24.1	*5*	*75.0*	47.2	*6*	24.8	*6*	*68.0*	−11.9	2.7
Budapest	28.6	*14*	10.8	*20*	*88.9*	41.7	*7*	17.8	*8*	*83.3*	45.8	64.4
Stockholm	50.0	*7*	22.9	*7*	*73.7*	36.1	*8*	18.8	*7*	*68.4*	−27.8	−17.8
Athens	28.6	*14*	12.0	*16*	*80.0*	33.3	*9*	15.8	*10*	*75.0*	16.7	31.5
Zürich	35.7	*11*	13.3	*14*	*90.9*	33.3	*9*	13.9	*14*	*85.7*	6.7	4.6
Copenhagen	42.9	*8*	16.9	*13*	*85.7*	30.6	*11*	16.8	*9*	*64.7*	−28.7	−0.2
Zagreb	10.7	*34*	4.8	*35*	*75.0*	27.8	*12*	9.9	*17*	*100.0*	159.3	105.4
Hamburg	17.9	*22*	12.0	*16*	*60.0*	25.0	*13*	11.9	*15*	*75.0*	40.0	−1.4
Prague	39.3	*9*	13.3	*14*	*100.0*	25.0	*13*	8.9	*21*	*100.0*	−36.4	−32.8
Brussels	39.3	*9*	21.7	*8*	*61.1*	22.2	*15*	11.9	*15*	*66.7*	−43.4	−45.2
Madrid	28.6	*14*	10.8	*20*	*88.9*	22.2	*15*	14.9	*12*	*53.3*	−22.2	37.0
Warsaw	17.9	*22*	9.6	*24*	*62.5*	22.2	*15*	9.9	*17*	*80.0*	24.4	2.7
Stuttgart	3.6	*56*	1.2	*60*	*100.0*	22.2	*15*	8.9	*21*	*88.9*	522.2	639.6
Geneva	25.0	*18*	10.8	*20*	*77.8*	19.4	*19*	9.9	*17*	*70.0*	−22.2	−8.7
Barcelona	17.9	*22*	6.0	*31*	*100.0*	19.4	*19*	6.9	*24*	*100.0*	8.9	15.0
Tallinn	10.7	*34*	3.6	*40*	*100.0*	19.4	*19*	7.9	*23*	*87.5*	81.5	119.1
Bratislava	21.4	*19*	8.4	*25*	*85.7*	16.7	*22*	5.9	*27*	*100.0*	−22.2	−29.6
Bucharest	14.3	*30*	7.2	*28*	*66.7*	16.7	*22*	6.9	*24*	*85.7*	16.7	−4.1
Düsseldorf	10.7	*34*	3.6	*40*	*100.0*	13.9	*24*	5.9	*27*	*83.3*	29.6	64.4
Lisbon	21.4	*19*	18.1	*11*	*40.0*	13.9	*24*	15.8	*10*	*31.3*	−35.2	−12.3
Oslo	35.7	*11*	21.7	*8*	*55.6*	13.9	*24*	6.9	*24*	*71.4*	−61.1	−68.0
Belgrade	10.7	*34*	4.8	*35*	*75.0*	13.9	*24*	5.0	*31*	*100.0*	29.6	2.7
Nicosia	10.7	*34*	3.6	*40*	*100.0*	13.9	*24*	5.0	*31*	*100.0*	29.6	37.0
Sofia	28.6	*14*	12.0	*16*	*80.0*	13.9	*24*	5.0	*31*	*100.0*	−51.4	−58.9
Ljubljana	17.9	*22*	6.0	*31*	*100.0*	13.9	*24*	5.0	*31*	*100.0*	−22.2	−17.8

Note: E.c. = European cities; a.c. = all cities; * based on normalized centralities.

for the 30 most central European cities and for the binary network. The whole table can be found in the Appendix to this chapter. Centralities have been calculated both for the overall network and for the intra-European one for the years 2001 and 2006. For the needs of this table the results have been normalized and for each different case the maximum degree centrality, or in other words the maximum number of the backbone connections

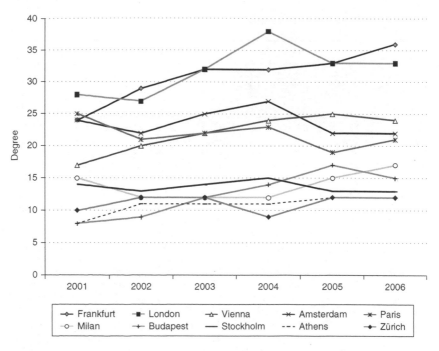

*Figure 4.5   Degree centrality 2001–06 for the ten most central cities in
            2006*

that a city shares with other cities, is equal to 100. In addition, the ranks
are presented as well as the overall change over time.

The table is ranked according to the 2006 degree centrality for the
intra-European network. For presentation reasons, the cities' centralities are analyzed in blocks of ten following the rank of Table 4.4. The
non-normalized degree centralities 2001–06 for the ten most central
cities in 2006 are presented in Figure 4.5. In 2006, Frankfurt is the most
centralized city since it is connected with 36 European cities. Very close
is London, with 91.7 percent of Frankfurt's connections. Interestingly
enough, some cities which are located in the periphery of Europe are also
found among the first ten. Vienna is the most characteristic case since it
shares 24 backbone connections with the rest of European cities in 2006,
reaching 66.7 percent of Frankfurt's centrality, which enables it to be the
third most central city according to this indicator. Along with Budapest,
these two cities seem to play the role of gateway cities for Eastern Europe
(Rutherford et al. 2004). Apart from them, Athens and Milan represent
the South of Europe, while Stockholm seems to be the main node for the
North of Europe.

After considering the global connections, the picture is different. The five most connected cities change their positions among them. London is by far the most connected city in 2006 with 101 connections, while Frankfurt falls back to the second position with only 70.3 percent of London's degree centrality, and it is followed by Paris, Amsterdam and Vienna. This big difference between the first and the second city denotes London's importance for the global IBN. The main change in the first tier of the ten most connected cities is Zürich, which falls to the 14th position and is replaced by Copenhagen when the global connections are taken into consideration. The above differences in centralities can be further explained by the relevant column in Table 4.4, which presents the percentage of the intra-European connections of each city. The global character of London in particular, but also Paris, is highlighted by the fact that only 32.7 percent and 42.9 percent of their total connections are towards Europe, contrary to the high European orientation of the peripheral gateway cities such as Vienna and Budapest and also Zürich. Somewhere in-between the two extremes of the spectrum, the Northern and Southern European hubs can be found.

Retrospectively and in terms of the degree centrality, most of the cities presented in Figure 4.5 gain in actual connections. It is important though to highlight the fact that Amsterdam, Paris and Stockholm lost connectivity over time in relative terms. Looking at the change of the normalized centrality, Budapest and Frankfurt gain mostly in this time period. Interestingly enough Budapest was not part of the first tier of cities in 2001.

Analyzing further the second tier of cities regarding their degree centralities, cities of both the centre and the periphery of Europe can be found (Figure 4.6). Despite the institutional importance of Brussels as the headcounter of the European Union, the Belgian capital lost six places in connectivity ranking. Although the majority of its connections are with other European cities, Brussels is still served by some valuable global links. On the contrary, Stuttgart's normalized degree centrality increased by 523 percent for the European links and 640 percent after including the non-European ones during the period 2001–06. In terms of the number of connections, Stuttgart had just one in 2001 and the number grew steadily until 2006, when it reached eight intra-European and nine total links in 2006. Prague is overtaken by Vienna as the former performed a gateway role for Eastern Europe in 2001. During the six-year period, it lost 36.4 percent of its degree centrality in relative terms and its actual European connections decreased from 11 to nine. During the whole time period, its degree centrality was not stable at all, as can be seen in Figure 4.6. It should also be highlighted here that Prague never managed to attract a

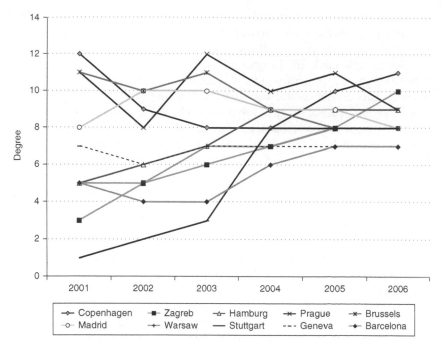

Figure 4.6   Degree centrality 2001–06 for the 11th–20th most central cities in 2006

direct extra-European connection, contrary to its competitor in Eastern Europe, Vienna, a fact which might explain why the latter grew in terms of connectivity while the former did not.

The urban nature of the international Internet backbone connectivity can be highlighted by the Spanish example. Both of the two most important cities in Spain, Madrid and Barcelona, can be found in this second tier of European cities. Apart from the fact that the capital city is the best-connected one and the relation between them seems to be competitive according to Figure 4.6, Barcelona was not being served in either 2001 or 2006 by any extra-European backbone link, while 47.7 percent of Madrid's connections are with non-European cities, reflecting Madrid's dominant role in Spain's extra-European IP communications. Comparing the above with the fact that 17 German cities[16] had (at least for one year in the study period) one international backbone connection, and the fact that the three most central had a percentage of extra-European connections varying from 50.7–88.9 percent, we can identify a similarity between the topology of the urban networks and spatial structure of the international IP backbone networks. In simple terms, the polycentric German urban develop-

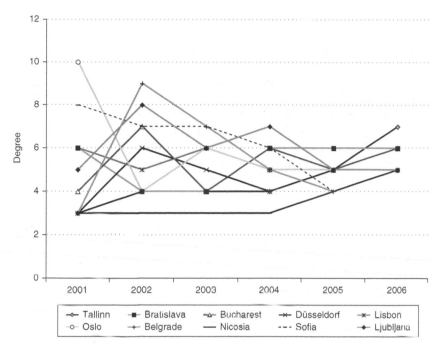

Figure 4.7   Degree centrality 2001–06 for the 21st–30th most central cities in 2006

ment pattern and the dominance of Madrid and (secondarily) Barcelona in Spain are reflected in the allocation of the Internet backbone nodes (see also Rutherford et al. 2004).

What is also interesting in this second tier of cities is the position of Zagreb. The Croatian capital experienced a vast growth in the European degree centrality (159.3 percent in 2001–06) and managed to be the 12th most connected city in terms of binary connections in Europe. Following the above argumentation, Zagreb started playing the role of a hub city in the Balkan region, with Athens being the main one, not only because of its greater centrality over time but mostly because of the higher bandwidth accumulation, as we will see later in the weighted degree centrality.

The third tier of cities mainly consisted of peripheral ones. We can identify a cluster of Eastern and South-Eastern European cities such as Bratislava, Bucharest, Belgrade, Sofia, Ljubljana and also Nicosia. Some of them lost in degree centrality over time (Bratislava, Sofia and Ljubljana) and some of them gained (Bucharest, Belgrade and Nicosia). After comparing Figure 4.7, which presents the degree centrality 2001–06 of the third tier of cities, with Figure 4.5, the instability of the evolution of bandwidth accumulation – at least for the less centralized nodes – becomes apparent. This indicates the easiness of rewiring or (re)lighting such networks in order to meet changes in demand (Gorman and Kulkarni 2004). Apart from Düsseldorf, some of the most remote cities of Europe are also included in this cluster: Oslo and Tallinn represent Europe's northern frontier and Lisbon its western edge. The peripheral location of these cities is probably one of the reasons explaining the high percentage of their extra-European connections, with Lisbon being the most interesting case, since in 2006, 68.7 percent of its links were with cities outside Europe. The geography of the extra-European links is analyzed further below.

Regarding the rest of the cities, the very low position of Rome and Berlin should be mentioned. They shared the 60th position in 2006 and both of them were served by only one international Internet backbone connection. Despite their importance in the European and the national urban systems, these cities did not act as national hubs for global IP communications. Apparently, the demand for such connectivity in Rome and Berlin was met using domestic links with these cities which hosted international backbone links in Italy and Germany, respectively.

The degree centrality illustrates the significance of each city, taking into consideration only the number of cities with direct connections. What is not included in this indicator is the capacity of this infrastructure. In order to take this into consideration, degree centrality for the weighted network and for the 30 most central cities is presented in Table 4.5. The whole table can be found in the Appendix of this chapter.

For presentation reasons, just as before, the cities' centralities will be analyzed in blocks of ten following the rank of Table 4.5. Taking into consideration the capacity of the links, the first tier of the most central cities is slightly changed in comparison to the centrality measures for the binary network. In 2006, the same four cities according to the binary degree centrality are the most central ones, but in this case London instead of Frankfurt is the most central city, followed by Paris, with Amsterdam found in fourth position. Although Frankfurt has more connections with European cities, London attracted higher-capacity links. Analyzing further the first tier of central cities, cities such as Athens and Budapest as well as Zürich appear to be less central when the capacity of the links is taken into consideration. The above cities have been replaced in the first tier by Copenhagen, Hamburg and Madrid. So, if the analysis of the centrality of the first tier of cities based on the binary network brought into sight a pan-European pattern with peripheral cities performing hub roles in the Internet backbone infrastructure, then the analysis of the same tier of cities based on capacity better reflects a more centralized pattern of the bandwidth allocation in Europe.

Table 4.5   *Weighted degree centrality 2001–06*

	2001 E.c.		a.c.		% Eur. links	2006 E.c.		a.c.		% Eur. links	Change 2001–06 for E.c. (%)	Change 2001–06 for a.c. (%)
London	96.8	*2*	100.0	*1*	*64.0*	100.0	*1*	100.0	*1*	*63.7*	3.3	0.0
Paris	100.0	*1*	75.6	*2*	*87.4*	84.9	*2*	66.4	*2*	*81.4*	−15.1	−12.1
Frankfurt	96.5	*3*	67.8	*4*	*94.1*	81.0	*3*	58.2	*3*	*88.6*	−16.0	−14.1
Amsterdam	93.2	*4*	71.9	*3*	*85.6*	64.7	*4*	49.6	*4*	*83.0*	−30.6	−31.0
Stockholm	35.7	*6*	24.5	*6*	*96.4*	29.2	*5*	20.2	*5*	*92.3*	−18.2	−17.7
Madrid	12.3	*10*	9.2	*9*	*88.5*	24.5	*6*	16.2	*7*	*96.1*	99.5	77.1
Copenhagen	21.1	*7*	18.4	*7*	*75.9*	24.2	*7*	18.1	*6*	*85.4*	14.9	−1.6
Vienna	11.3	*12*	7.5	*13*	*99.9*	21.4	*8*	13.7	*8*	*99.7*	89.2	82.7
Hamburg	11.0	*14*	7.6	*12*	*95.4*	19.4	*9*	12.7	*10*	*97.3*	75.9	66.3
Milan	18.2	*8*	12.5	*8*	*95.6*	19.0	*10*	12.8	*9*	*94.1*	4.4	2.3
Brussels	48.2	*5*	32.2	*5*	*99.0*	18.5	*11*	11.8	*11*	*100.0*	−61.6	−63.3
Düsseldorf	8.3	*15*	5.5	*15*	*100.0*	11.6	*12*	8.0	*12*	*92.5*	40.7	46.7
Geneva	11.2	*13*	7.5	*14*	*99.1*	10.2	*13*	7.9	*13*	*82.8*	−8.7	5.3
Zürich	12.2	*11*	8.3	*11*	*97.2*	10.2	*14*	6.7	*14*	*96.8*	−16.6	−19.2
Warsaw	1.4	*32*	0.9	*32*	*96.0*	8.7	*15*	5.6	*15*	*99.1*	531.3	489.5
Bratislava	4.4	*20*	2.9	*20*	*99.9*	7.7	*16*	4.9	*16*	*100.0*	77.3	70.8
Prague	7.3	*16*	4.8	*16*	*100.0*	7.4	*17*	4.7	*18*	*100.0*	0.6	−3.0
Helsinki	4.8	*19*	3.3	*18*	*95.4*	7.3	*18*	4.7	*19*	*100.0*	53.6	41.3
Oslo	13.7	*9*	9.1	*10*	*99.0*	6.9	*19*	4.9	*17*	*90.7*	−49.2	−46.5
Dublin	2.5	*24*	1.8	*24*	*92.6*	6.3	*20*	4.2	*20*	*96.4*	152.7	134.1
Budapest	1.9	*27*	1.3	*27*	*98.5*	5.5	*21*	3.5	*21*	*98.9*	191.2	179.8
Munich	6.0	*17*	4.0	*17*	*98.6*	4.4	*22*	2.8	*22*	*100.0*	−26.7	−30.3
Barcelona	2.4	*25*	1.6	*25*	*100.0*	3.9	*23*	2.5	*24*	*100.0*	64.7	58.8
Athens	0.6	*35*	0.5	*35*	*73.2*	3.4	*24*	2.8	*23*	*79.2*	510.9	444.2
Lisbon	2.0	*26*	1.5	*26*	*90.8*	3.3	*25*	2.2	*25*	*96.0*	62.4	48.0
Brno	0.0	*63*	0.0	*64*	*100.0*	2.8	*26*	1.8	*26*	*100.0*	109 309.7	105 388.1
Tallinn	0.3	*37*	0.2	*38*	*100.0*	1.7	*27*	1.1	*29*	*98.3*	431.2	421.0
Bucharest	0.9	*33*	0.6	*33*	*99.6*	1.7	*28*	1.1	*30*	*99.6*	88.8	82.0
Ljubljana	0.2	*39*	0.1	*40*	*100.0*	1.6	*29*	1.0	*31*	*100.0*	800.1	767.8
Marseille						1.2	*30*	0.8	*32*	*100.0*		

Note: E.c. = European cities; a.c. = all cities.

From a retrospective point of view, in 2001 only two cities were not part of the first tier: that is, Vienna and Hamburg. These cities experienced significant increase in centrality through the six-year period (89.2 percent and 75.9 percent, respectively), while the increase of the non-normalized centrality, or in other words the increase of the aggregated bandwidth at city level, reached 1177 percent and 1088 percent, correspondingly.[17] Nonetheless, Madrid experienced the highest increase in centrality during

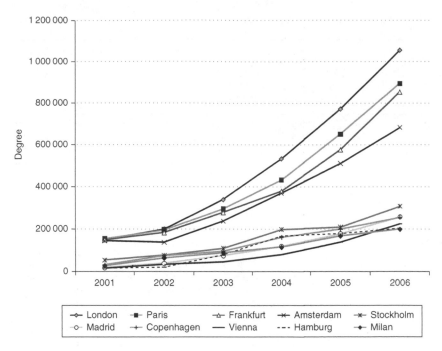

*Figure 4.8   Degree centrality (w) 2001–06 for the ten most central cities
              in 2006*

the time period (99.5 percent). Interesting also is the fact that for some
of the most central cities, such as Paris, Frankfurt, Amsterdam and
Stockholm, a decrease in normalized centrality was observed, but of
course not in the absolute bandwidth accumulation. London managed
to increase its normalized degree centrality slightly and this is why from
2002 onwards it is the most centralized city. Figure 4.8 presents the change
in bandwidth (non-normalized centrality) in 2001–06. It can be seen that
bandwidth allocation has increased exponentially over time. What is also
important is the unprompted division of these cities into two clusters: the
four most connected ones and the remaining six. The change of each city's
bandwidth is highly related to the cluster it belongs to.

   The ranking of the first-tier cities according to the weighted network
centralities do not change when the extra-European connections are taken
into consideration. What changes though is London's importance. Paris,
which is the second most central city, has a degree centrality equal to 84.9
percent of London's centrality when only the intra-European links are
included. However, when the extra-European links are taken into consideration, then Paris reaches only 66.4 percent of London's aggregated

bandwidth. This difference between London and the second city is greater for the weighted network than the binary one, indicating a greater dominance of London in bandwidth allocation. The above is in accordance with the percentage of bandwidth dedicated to European links: 36.3 percent of London's aggregated bandwidth serves extra-European connections while only 18.6 percent of Paris bandwidth is dedicated to such links. Close to Paris is Amsterdam, indicating again its international role, while the rest of the first-tier cities use less than 15 percent of their bandwidth for extra-European communications. Regarding 2001, the main difference was Copenhagen, which at this point appeared to be more globalized, since 24.1 percent of its aggregated bandwidth was due to extra-European links. During the six-year period, Copenhagen's bandwidth dedicated to intra-European links increased proportionally more than the bandwidth for extra-European links.

In the second tier of cities, the differences between the binary degree centralities geography and the weighted degree centrality geography emerge. Only four cities are located in the second tier according to both centrality measures. Dusseldorf and Dublin manage to increase their relative position 12 and 15 places respectively, while Zürich and Prague lose four and three places. Dublin's different performance in the two indicators reflects the fundamental difference between the two centrality measures; while the degree centrality based on the binary network reflects hub structures and up to a certain extent the topology of the IBN, the aggregated bandwidth at city level or in other words the degree centrality of the weighted network seems to be related more with economic attributes. This is why the capital city of the Irish Tiger accumulates in relative terms much more bandwidth than links to other cities.

Going further, Copenhagen used to be part of the second tier of cities when the binary degree centralities were taken into consideration. However, as was stated above, Copenhagen is part of the first tier according to the weighted degree centrality. In addition, two cities from Scandinavia are included in this tier – Helsinki and Oslo – increasing the centrality of the northern cities and gaining six and five places. Bratislava also gained six places in the relative ranking because of the inclusion of bandwidth in the centrality measure. It could be said that Bratislava has a competitive role against Budapest; the former is more central when the actual weights are taken into consideration, while the latter is more central for the binary network.

Figure 4.9 presents the evolution of the degree centrality in real terms (bandwidth) in the period 2001–06 for the second tier of cities. The picture is not as clear as it was in Figure 4.8 for the first tier because the hierarchies change over time. What is obvious though is the fact that Brussels

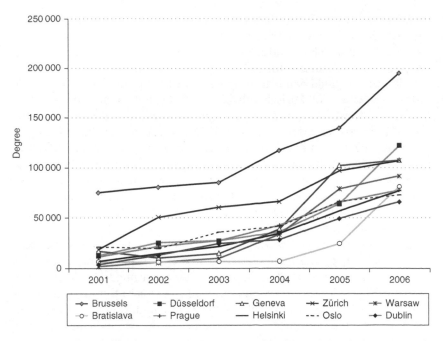

*Figure 4.9　Degree centrality (w) 2001–06 for the 11th–20th most central
cities in 2006*

seems to fit better to the first tier than to the second one, because of the
high agglomeration of bandwidth. Over time, the European Union's headquarters, the two main cities of Switzerland and the Norwegian capital,
lost centrality in relative terms. On the contrary, Warsaw had an immense
increase in 2001–06 of 531 percent which enabled the Polish capital to
increase its relative position from 32nd position to 15th. Dublin also experienced a great increase of 153 percent during the same time.

Looking to the centrality ranking when the extra-European connections
are included in the analysis, the two ranks seem to be almost identical,
with minor differences between them, contrary to what applies for the
binary network. This happens because the bulk of the bandwidth which is
aggregated in the European cities is dedicated to intra-European connections with very few exceptions, such as London and, to a certain extent,
Paris and Amsterdam from the first tier. In the second tier, Geneva is the
only city in which more than 10 percent of its aggregated bandwidth is
due to extra-European links. It should be noted here that Geneva's global
character can also be identified by its binary connections, 30 percent of
which were with cities outside Europe. What is interesting here is the

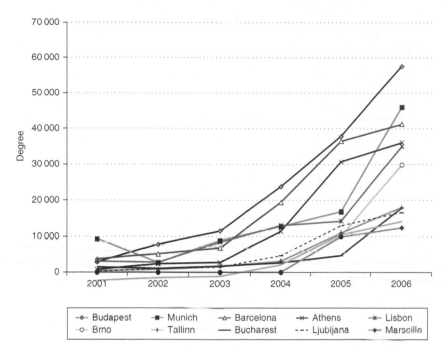

Figure 4.10 Degree centrality (w) 2001–06 for the 21st–30th most central cities in 2006

different connectivity profiles of Switzerland's two main cities: Zürich is more central in terms of actual connections, while Geneva agglomerates slightly more bandwidth and is the most extroversive one.

The third tier of cities, which is presented in Figure 4.10, mainly consists of cities which are located on the periphery of Europe. There is a cluster of cities from Central, South-East and East Europe such as Budapest, Athens, Brno, Tallinn, Bucharest and Ljubljana, and a cluster of cities from the South West such as Barcelona, Lisbon and Marseille. Munich is the only city from Europe's pentagon. The reader is reminded that the third tier of cities for the case of the binary degree centrality consists mostly on peripheral cities. However, again only four out of ten cities are the same in the third tier of the two different centrality measures. Budapest is the most central city of this tier. It is notable though that when the bandwidth is taken into consideration, Budapest gains 14 places in the rank. Athens is also very low ranked compared to the binary connectivity since it lost 15 places. On the contrary, the Czech city of Brno gained 18 places.

Figure 4.10 presents the evolution of degree centrality of the third tier of cities for the weighted network. It could be said that it is more homogenous than the previous tier. What is interesting is the steady growth of Budapest through the six-year time period, which was followed by Barcelona until 2005. Munich is another interesting case. In 2002 the aggregated bandwidth was decreased, but this decline only lasted for a year. From 2003 onwards, Munich's degree centrality kept on growing. Brno and Marseille followed very similar growth patterns. The former was only served by two backbone links with total bandwidth of 4.048 Mbps and degree centrality equal to 0.003 (maximum equals to 100) in 2001, while the latter had no such links. Although over time both of them grew similarly, Brno appears to have a vast increase because of its very low initial degree, and therefore gained 38 places in the ranking. Ljubljana, Athens and Tallinn also experienced a great increase in the accumulated bandwidth, contrary to Munich which lost in terms of relative centrality.

In terms of the percentage of the bandwidth that is accumulated because of the extra-European links, the only interesting case is Athens: 21.8 percent of the agglomerated bandwidth in the Greek capital in 2006 was because of the 16 extra-European backbone links that were present in this year, justifying its hub role in South-Eastern Europe. Apart from this, Lisbon is also interesting since in 2001, 9.2 percent of its weighted degree centrality was due to the connections with non-European cities.

However, Lisbon is a very interesting case when the discussion turns to the extra-European links, as is analyzed below. Tables 4.6 and 4.7 present the percentage of each city's degree centrality because of its connections with extra-European cities, based on the binary and weighted (bandwidth) network. The tables identify the most extroversive cities. However, the definition of extroversion is rather arbitrary. For the case of the binary network and because of the greater diffusion of connections, cities are defined as extroversive when at least 20 percent of their backbone connections are with non-European cites. On the contrary, as was mentioned above, the weighted backbone network is much more centralized, or in simple terms the bulk of bandwidth is concentrated in a small number of cities. Because of the above attribute, cities with more than 5 percent of their accumulated bandwidth bound to extra-European links are also defined as extroversive. The cities included in Tables 4.6 and 4.7 satisfy at least one of these two attributes.

Two different percentages are presented for each city and for each continent; the columns numbered with odd numbers refer to the importance of each continent for each city's connectivity and the sum of these columns is equal to 100 percent for each city and for each year. The remaining columns (numbered with even numbers) refer to the city's importance in Europe's total connectivity with each continent and the sum of each column is equal to 100 percent. Both tables are ranked according to 2006 degree centrality.

In general, cities perform differently in these two measures of extroversion. London for instance seems to be more globalized according to the binary connections than the weighted ones. The reason behind this lies in the diffusion of new technology high-capacity links and the demand for telecommunications services and interaction between any two cites. In 2006, apart from the 33 percent of intra-European links, only 6 percent of all London's connections terminated in US and Canadian cities while 31 percent terminated in Africa and 28 percent in the Asia and Pacific region. On the contrary, 34 percent of its accumulated bandwidth in 2006 was because of links which terminated in the US and Canada, while less than 1 percent of bandwidth terminated in Africa and 1 percent terminated with the Asia and Pacific region. This reflects the fact that the links with Africa and Asia are characterized by very low capacity, contrary to very high bandwidth (submarine) links with US and Canadian cities. So, on one hand there is a demand for a few but high-capacity transatlantic links, and on the other hand there is a demand for a lot of low capacity links with numerous cities in Africa and the Asia and Pacific region. As a result, there is a high demand for data exchange between London and a few specific US and Canadian cities (the link between London and New York is for every year of the study period the highest-capacity link) and a much lower demand between London and several cities in Africa and Asia and the Pacific. What is interesting though is to try to explain these different demands. The links between London and North America are more straightforward to explain since they interconnect the two most developed regions of the planet, Europe and North America, and they represent the interaction that takes place between them and, up to a point, the interaction that takes place between the two global cities of London and New York. In addition, it highlights the role of London as a gateway to North America for the rest of the European cities and its great importance in the geography of the Internet. The links with Africa and Asia though are more complicated. Firstly, they represent the global need for universal connectivity. The lack of Internet infrastructure in Africa makes the use of international (and expensive) backbone links essential even for intra-Africa data exchange (ITU 2004). And because of London's importance in the Internet geography, cities from Africa and Asia are connected to London in order to achieve global and regional Internet connectivity. A second reason lies in London's role as a global city. Its predominant position in the world cities hierarchy is a significant pull factor in attracting backbone links from remote cities, underlining the extensive and geographically dispersed demand for data exchange and consequently interaction with one

The geography of the Internet

Table 4.6 *Geographic allocation of backbone connections, % of binary links*

	2001											
	Africa		Asia and Pacific		Europe		Latin America and Caribbean		Rest of Europe		USA and Canada	
	(1)	(2)	(3)	(4)	(5)	(6)	(7)	(8)	(9)	(10)	(11)	(12)
London	22	30	36	45	34	7	0	0	5	15	4	6
Paris	33	30	18	15	45	6	0	0	0	0	4	4
Frankfurt	3	2	11	6	65	6	0	0	8	11	14	9
Amsterdam	9	5	9	4	73	6	0	0	3	4	6	4
Milan	0	0	15	4	75	4	0	0	0	0	10	4
Stockholm	0	0	5	1	74	4	0	0	16	11	5	2
Brussels	17	5	0	0	61	3	0	0	6	4	17	6
Oslo	17	5	11	3	56	3	0	0	11	7	6	2
Palermo	19	5	31	7	19	1	13	67	13	7	6	2
Lisbon	33	8	0	0	40	2	7	33	0	0	20	6
Munich	7	2	20	4	60	2	0	0	0	0	13	4
Copenhagen	0	0	0	0	86	3	0	0	7	4	7	2
Athens	0	0	0	0	80	2	0	0	0	0	20	4
Hamburg	0	0	10	1	60	2	0	0	10	4	20	4
Leuk	50	8	30	4	10	0	0	0	0	0	10	2
Sofia	0	0	0	0	80	2	0	0	0	0	20	4
Madrid	0	0	0	0	89	2	0	0	0	0	11	2
Geneva	0	0	0	0	78	2	0	0	0	0	22	4
Helsinki	0	0	0	0	67	2	0	0	22	7	11	2
Warsaw	0	0	0	0	63	1	0	0	13	4	25	4
Nittedal	0	0	0	0	57	1	0	0	43	11	0	0
Luxembourg	14	2	0	0	71	1	0	0	0	0	14	2
Bucharest	0	0	0	0	67	1	0	0	0	0	33	4
Zagreb	0	0	0	0	75	1	0	0	0	0	25	2
Dublin	0	0	0	0	75	1	0	0	0	0	25	2
Belgrade	0	0	0	0	75	1	0	0	0	0	25	2
Lausanne	0	0	0	0	75	1	0	0	0	0	25	2
Rotterdam	0	0	0	0	100	1	0	0	0	0	0	0
Tirana	0	0	0	0	33	0	0	0	0	0	67	4
Düsseldorf	0	0	0	0	100	1	0	0	0	0	0	0
Gdansk	0	0	0	0	50	0	0	0	0	0	50	2
Tartu	0	0	0	0	50	0	0	0	50	4	0	0
Thessaloniki												
Graz												
Hannover												
Total	10	100	11	97	65	67	0	100	4	93	9	91

Notes:
(1) + (3) + (5) + (7) + (9) + (11) = (13) + (15) + (17) + (19) + (21) + (23) = 100%.
The cities included here fulfill at least one of the following criteria: % of extra-European links > = 20%, and % of total bandwidth because of extra-European links >= 5%.

Source: Adapted from Tranos and Gillespie (2011).

Table 4.6   (continued)

	2006											
	Africa		Asia and Pacific		Europe		Latin America and Caribbean		Rest of Europe		USA and Canada	
	(13)	(14)	(15)	(16)	(17)	(18)	(19)	(20)	(21)	(22)	(23)	(24)
London	31	**31**	28	**35**	33	7	0	0	3	**13**	6	**16**
Paris	37	**18**	14	9	43	5	2	**33**	0	0	4	5
Frankfurt	18	**13**	20	**18**	51	8	0	0	7	**22**	4	8
Amsterdam	3	1	9	4	69	5	0	0	6	9	13	**11**
Milan	12	3	12	4	68	4	0	0	0	0	8	5
Stockholm	5	1	16	4	68	3	0	0	11	9	0	0
Brussels	17	2	8	1	67	2	0	0	0	0	8	3
Oslo	14	1	0	0	71	1	0	0	0	0	14	3
Palermo	20	3	53	**10**	20	1	0	0	0	0	7	3
Lisbon	56	9	0	0	31	1	6	**33**	0	0	6	3
Munich	17	1	0	0	83	1	0	0	0	0	0	0
Copenhagen	6	1	0	0	65	2	0	0	18	**13**	12	5
Athens	0	0	19	4	75	3	0	0	0	0	6	3
Hamburg	0	0	8	1	75	2	0	0	0	0	17	5
Leuk	50	1	50	1	0	0	0	0	0	0	0	0
Sofia	0	0	0	0	100	1	0	0	0	0	0	0
Madrid	20	3	7	1	53	2	7	**33**	0	0	13	5
Geneva	0	0	0	0	70	2	0	0	0	0	30	8
Helsinki	0	0	0	0	100	1	0	0	0	0	0	0
Warsaw	0	0	0	0	80	2	0	0	20	9	0	0
Nittedal	100	**10**	0	0	0	0	0	0	0	0	0	0
Luxembourg	0	0	0	0	100	1	0	0	0	0	0	0
Bucharest	0	0	0	0	86	1	0	0	14	4	0	0
Zagreb	0	0	0	0	100	2	0	0	0	0	0	0
Dublin	0	0	0	0	80	1	0	0	0	0	20	3
Belgrade	0	0	0	0	100	1	0	0	0	0	0	0
Lausanne	0	0	0	0	75	1	0	0	0	0	25	3
Rotterdam	0	0	0	0	50	0	0	0	0	0	50	3
Tirana	0	0	0	0	100	1	0	0	0	0	0	0
Düsseldorf	0	0	0	0	83	1	0	0	0	0	17	3
Gdansk												
Tartu												
Thessaloniki	0	0	25	1	75	1	0	0	0	0	0	0
Graz	0	0	0	0	0	0	0	0	100	4	0	0
Hannover	0	0	0	0	0	0	0	0	0	0	100	3
Total	14	98	11	94	65	62	0	100	3	83	5	95

Table 4.7   Geographic allocation of backbone connections, % of bandwidth

	2001											
	Africa		Asia and Pacific		Europe		Latin America and Caribbean		Rest of Europe		USA and Canada	
	(1)	(2)	(3)	(4)	(5)	(6)	(7)	(8)	(9)	(10)	(11)	(12)
London	0	18	0	54	64	15	0	0	0	10	36	53
Paris	0	48	0	29	87	15	0	0	0	0	12	14
Frankfurt	0	0	0	3	94	15	0	0	0	13	6	6
Amsterdam	0	3	0	3	86	14	0	0	0	0	14	15
Milan	0	0	0	0	96	3	0	0	0	0	4	1
Stockholm	0	0	0	0	96	6	0	0	1	52	2	1
Brussels	0	1	0	0	99	7	0	0	0	1	1	0
Oslo	0	1	0	3	99	2	0	0	0	1	1	0
Palermo	13	25	4	3	9	0	2	67	1	0	71	0
Lisbon	0	1	0	0	91	0	0	33	0	0	9	0
Munich	0	0	0	3	99	1	0	0	0	0	1	0
Copenhagen	0	0	0	0	76	3	0	0	0	3	24	6
Athens	0	0	0	0	73	0	0	0	0	0	27	0
Hamburg	0	0	0	0	95	2	0	0	0	0	5	1
Leuk	11	2	4	0	42	0	0	0	0	0	42	0
Sofia	0	0	0	0	94	0	0	0	0	0	6	0
Madrid	0	0	0	0	89	2	0	0	0	0	11	2
Geneva	0	0	0	0	99	2	0	0	0	0	1	0
Helsinki	0	0	0	0	95	1	0	0	3	15	2	0
Warsaw	0	0	0	0	96	0	0	0	0	0	4	0
Nittedal	0	0	0	0	48	0	0	0	52	2	0	0
Luxembourg	0	0	0	0	96	0	0	0	0	0	3	0
Bucharest	0	0	0	0	100	0	0	0	0	0	0	0
Zagreb	0	0	0	0	26	0	0	0	0	0	74	0
Dublin	0	0	0	0	93	0	0	0	0	0	7	0
Belgrade	0	0	0	0	54	0	0	0	0	0	46	0
Lausanne	0	0	0	0	75	0	0	0	0	0	25	0
Rotterdam	0	0	0	0	100	0	0	0	0	0	0	0
Tirana	0	0	0	0	40	0	0	0	0	0	60	0
Düsseldorf	0	0	0	0	100	1	0	0	0	0	0	0
Gdansk	0	0	0	0	50	0	0	0	0	0	50	0
Tartu	0	0	0	0	67	0	0	0	33	0	0	0
Thessaloniki	0	0	0	0	0	0	0	0	0	0	0	0
Graz	0	0	0	0	0	0	0	0	0	0	0	0
Hannover	0	0	0	0	0	0	0	0	0	0	0	0
Total	0	100	0	99	86	91	0	100	0	98	14	100

Notes:
(1) + (3) + (5) + (7) + (9) + (11) = (13) + (15) + (17) + (19) + (21) + (23) = 100%.
The cities included here fulfill at least one of the following criteria: % of extra-European
links > = 20%, and % of total bandwidth because of extra-European links >= 5%.

Source: Adapted from Tranos and Gillespie (2011).

Table 4.7 (continued)

	Africa		Asia and Pacific		Europe		Latin America and Caribbean		Rest of Europe		USA and Canada	
	(13)	(14)	(15)	(16)	(17)	(18)	(19)	(20)	(21)	(22)	(23)	(24)
London	0	41	1	41	64	17	0	0	1	24	34	49
Paris	0	22	0	9	81	14	0	1	0	0	18	17
Frankfurt	0	1	1	12	89	13	0	0	1	17	10	8
Amsterdam	0	2	0	4	83	11	0	0	0	1	17	12
Milan	0	1	1	3	94	3	0	0	0	0	5	1
Stockholm	0	0	0	0	92	5	0	0	8	51	0	0
Brussels	0	0	0	0	100	3	0	0	0	0	0	0
Oslo	0	0	0	0	91	1	0	0	0	0	9	1
Palermo	14	19	43	18	4	0	0	0	0	0	39	1
Lisbon	1	2	0	0	96	1	0	1	0	0	3	0
Munich	0	0	0	0	100	1	0	0	0	0	0	0
Copenhagen	0	0	0	0	85	4	0	0	0	2	14	4
Athens	0	0	15	12	79	1	0	0	0	0	5	0
Hamburg	0	0	0	0	97	3	0	0	0	0	3	0
Leuk	17	0	83	0	0	0	0	0	0	0	0	0
Sofia	0	0	0	0	100	0	0	0	0	0	0	0
Madrid	1	11	0	0	96	4	0	98	0	0	3	1
Geneva	0	0	0	0	83	2	0	0	0	0	17	2
Helsinki	0	0	0	0	100	1	0	0	0	0	0	0
Warsaw	0	0	0	0	99	1	0	0	1	2	0	0
Nittedal	100	1	0	0	0	0	0	0	0	0	0	0
Luxembourg	0	0	0	0	100	0	0	0	0	0	0	0
Bucharest	0	0	0	0	100	0	0	0	0	0	0	0
Zagreb	0	0	0	0	100	0	0	0	0	0	0	0
Dublin	0	0	0	0	96	1	0	0	0	0	4	0
Belgrade	0	0	0	0	100	0	0	0	0	0	0	0
Lausanne	0	0	0	0	75	0	0	0	0	0	25	0
Rotterdam	0	0	0	0	50	0	0	0	0	0	50	0
Tirana	0	0	0	0	100	0	0	0	0	0	0	0
Düsseldorf	0	0	0	0	92	2	0	0	0	0	8	1
Gdansk	0	0	0	0	0	0	0	0	0	0	0	0
Tartu	0	0	0	0	0	0	0	0	0	0	0	0
Thessaloniki	0	0	7	0	93	0	0	0	0	0	0	0
Graz	0	0	0	0	0	0	0	0	100	1	0	0
Hannover	0	0	0	0	0	0	0	0	0	0	100	2
Total	0	100	1	99	83	88	0	100	1	99	15	100

of the main nodes of the globalized informational economy. Last but not least, it could also be observed that London's backbone links with Africa as well as with Asia and the Pacific region also reflect Britain's past Empire.

At the same time, irrespective of the very small share of African and Asian connections to London's total bandwidth, London remains the city with the greatest capacity towards Africa (Table 4.7, column 14) and the Asia and the Pacific region (column 16) and of course towards the US (column 23) and the rest of the European cities (column 18). In other words, because of London's vast accumulated bandwidth, even the routes which represent a very small share of its total degree centrality are enough to give London the role of the dominant city in the IP communications with other continents. The above once more highlights London's importance in the geography of the Internet infrastructure.

However, its dominance in Africa's Internet connectivity was not constant through time. In 2001 and in terms of binary links, both London and Paris had a share of 30 percent each in Europe's total links with Africa (column 2 in Table 4.6). What is interesting though is that Paris's links with Africa were at higher capacity than London's and as a result Paris was the dominant city in connecting with Africa in terms of capacity, since it represented 48 percent of Europe's total capacity towards Africa (column 2 in Table 4.7). The above can be interpreted as a competition over time between London and Paris to become Europe's main Internet infrastructure hub, and also as a competition to be the gateway city for communications with other continents such as Africa. From an Internet service provider (ISP) perspective, the latter can be translated as a competition for selling universal (and regional) connectivity to a continent with very low infrastructural capacity and strong colonial relations both with London and Paris. Over time, London seems to have succeeded in this competition and gain the role as the main gateway city both for Africa and for Asia and Pacific region.

In general, Paris's extra-European links seem to have a similar spatial structure to London's, but because of their lower capacity, Paris's importance at the European level is lower than London's. Apart from its links with Africa, 14 percent of its binary degree centrality is due to connections with Asia and the Pacific region, reflecting again the demand for extensive (in geographical range) but not intensive (in terms of bandwidth) post-colonial digital links. It should be noted here that 18 percent of the accumulated bandwidth in Paris is dedicated to communications with the US and Canada, almost half of London's percentage, again indicating London's dominance in Europe's Internet geography.

Regarding the other two highly central cities, Frankfurt and Amsterdam, their global character is mainly reflected in the binary degree centrality. In general, Frankfurt has a more balanced division of its extra-European links and Amsterdam is more tied with the US and Canada. A significant share of Frankfurt's binary degree connectivity is because of its links with Asia and the Pacific, and Africa. In addition, Frankfurt is the dominant gateway city in terms of binary backbone links with the rest of Europe (17 percent of Europe's total links with the rest of Europe region), which includes countries such as Russia, Ukraine, Belarus and also Iceland and Greenland. However, Frankfurt's links towards the cities of the rest of Europe are rather low capacity, since Frankfurt is only responsible for 17 percent of Europe's total bandwidth towards this region. The dominant city in terms of bandwidth bound for Internet links with the rest of the Europe is Stockholm, which carries 51 percent of Europe's total bandwidth towards the cities of the rest of Europe. In more detail, the above high-capacity backbone links, which enable Stockholm to have such a dominant role in 2006, are towards Moscow and St Petersburg, while Frankfurt's links are also with Moscow and St Petersburg and in addition with Kiev, Lvov and Minsk. Looking retrospectively, Frankfurt also managed to increase its importance over time in providing connectivity to Africa and the Asia and Pacific region. Amsterdam on the other hand is more focused to European Internet backbone links. The main share of Amsterdam's links with non-European cities is cities from North America. More specifically, 13 percent and 17 percent of its degree centrality (binary and weighted) are due to US and Canadian links. The above enables Amsterdam to control 11 percent and 12 percent of Europe's binary links and bandwidth to North America.

Going further down in Table 4.6, apart from Stockholm, Copenhagen and also Warsaw and Bucharest are interesting cases because of their large share of links with the rest of Europe. What is also interesting is the complementarities between them: while Stockholm decreased its share of connections with these countries, Copenhagen increased it over time. However, its links are not of high capacity as can be seen in Table 4.7. Interestingly enough, though, for the case of Warsaw and Bucharest, the extra-European links refer only to cities in the rest of Europe. The geographic proximity between the cities of Central and Eastern Europe explains why the above cities, which do not have other extra European links, are well connected with the cities of what is defined here as the "rest of Europe".

Brussels is also a unique case. It is the only city which can be found at such a high rank in both centrality measures, but in which almost 100 percent of its already accumulated bandwidth is due to intra-European links. Although 33 percent of Brussels binary degree centrality is because of its links with non-European cities, these links are of low capacity and this is the reason why they result in an insignificant share of external links in terms of bandwidth. It could be said that the above reflects the city's unique role: hosting the European Union's headquarters makes it important, but its importance is almost exclusively intra-European in terms of the IBN function.

The next interesting case is Lisbon: 56 percent of its total binary connectivity is towards Africa and 6 percent towards Latin America. The above shares are equal to 9 percent and 33 percent of Europe's total connectivity with Africa and Latin America and the Caribbean region, which enables Lisbon to be the fifth most dominant city for African connectivity and to share the first place for Latin America and the Caribbean region. However, in Europe in total there are only three links with the latter region, one of which terminated in Lisbon in 2001. This is not surprising, though, because Latin America and the Caribbean region mainly gain universal IP connectivity through the US and more specifically through their gateway city, Miami (Garcia 2000; Grubesic and O'Kelly 2002). And this is obviously the reason why Lisbon (along with Madrid, Milan and Palermo) has a direct link with Miami.

In total, the capacity of links with Africa and Latin America is very low as can be seen in Table 4.7. This reflects the low demand for Internet services in these regions, but at the same time the need for universal connectivity. In addition, the importance of geography in submarine backbone networks roll-out is also reflected in these links. The location of Lisbon facing the Atlantic is a competitive advantage for setting up backbone fiber links with Africa because of the way these links are rolled out: the fiber is installed by a special ship, which follows a route near the coast of Portugal and Africa. Lisbon is a very suitable location for setting up such links, but it cannot be claimed that this is the main reason why Lisbon is highly connected with Africa. Lisbon is also a suitable location for setting up links with the US, but its share of connectivity with the US is very low (6 percent), highlighting the multidimensional interpretation of the backbone Internet geography. The main reason behind the extensive links with Africa is Portugal's colonial past, which is reflected once more in the geography of the backbone networks.

A similar case to Lisbon is that of Madrid. Almost half of the Spanish capital's connections in 2006 were with non-European cities. More specifically 20 percent of its binary degree centrality was due to links with Africa, 7 percent with Asia and the Pacific, 7 percent with Latin America, having one of the three backbone links that Europe shares with this continent. In terms of capacity, Madrid is the main nodal point for links with Latin America and the Caribbean since 98 percent of Europe's dedicated bandwidth for this continent passes through Madrid. However, this is a recent development because in 2001 Madrid only had links with European cities and North America. Madrid is also an important node for communications with Africa; 11 percent of Europe's bandwidth to this continent comes through the Spanish capital. Once again, a multilevel interpretation of the geography of the IBNs can be observed: Madrid's extra-European backbone links seem to be defined both by the city's location at the southwest tip of Europe, but also by its historical relations with Latin America.

Palermo is another fascinating case: 80 percent of its binary degree connectivity results from backbone links which terminate in cities outside Europe. More specifically, in 2006, 20 percent of the city's 13 links were with African and 53 percent with Asian and Pacific cities. Even more interesting is its share of links with Latin America and the Caribbean region in 2001, which reached 13 percent and enabled it to be the most important European node for backbone connections with Latin America. Its global character is even more obvious when the discussion turns to the weighted degree centrality. In 2006, 14 percent of its accumulated bandwidth was because of its links with African cities, 43 percent because of the Asia and the Pacific backbone networks and only 4 percent because of the intra-European links. From the dominance point of view, 14 percent of Europe's bandwidth to Africa and 18 percent towards Asia and the Pacific region pass through Palermo. In addition in 2001 67 percent of Europe's capacity towards Latin America and the Caribbean was passing through Palermo. Furthermore, 39 percent of its total bandwidth terminates in Northern America. All in all, Palermo is an Internet node of global importance. The reason behind this is its geographical location. It is located in Sicily, in the middle of the Mediterranean Sea, which was always an area with great trade activity between Europe, the Middle East and Africa. It seems that nowadays the trade activity in the area takes place not only on the sea's surface but also on the sea floor; the trade past of the Mediterranean Sea is replicated in the numerous fiber optic cables of the IBNs, which are laid on the floor of the Mediterranean Sea, and Palermo is a nodal point for these corridors of the digital economy.

When the discussion focuses on the determinant role of geography and physical distance in the allocation of the extra-European links, then Athens is also a good example: 19 percent of its binary and 15 percent of its weighted degree centrality is because of its links with Asia and the Pacific region, and more specifically with the neighboring countries of Turkey and Israel. The above capacity represents 12 percent of Europe's total capacity towards this continent.

On the other hand, for some cases geographic proximity is not a determinant factor at all. Leuk (Switzerland) and Nittedal (Norway) for instance do not have any intra-European links. Leuk is only served by two international backbone links which terminate to Africa and to Asia and the Pacific region. Nittedal had a degree centrality of 10 in 2006 and all of the links are with Africa. So, for these cities geographic proximity is not a determinant factor for their Internet backbone connectivity.

A different case is the Swiss cities of Geneva and Lausanne as well as Dublin. They shared, respectively, 30, 25 and 20 percent of their backbone links, and 17, 25 and 4 percent of their accumulated bandwidth, with the US and Canada in 2006, while the rest of their connections are only with European cities. The above pattern highlights the unique international character of Switzerland and the demand for interaction with specific cities; the link between New York and Geneva might reflect to a certain extent the location of the United Nations (UN) headquarters in the former, and the concentration of the UN's agencies in the latter (Sassen 2008). In addition, Dublin has well-established socio-economic relations with the US, with significant bidirectional migration flows (e.g. Walsh 2007) and in addition is located on the western tip of Europe.

Contrary to the interpretation of the above cities' Internet backbone links with North America, back in 2001 a different group of cities used to be highly connected with US cities, and for very different reasons. Cities such as Bucharest, Zagreb, Belgrade, Tirana and, to a certain extent, Athens used to be highly dependent upon the US in order to gain universal connectivity. Even at this time a significant part of the intra-European data traffic was through the US (Townsend 2003). Countries with low connectivity did not have any other choice but to use the expensive transatlantic backbone networks even for short intra-European data transfers. The US took advantage of its primacy in the development of the Internet to vend such services across the globe in ways similar to London's, and to a certain degree Lisbon's, attempt to provide global connectivity to their past colonies.

Retrospectively, the allocation of the connections from Europe towards the rest of the world seems to be quite stable, with the only differences in the connections with Africa and the US and Canada. Regarding the allocation of the capacity, the changes over time are minor and the vast majority of the extra-European bandwidth is because of links with North America.

4.5.2 Betweenness and Eigenvector Centrality

Continuing the analysis of centrality scores according to different measures, Table 4.8 presents the betweenness centrality scores for the 30 most central European cities. The whole table can be found in the Appendix of this chapter. As was stated above, this centrality measure is based on the binary network and it is a representation of how common it is to find a city as an internal (not origin or destination) part of a geodesic; or using the Internet terminology, how common it is for a city to be one of the different hops which consist of a data packet route between any potential origin and destination, without taking into consideration the centrality of the origin and the destination. Apparently, the number of connections that each city has does not affect this measure. Betweenness centrality does not reflect infrastructural supply, as could be assumed for the degree centrality which measures the accumulated binary connections or the accumulated bandwidth. On the contrary, it is a representation of the importance of a city in the Internet data transport system. As a result of this structural difference between the two indicators the cities' hierarchy presented in Table 4.8 is very different from the one which emerged from the degree centrality.

For presentation reasons, the same method as above is adopted here and the cities' centralities are analyzed in blocks of ten following the centrality ranking. The first tier of the ten most central cities has been changed with respect to the degree centrality measures. The most important change refers to the well-established, up to now, four most central cities. According to this measure the cluster of London, Paris, Frankfurt and Amsterdam does not exist any more. Just like the binary degree centrality measure, Frankfurt is the most central city according to betweenness centrality of the intra-European network, and is followed by London, Vienna and Milan, with the latter being the one which is mostly relatively favoured by this measure. Further below, Paris and Amsterdam are found in fifth and sixth place and interestingly enough the rest of this tier's cities are located in the Eastern and South-Eastern part of Europe: Zagreb, Budapest, Warsaw and Athens, with the Croatian and Polish capitals being favored by this measure. Looking at betweenness centrality retrospectively, notable changes took place during the six-year study period. In 2001, apart from the changes in the top rank positions, with London being the most central city followed by Frankfurt and Amsterdam, the most notable changes were for the cities of Eastern and South-Eastern Europe: Budapest, Warsaw and Athens were replaced by Stockholm, Geneva and Lisbon. In terms of centrality change, apart from Frankfurt, these Eastern European cities were the only ones that experienced centrality increase during the study period, with Warsaw having the greatest increase. It can be easily observed that over time there is a noteworthy geographical pattern of change in Europe: because of the development of the Internet infrastructure in Eastern and South-Eastern European cities and their steady disengagement from the US in order to gain universal Internet connectivity, cities from this area managed to integrate in the IBN in Europe. Most importantly, they integrated well enough to appear more central

The geography of the Internet

Table 4.8   Betweenness centrality 2001–06

	2001				2006				E.c. change 2001–06 (%)	a.c. change 2001–06 (%)
	E.c.		a.c.		E.c.		a.c.			
Frankfurt	73.1	2	22.0	3	100.0	1	63.7	2	36.8	189.8
London	100.0	1	100.0	1	62.5	2	100.0	1	−37.5	0.0
Vienna	59.4	4	12.0	9	49.2	3	14.0	4	−17.2	16.2
Milan	45.7	6	12.4	8	39.6	4	12.2	6	−13.4	−1.1
Paris	57.6	5	49.3	2	36.4	5	34.8	3	−36.9	−29.3
Amsterdam	72.7	3	17.3	4	30.3	6	12.5	5	−58.4	−27.6
Zagreb	24.6	9	4.6	18	30.1	7	7.5	10	22.5	62.3
Budapest	5.9	28	0.9	37	19.3	8	6.3	12	227.1	583.0
Warsaw	1.4	35	2.5	21	18.6	9	5.6	13	1193.3	120.6
Athens	5.0	29	1.5	33	13.7	10	5.4	14	171.0	269.5
Copenhagen	18.0	12	5.4	13	11.7	11	7.7	9	−34.7	42.4
Hamburg	0.0	48	3.6	19	10.8	12	3.1	17		−13.1
Prague	14.4	15	2.3	24	10.6	13	2.9	18	−26.2	23.2
Marseille					8.6	14	2.2	19		
Dublin	12.5	20	2.3	26	8.6	15	2.2	20	−31.5	−4.3
Monaco	1.0	37	0.2	44	8.6	15	2.2	20	746.8	857.4
Ostrava					8.6	15	2.2	20		
Zürich	22.6	11	4.6	17	7.9	18	1.9	23	−64.8	−59.1
Belgrade	0.2	43	1.4	34	6.1	19	1.6	26	2608.7	13.6
Ljubljana	12.8	17	2.0	32	4.2	20	1.7	25	−66.8	−11.1
Stockholm	26.9	7	9.1	10	3.8	21	1.8	24	−85.8	−80.5
Madrid	10.9	26	2.4	23	3.8	22	4.4	15	−65.3	85.0
Barcelona	4.8	30	1.0	36	2.6	23	0.8	29	−46.1	−14.9
Stuttgart	0.0	48	0.0	52	2.3	24	1.1	27		
Nicosia	0.0	48	0.0	52	2.2	25	1.0	28		
Skopje	1.8	33	0.4	39	1.1	26	0.1	41	−37.3	−59.7
Pristine					1.1	27	0.2	38		
Tirana	0.0	48	0.3	41	1.1	28	0.3	33		−4.4
Bratislava	0.3	42	0.4	40	1.0	29	0.3	36	311.5	−21.4
Podgorica					1.0	30	0.1	42		

Note: E.c. = European cities; a.c. = all cities.

than some of the cities of the West, with greater presence in the informational economy.

What is interesting though is to verify the above for the overall network and not only for its intra-European extraction. When all the links are included in the analysis, in 2006 London was the most central city, once again demonstrating its global importance in the geography of the Internet. Paris and Amsterdam overtook Milan, and Vienna remained in the same position. The three cities from Eastern Europe, that is Budapest, Warsaw and Athens, were replaced by Copenhagen, Palermo and Lisbon because of their geographically extensive linkages with non-European cities, which enable them to be part of many different geodesics. Back in 2001, betweenness centrality for the whole network was even more biased toward the Western part of Europe. London, Paris, Frankfurt and Amsterdam were the three most central cities. Vienna was the only gateway city for Eastern Europe and the rest of the South-Eastern countries were replaced by Stockholm, Brussels, Palermo and Lisbon, reflecting to some extent the degree centrality for all the cities in Table 4.4.

The second tier of cities seems to be much differentiated by the same tier of Table 4.4; only three of ten cities are common in the second tiers of the two binary centrality measures: that is, Copenhagen, Hamburg and Prague. Apart from the Czech capital, Ostrava, Belgrade and Ljubljana constitute a cluster of Eastern and Southern cities. Cities such as Ostrava and also Dublin and Monaco climbed in the hierarchy while Zürich's centrality is undermined by this measure. If the overall network is taken into consideration, a few changes would have taken place in this tier. Apart from the cities of South-Eastern Europe mentioned above, Madrid would also be part of this tier, again because of its extroversive connectivity profile.

Looking backwards, many changes took place in the six-year study period. Belgrade and Monaco gained a lot in terms of betweenness centrality. In general, only four out of ten cities were of this tier in 2001. The changes are even more radical when the overall network is taken into consideration. Cities such as Marseille and Ostrava would be further below, sharing the 52nd place, and cities such Geneva, Oslo, Nittedal and Leuk would be part of this tier because of their external links.

Looking at the remaining cities of Table 4.8, many differences with the degree centrality can be observed. Important cities in terms of degree centrality such as Stockholm, Brussels, Geneva and Lisbon lost position in betweenness rank, while a cluster of cities from South-Eastern Europe consisting of Skopje, Pristine, Tirana, Podgorica and Thessaloniki appears to be more important using this measure. These changes denote the differentiated hub roles observed in the European IBN. The increase in Internet penetration in Eastern Europe at the end of the study period generated the need for Internet hubs in this area, and this is what the above changes reflect.

Indeed, betweenness centrality provides another view of how cities act

as nodes in the IBN. It could be compared with the binary degree centrality, because both of them are based on the binary network. While degree
centrality is a connectivity indicator providing valuable information on
the number of the cities that a city is directly connected with, betweenness
centrality is an indicator of how important the location of a city is, not in
geographical but in network terms.

The last centrality measure analyzed here is the eigenvector centrality for the weighted network, which is presented in Table 4.9. As it was
stated above, this centrality measure is useful because the centrality score
of a city is based on the centrality of its neighbors. Again, for comparison
reasons, the last column of the table presents the rank of the degree centrality for the weighted network of the intra-European international links.
The same strategy applies here and the eigenvector centrality analysis is
based on city blocks of ten. Just like the weighted degree centrality, the
cluster of the first four highly important cities emerged again: London is
the most central node and is followed by Paris, Frankfurt and Amsterdam.
What is interesting here is the fact that the difference between the first and
second city in terms of the normalized score is the smallest compared with
the other centrality measures. Obviously, because this indicator takes into
consideration the importance of neighbors, the differences in centrality
measures are smoother than the more direct approach of degree centrality. The cities which are included in the first tier of eigenvector and not
in the first tier of weighted degree centrality are Brussels, Düsseldorf and
Geneva. The reason why these cities were advanced under this centrality
measure is because of their intensive linkages with the cluster of the four
most central cities. The explanation for the above intensive connectivity is twofold: all of the above-mentioned cities are included in Europe's
pentagon, so not only the small physical distance, but also their intensive
socio-economic links define this connectivity pattern. This is the reason
why cities such as Copenhagen, Stockholm and Vienna, which accumulated enough bandwidth to be part of the first tier of cities regarding the
weighted degree centrality, ended up being part of the second tier of cities
for this measure. Apparently their connectivity pattern with the highly
centralized cluster of cities was not intensive enough to enable them to
remain in their positions according to the accumulated bandwidth, which
is due to their roles as gateway cities to the North and East of Europe.

Changes because of the inclusion of the extra-European links as well
as changes over time are minor for this indicator. When the backbone
connections with non-European cities are taken into consideration the
main change is that Copenhagen and Dublin appear to be more central,
obviously because of their high-capacity links with New York. In general,
changes because of the external links are negligible as almost all of the

Table 4.9   Weighted eigenvector centrality 2001–06

	2001				2006				E.c. change 2001–06 (%)	a.c. change 2001–06 (%)
	E.c.		a.c.		E.c.		a.c.			
London	98.4	2	100.0	1	100.0	1	100.0	1	1.6	0.0
Paris	100.0	1	77.4	2	92.3	2	70.4	2	−7.7	−9.0
Frankfurt	88.5	3	58.7	4	79.9	3	55.3	3	−9.7	−5.8
Amsterdam	85.0	4	66.3	3	65.1	4	52.0	4	−23.4	−21.6
Madrid	11.7	8	7.8	9	33.5	5	21.6	5	186.8	178.7
Brussels	59.0	5	40.9	5	24.9	6	16.7	6	−57.8	−59.2
Milan	14.1	6	8.6	8	15.1	7	9.4	8	7.1	9.7
Düsseldorf	9.3	11	5.8	10	12.0	8	8.9	9	29.0	53.6
Geneva	9.7	10	5.8	11	11.3	9	7.4	12	16.4	28.4
Hamburg	5.3	13	3.9	13	10.9	10	7.6	11	104.5	98.0
Copenhagen	9.9	9	11.1	6	10.6	11	10.0	7	6.8	−9.7
Dublin	2.8	16	2.3	15	10.2	12	7.9	10	268.5	244.6
Zürich	8.1	12	4.8	12	8.8	13	5.2	14	8.2	9.0
Warsaw	0.4	26	0.2	27	8.8	13	4.7	15	2117.3	1868.2
Stockholm	13.7	7	9.6	7	8.6	15	5.4	13	−37.0	−44.1
Vienna	2.6	17	1.4	18	7.3	16	3.9	16	185.4	186.3
Prague	1.0	19	0.5	25	5.4	17	3.0	18	443.0	473.1
Barcelona	1.0	19	0.7	19	5.0	18	3.1	17	406.8	325.7
Lisbon	0.8	24	0.6	24	3.9	19	2.7	19	397.8	391.7
Oslo	4.6	14	3.0	14	2.9	20	2.6	20	−37.0	−13.3
Budapest	0.4	26	0.3	26	2.2	21	1.1	22	443.0	313.3
Athens	0.6	25	0.7	20	2.0	22	1.5	21	231.8	125.3
Bucharest	0.2	29	0.1	34	1.6	23	0.8	24	714.5	931.9
Bristol					1.4	24	0.9	23		
Helsinki	1.0	19	0.6	21	1.1	25	0.5	27	8.6	−18.5
Munich	1.0	19	0.6	23	0.9	26	0.5	28	−9.5	−11.7
Bratislava	0.2	29	0.1	29	0.9	26	0.4	30	352.5	227.6
Tallinn	0.2	29	0.1	30	0.7	28	0.5	29	262.0	365.2
Basel	0.0	34	0.0	39	0.7	28	0.4	31		1082.7
Kolding					0.5	30	0.3	33		

Note: E.c. = European cities; a.c. = all cities.

non-European cities appeared to have very low centrality because only
their backbone links with European cities are included.[18] Retrospectively,
Stockholm and Copenhagen used to be more central for both versions
of the network. Madrid and Hamburg experienced the highest centrality

increase and Brussels the highest decrease through the six-year study period.

The second tier of cities consists of the more peripheral (in geographical terms) cities, which perform a significant role in the geography of the Internet in Europe. The hub cities of North Europe, Copenhagen, Stockholm and Oslo, as well as these of the Eastern and South-Eastern Europe such as Warsaw, Vienna and Prague, are included here. In addition, Dublin and Barcelona because of their high-capacity links with London and Paris, respectively, are found in this tier. Finally Zürich appears to be a peripheral city in the geography of the Internet, despite locating in Europe's core.

Again the changes because of the extra-European links as well as the changes over time are minor, with Warsaw gaining the most centrality increase. Interestingly enough, despite Lisbon's external links, its centrality because of the inclusion of extra-European linkages did not change simply because its links are of low bandwidth and with cities which appear to be of low importance.

The third tier contains even more peripheral cities. From the Eastern and South-Eastern part of Europe Budapest, Athens, Bucharest and Bratislava are part of this tier, while from the North, Helsinki, Tallinn and Kolding can be found here. From Central Europe, Munich and Basel, despite their geographic proximity to the most connected cities, are characterized by low eigenvector centrality. Differences over time and after the inclusion of the non-European links are again minor.

All the above centrality measures provide different but equally valuable understandings about the distinctive roles of the European cities in the IBN, helping to better understand the geography of the Internet infrastructure in Europe. Binary and weighted degree centralities represent the infrastructural supply, with the latter better highlighting the economic geography of Europe and the former being associated with political as well as physical geography. On the contrary, the other two centrality measures are more related with the technological nature of the Internet backbone: betweenness centrality highlights the potential utility of the city in the IP data transfer because of its location in the network space, while eigenvector centrality highlights cities' importance based on its indirect weighted links, in a way similar to the Internet's function.

4.5.3   Summary of Different Centrality Measures

In order to summarize the above centrality measures, cluster analysis is applied. As the main goal here is to cluster cities based on their performance on the centrality indicators, cluster analysis is an appropriate method as its usefulness in classifying relatively "raw" data in an exploratory comparative framework is well established (Nijkamp et al. 1999). Based on the above analysis, the resulting clusters, apart from distinguishing the obvious most centralized cities, also provide interesting insights concerning the least central cities. In order to achieve this, the empirical method of k-means is utilized. In simple terms, this non-hierarchical method results in k new clusters, with k being a priori defined (Rogerson 2006). All the centrality indicators were included in this analysis as they highlight different facets of the Internet infrastructure: the binary and weighted degree centrality, the betweenness and eigenvector centrality, with and without the extra-European links. This method was applied for both 2001 and 2006. In order to avoid a two-cluster solution with the most central cities (usually London, Frankfurt, Paris and Amsterdam) forming one cluster and having the rest of the cities crowded in a second cluster, calibration tests were initially applied in order to select a k suitable for the analysis. According to these tests, the most suitable k for better explaining the pattern of centrality was equal to 7. Table 4.10 presents the allocation of the European cities to the new clusters.

In total, the four leading cities form the "golden diamond" of the Internet infrastructure (Tranos and Gillespie 2011) as they are almost always found in the top of the European hierarchy. And most importantly, their hegemony is stable over time. While London and Paris have a unique character and for both years they shaped individual clusters, London is the most central city. This can be attributed to London's character as a global city and as the main European gateway. The above is in accordance with previous results from world city research: despite the different approaches, concepts, methodologies and data sources (Derudder and Witlox 2005), all the relevant studies identify London, along with New York, Tokyo and Paris, at the top of the global urban hierarchy (Taylor 2004). Indeed, IBNs, but also other networks such as aviation (see Chapter 5), provide London with the essential infrastructural layer, underpinning the global city process. Based on the well-accepted argument that the flows through world cities are more important structural elements for these cities than what is contained within them (Derudder and Witlox 2005), it can reasonably be advanced that London's dominance in the (European) IBN is integrally associated with its leading position in the global urban hierarchy. In addition, transatlantic communication links connecting London with the East Coast of the US traditionally attracted the attention of investors for new developments. Malecki and Wei (2009) highlight the fact that during the 1890s, a telegraph from Paris to London was transmitted faster through New York than directly between the two cities, because of the technological advance of submarine cables (Headrick 1991). Interestingly

Table 4.10 Cluster analysis based on the centrality measures for 2001 and 2006

	1	2	3	4	5	6	7
2001	London	Paris	Amsterdam, Frankfurt	Milan, Vienna	Brussels	Copenhagen, Geneva, Lisbon, Madrid, Munich, Oslo, Prague, Sofia, Stockholm, Zürich	Andorra, Antwerp, Athens, Banja Luka, Barcelona, Basel, Belgrade, Berlin, Bratislava, Brno, Bucharest, Budapest, Cologne, Dortmund, Dublin, Düsseldorf, Ehingen, Gdansk, Hamburg, Helsinki, Karlsruhe, Lausanne, Leuk, Ljubljana, Luxembourg, Lyon, Manchester, Monaco, Mostar, Msida, Nice, Nicosia, Nittedal, Palermo, Plovdiv, Portsmouth, Riga, Rome, Rotterdam, San Marino, Sarajevo, Skopje, Split, Strasbourg, Stuttgart, Tallinn, Tartu, Tirana, Turin, Vilnius, Warsaw, Zagreb
2006	London	Paris	Amsterdam	Frankfurt	Milan, Vienna	Athens, Brussels, Budapest, Copenhagen, Düsseldorf, Geneva, Hamburg, Madrid, Prague, Stockholm, Warsaw, Zagreb, Zürich	Andorra, Banja Luka, Barcelona, Basel, Belgrade, Berlin, Bielsko-Biala, Bratislava, Bristol, Brno, Bucharest, Cluj, Dublin, Ehingen, Eindhoven, Gothenburg, Gyor, Helsinki, Hilden, Klagenfurt, Kolding, Lausanne, Lisbon, Ljubljana, Luxembourg, Malmö, Manchester, Maribor, Marseille, Monaco, Mostar, Msida, Munich, Nice, Nicosia, Nuremberg, Oslo, Ostrava, Palermo, Podgorica, Poznan, Pristine, Riga, Rome, Rotterdam, Sarajevo, Skopje, Sofia, Stuttgart, Tallinn, Thessaloniki, Timisoara, Tirana, Turin, Venice, Vilnius, Wroclaw

Table 4.11   Cluster centers

		1	2	3	4	5	6	7	
2001	Degree	100	89	86	57	39	34	11	
	degree (w.)	97	100	95	15	48	12	1	
	degree (ac)	100	66	42	24	22	16	5	
	degree (w.-a.c.)	100	76	70	10	32	9	1	
	betweenness	100	58	73	53	17	17	3	
	betweenness (a.c.)	100	49	20	12	13	6	1	
	eigenvector (w.)	98	100	87	8	59	6	1	
	eigenvector (w.-a.c.)	100	77	63	5	41	4	0	
	N	*1*	*1*	*2*	*2*	*1*	*10*	*52*	*69*
2006	Degree	92	58	61	100	57	27	8	
	degree (w.)	100	85	65	81	20	13	1	
	degree (ac)	100	49	32	70	26	13	4	
	degree (w.-a.c.)	100	66	50	58	13	9	1	
	betweenness	63	36	30	100	44	10	1	
	betweenness (a.c.)	100	35	13	64	13	4	1	
	eigenvector (w.)	100	92	65	80	11	11	1	
	eigenvector (w.-a.c.)	100	70	52	55	7	7	0	
	N	*1*	*1*	*1*	*1*	*2*	*13*	*57*	*76*

Note: w. = weighted; a.c. = all the cities.

enough, the same used to happen to intra-European Internet traffic even in the early 2000s, as a significant proportion was transmitted via the US (Townsend 2003). In addition, even in 2006 the link with the highest capacity involving a European city was the one between London and New York. It can be said that London was always favored by a surplus of communication links with the US, which enabled London to perform a gateway role for the European cities in terms of transatlantic communications. To sum up, for various economic, historical and geographic reasons including its hegemony in the transnational urban network, London is not only the leading city in terms of Internet connectivity in Europe, but it also performs a vital hub role, acting as a gateway following historical patterns.

Following the European urban hierarchy, Paris is the second most central city in the European Internet backbone. According to Table 4.11, which presents the centers of the new clusters and their main characteristics, Paris appears to be more central when capacity is taken into consideration. This can be translated to a connectivity pattern based more on links of higher rather than of lower capacity.

Different connectivity patterns, but similar roles, can be identified for the other two cities of Europe's Internet diamond, Frankfurt and Amsterdam. While Frankfurt is more central according to the binary centrality measures (degree and betweenness) revealing a relatively high number of low-capacity links, Amsterdam – like Paris – is favored by fewer high-capacity Internet backbone links. However, both of them perform hub roles. Frankfurt's high betweenness centrality illustrates this function, as its central location in the middle of Europe enables it to share direct links with a great number of cities located in both Western and Eastern Europe. On the other hand, Amsterdam's hub role in the European IBN is illustrated not only by its high centrality measures, but also by the fact that it hosts the most important Internet Exchange Point (IXP) in Europe in terms of Internet traffic (Euro-IX 2006).

Nevertheless, cluster analysis reveals new information when the discussion moves away from the four most central cities. More specifically, the fifth cluster is formed by Milan and Vienna for both 2001 and 2006 and is characterized by high binary degree centrality measures, intermediate weighted degree and betweenness centrality and very low eigenvector centrality. The above characteristics reflect cities with quite central locations (betweenness) which are linked with a large number of other cities (binary degree) with relatively low-capacity links (weighted degree). Vienna and Milan are the two cities allocated to this cluster. The former is the main gateway city for Central and Eastern Europe, and is the fifth and fourth most central city in regards to binary degree and betweenness centrality. However, these links are of low capacity as is reflected in the lower weighted degree centrality (eighth most central). Milan on the other hand is Italy's main node, but it also performs a hub role for the South of Europe. Interestingly enough, Milan's high-capacity links are with Northern cities, but the majority of its links are with Southern cities and all of them are of low capacity.

The sixth cluster consists of moderate central cities, but still important for Europe's Internet backbone geography for both years. This cluster includes the hub cities of Northern Europe, Stockholm, Copenhagen (as well as Oslo in 2001) and Hamburg, as well as Madrid (and Lisbon in 2001) and the secondary – after Vienna – hub cities of the Eastern and South-Eastern Europe such as Athens, Budapest, Prague, Warsaw and Zagreb. Interestingly enough, the Northern European cities are very well connected in terms of their installed capacity and links with the rest of the world and consequently act as hub cities for Internet backbone connectivity in their hinterlands. However, because of their peripheral location, these cities cannot perform important roles for the function of the overall network, as is reflected in their low betweenness and eigenvector centrality measures. In 2001, Prague and Sofia were the only cities in this cluster from that area, a fact which indicates the radical increase of the Internet backbone connectivity in Eastern and South-Eastern Europe during the six-year study period. In addition, this cluster also includes some central (in geographical terms) cities, such as Brussels, Geneva and Zürich (Munich in 2001), for which, despite their location in Europe's pentagon, their Internet backbone centrality measures are not high enough to enable them to be part of Europe's first tier. Finally, for both years the most extensive cluster is the one which refers to the least central cities: 75 percent of the connected cities for both years are found in this cluster, indicating the highly centralized character of the IBN in Europe.

4.6 CONCLUSIONS

Summing up the above analysis, the first point which should be mentioned is the highly skewed distribution of the backbone links when their capacity is taken into consideration. There is a small number of links which can be characterized as outliers because their capacity is much greater than the average. What is interesting from a geography point of view is that these outliers are mainly concentrated in Europe's core area, known as the pentagon. Additionally, over time there is a trend towards a decrease in the variation of the capacity of the backbone links. Technological improvements and cost reductions enabled this cohesion trend in the capacity distribution: while the maximum capacity link was increased by a factor of six (from 77 768 to 467 671 Mbps) during 2001–06, the lowest-capacity link was increased by a factor of 31 (from 0.064 to 2Mbps). Apart from this, specific reasons should explain the skewed distribution of the high-capacity backbone links among cities such as London, Paris, Amsterdam and Frankfurt. An attempt to explain this takes place in Chapter 6 of this book.

Also interesting are the results of the centralization measures in order to better realize the network's big picture. According to degree centralization, there is a clear tendency for a more centralized network over the six-year study period. The trend is similar when the betweenness centralization is calculated. However, according to this measure, which is a better proxy of the IP data packet transport system, the European international IBN is less centralized compared to the previous measure, which is more related to the infrastructural capital. The centralization of the network, though, appears to be higher regarding the eigenvector centrality, which also takes into consideration the indirect links. But the network seems even more centralized when the capacity of the backbone links is included in eigenvector centrality calculation. All in all, it could be said that the

European extraction of the international IBN is in general moderately centralized, but when the capacity is included in the analysis the network appears to be more centralized.

Even more interesting from a geography standpoint are the different centrality measures. These local statistics reveal the distinctive roles cities perform in the Internet function. Firstly, London is by some margin Europe's leading world city, expressed both in terms of its very high levels of binary and weighted centrality within the Internet and by its high level of connectivity with cities in other regions of the world. The other three European cities with demonstrable world city status are Paris, Frankfurt and Amsterdam. Paris is the second most important city in terms of its centrality weighted by bandwidth, and Frankfurt in terms of the number of cities it is connected with. Amsterdam is behind both of these cities, but it is characterized by substantial bandwidth accumulation and displays a high level of connectivity with North American world cities. In total, 55 percent of the intra-European bandwidth and 59 percent of the whole bandwidth of the European cities is allocated among London (17 percent and 22 percent respectively), Paris (14 percent and 14 percent), Frankfurt (13 percent and 13 percent) and Amsterdam (11 percent and 11 percent).

All of the other major cities in Europe are substantially behind the Internet diamond formed by these four cities. Stockholm, Copenhagen and Hamburg are well connected in terms of their installed capacity and direct binary linkages, but they seem to be much less central in terms of indirect links, reflecting the peripherality of the northern edge of the European urban system and the hub roles they perform in their hinterlands. Stockholm, however, does have high bandwidth links with the major Russian cities.

Amongst this second tier of major cities, Madrid and Brussels have relatively high levels of centrality in terms of bandwidth, both of them having high-capacity links with one or more of the cities constituting the Internet diamond, even though the number of cities they have direct links with is relatively modest. Vienna and Milan, in contrast, have a large number of low-capacity links. Vienna appears to be acting as a gateway or hub for cities in Central and Eastern Europe, while Milan is playing a similar role for Southern Europe; most of its direct links are with southern cities, though its few high-capacity links are with London, Paris and Frankfurt, but also with Vienna and Zürich.

Another tier down, a group of cities consisting of Zürich, Warsaw, Budapest, Athens, Lisbon and Palermo are characterized by relatively high numbers of direct connections, but predominantly in low bandwidth links. Most of these cities have connectivity patterns that are primarily external to Europe, at least in terms of the definition of Europe used here.

For Palermo and Athens, these links are primarily to the Near and Middle East, while for Lisbon they are primarily to Africa. Warsaw and Budapest, in contrast, are oriented towards Eastern and Central Europe, respectively. Zürich on the other hand appears to have all the "right connections" as it is connected with most of the high-centrality cities in Europe.

All in all, despite the fact that the network has been expanded mainly towards the East during the six-year period and some cities outside the core gained in terms of centrality, its core remained strong and the overall network appeared to be slightly more centralized.

Table 4A.1   *Different degree centrality measures and relevant rankings, 2001 and 2006*

	Binary degree		Weighted degree		Betweenness		Eigenvector	
	2001	2006	2001	2006	2001	2006	2001	2006
Amsterdam	40 *4*	32 *4*	72 *3*	50 *4*	17 *4*	13 *5*	66 *3*	52 *4*
Andorra	4 *40*	2 *52*	0 *51*	0 *76*	0 *52*	0 *48*	0 *48*	0 *62*
Antwerp	2 *47*		2 *23*		0 *52*		2 *17*	
Athens	12 *16*	16 *10*	1 *35*	3 *23*	2 *33*	5 *14*	1 *20*	2 *21*
Banja Luka	2 *47*	1 *60*	0 *62*	0 *67*	0 *50*	0 *48*	0 *60*	0 *64*
Barcelona	6 *31*	7 *24*	2 *25*	3 *24*	1 *36*	1 *29*	1 *19*	3 *17*
Basel	1 *60*	3 *45*	0 *30*	1 *37*	0 *52*	0 *48*	0 *39*	0 *31*
Belgrade	5 *35*	5 *31*	0 *56*	0 *50*	1 *34*	2 *26*	0 *58*	0 *44*
Berlin	7 *28*	1 *60*	3 *21*	0 *51*	0 *38*	0 *48*	0 *28*	0 *53*
Bielsko-Biala		1 *60*		0 *53*		0 *48*		0 *72*
Bijeljina								
Bratislava	8 *25*	6 *27*	3 *20*	5 *16*	0 *40*	0 *36*	0 *29*	0 *30*
Bristol		1 *60*		1 *35*		0 *48*		1 *23*
Brno	2 *47*	3 *45*	0 *64*	2 *26*	2 *26*	0 *48*	0 *60*	0 *42*
Brussels	22 *8*	12 *15*	32 *5*	12 *11*	13 *6*	0 *32*	41 *5*	17 *6*
Bucharest	7 *28*	7 *24*	1 *33*	1 *30*	0 *46*	0 *31*	0 *34*	1 *24*
Budapest	11 *20*	18 *8*	1 *27*	4 *21*	1 *37*	6 *12*	0 *26*	1 *22*
Cluj		1 *60*		0 *72*		0 *48*		0 *59*
Cologne	2 *47*		0 *52*		0 *52*		0 *43*	
Copenhagen	17 *13*	17 *9*	18 *7*	18 *6*	5 *13*	8 *9*	11 *6*	10 *7*
Dortmund	1 *60*		0 *54*		0 *52*		0 *44*	

Dresden	5	35	5	31	2	24	4	20	2	25	2	20	2	15	8	10
Dublin	4	40	6	27	6	15	8	12	0	52	0	45	6	10	9	9
Düsseldorf	2	47	1	60	0	61	0	77	0	49	0	48	0	60	0	72
Ehingen			1	60				72				48				59
Eindhoven	45		70		68		58		22		64		59		0	
Frankfurt	2	47		2		4		3		3		2		4	55	3
Gdansk	11	20	10	17	8	48	8	13	0	52	0	35	0	37	7	12
Geneva						14			5	16	0		6	11		48
Gothenburg			1	60				60			0	48				70
Graz			1	60				60			0	48				67
Gyor			1	60				72			0	48				11
Hamburg	12	16	12	15	8	12	13	10	4	19	3	17	4	13	8	25
Hannover			1	60			1	28			0	48			1	27
Helsinki	11	20	5	31	3	18	5	19	2	31	0	48	1	21	1	55
Hilden			3	45				44			0	48				
Imsbruck																
Karlsruhe	1	60			0	68			0	52			0	60		60
Katowice																
Klagenfurt			2	52				64			0	48				70
Kolding			2	52				42			0	48				33
Lausanne	5	35	4	39	0	43	0	43		47	0	48	0	33		32
Leuk	12	16	2	52	0	49	0	80		15	4	16	0	38		72
Lille																
Lisbon	18	11	16	10	2	26	2	25	15	5	9	8	1	24	3	19
Ljubljana	6	31	5	31	0	40	1	31	2	32	2	25	0	41		35
Lodz																
London	100	1	100	1	100	1	100	1	100	1	100	1	100	1	100	1
Luxembourg	8	25	3	45	1	34		38	0	42	0	48	1	22		34
Lyon	2	47			2	22	0		2	26			0	31	0	

Table 4A.1 (continued)

Each cell shows the centrality value followed by its rank (value rank).

	Binary degree		Weighted degree		Betweenness		Eigenvector	
	2001	2006	2001	2006	2001	2006	2001	2006
Madrid	11 20	15 12	9 10	16 7	2 23	4 15	8 9	22 5
Malmö		2 52		0 57		0 48		0 47
Manchester	1 60	1 60	0 37	0 47	0 52	0 48	0 47	0 51
Maribor		1 60		0 77		0 48		0 72
Marseille		5 31		1 32		2 19		0 39
Milan	24 5	25 6	13 8	13 9	12 8	12 6	9 8	9 8
Monaco	2 47	3 45	0 46	0 59	0 44	2 20	0 40	0 52
Mostar	2 47	1 60	0 65	0 67	2 26	0 48	0 60	0 72
Msida	2 47	3 45	0 50	0 56	0 43	0 34	0 55	0 54
Munich	18 11	6 27	4 17	3 22	3 20	0 44	1 23	1 28
Nice	2 47	1 60	0 48	0 70	0 48	0 48	0 49	0 72
Nicosia	4 40	5 31	0 59	0 55	0 52	1 28	0 50	0 49
Nittedal	8 25	10 17	0 53	0 69	5 14	7 11	0 60	0 72
Nuremberg		1 60		0 57		0 48		0 65
Oradea								
Oslo	22 8	7 24	9 11	5 17	9 11	0 40	3 14	3 20
Ostrava	19 10	2 52	0 36	1 33	13 7	2 20	0 57	0 42
Palermo		15 12		2 27		9 7		0 56
Paris	66 2	49 3	76 2	66 2	49 2	35 3	77 2	70 2
Plovdiv	1 60		0 65		0 52		0 53	
Podgorica		4 39		0 71		0 42		0 72
Portsmouth	1 60		0 67		0 52		0 60	
Pozman		1 60		0 51		0 48		0 58

City																
Prague	13	14	9	21	5	16	5	18	2	24	3	18	1	25	3	18
Pristine			4	39			0	69			0	38			0	68
Riga	6	31	5	31	0	41	1	36	2	25	0	43	0	45	0	37
Rijeka																
Rome	2	47	1	60	1	29	0	47	0	51	0	48	0	42	0	68
Rotterdam	5	35	2	52	1	28	0	41	0	45	0	48	0	32	1	26
Salzburg																
San Marino	1	60			0	60			0	52			0	58		
Sarajevo	6	31	2	52	0	55	0	66	1	35	0	46	0	60	0	72
Skopje	4	40	4	39	0	57	0	54	0	39	0	41	0	55	0	66
Sofia	12	16	5	31	0	43	0	45	6	12	0	47	0	36	0	38
Split	1	60			0	68			0	52			0	60		
Stockholm	23	7	19	7	25	6	20	5	9	10	2	24	10	7	5	13
Strasbourg	4	40			3	19			2	26			2	16		
Stuttgart	1	60	9	21	0	39	0	40	0	52	1	27	0	46	0	45
Tallinn	4	40	8	23	0	38	1	29	0	52	0	39	0	30	1	29
Tartu	2	47			0	57			0	52			0	60		
Thessaloniki			4	39			0	63			1	30			0	50
Timisoara			3	45			0	49			0	48			0	40
Tirana	4	40	4	39	0	63	0	65	0	41	0	33	0	53	0	63
Turin	1	60	1	60	1	30	0	72	0	52	0	48	0	52	0	59
Varna																
Venice			1	60			0	46			0	48			0	57
Vienna	24	5	28	5	8	13	14	8	12	9	14	4	1	18	4	16
Vilnius	7	28	6	27	0	47	1	34	3	22	0	37	0	51	0	36
Warsaw	10	24	10	17	1	32	6	15	3	21	6	13	0	27	5	15
Wroclaw			1	60			0	60			0	48			0	46
Zagreb	5	35	10	17	0	45	0	39	5	18	8	10	0	35	0	41
Zürich	13	14	14	14	8	11	7	14	5	17	2	23	5	12	5	14

5. Internet backbone and aviation networks: a comparative study

5.1 INTRODUCTION

This chapter compares the topology and the derived urban geographies of two infrastructural networks: the Internet backbone and the aviation network across European cities. While the latter consists of the international intercity aviation links, the former consists of the long-haul Internet Protocol (IP) links, which connect long-distance destinations and are responsible for the global character of the Internet (Malecki 2004). This analysis aims to explore how these networks are developed across European cities, understand their different topologies and compare the way the Internet backbone and the aviation networks interconnect the nodes of the European urban network. This topological exercise can feed a European urban geography discussion by providing insights to the different roles European cities perform in these networks. As Derudder et al. (2007) highlight, cities can derive functional centrality due to their roles in infrastructural networks.

Such a comparative analysis is crucial for this book, the main focus of which is the geography of the Internet infrastructure, for various reasons. Firstly, from an economic geography standpoint, both the Internet (Malecki 2002a) and the aviation network (Graham 1998) facilitate the knowledge-based economy (OECD 1996): while the Internet transports the informational goods (O'Kelly and Grubesic 2002), the aviation network transports the main actors of the knowledge economy, the people who form the managerial elites (Castells 1996; Beaverstock 2002), across the distributed centers of production and consumption in order to interact and acquire complex and tacit knowledge (Rimmer 1998). In reality, the "spatial organization of the new international division of labour" (Friedmann 1986, p. 69) is materialized by advances in these two networks. The spatial distribution of these facilitators might be reflected in or affect the agglomeration of specific – global – economic activities (Matsumoto 2007).

In addition, and from an urban geography perspective, both networks support the "world city process" (Castells 1996). Telecommunications just like transportation are "friction-reducing technologies", because of their ability to reduce the cost of distance (Cohen et al. 2002; Cohen-Blankshtain and Nijkamp 2004), and enable global interaction by facilitating global economic activity (Malecki and Wei 2009) and supporting the emergence of a world cities network. As Derudder (2006, p. 2029) highlights, "in a networked context, important cities derive their status from what flows between them rather than from what remains fixed within them" (Amin and Graham 1999; Allen 1999; Castells 2001). Both networks carry a significant part of these flows (Taylor 2004). Smith and Timberlake (2002 p. 139) recognize world cities as the "spatial articulations of the global flows that constitute the world economy" and Rimmer (1998, p. 439) identifies them "as junctions in flows of goods, information and people rather than as fixed locations for the production of goods and services". However, these flows are not transported in an abstract space, but rather on this specific infrastructural layer, identified by Castells (1996) as the first layer of the space of flows, which is (unequally) spread around the world following a network topology and mostly consists of the Internet and the aviation network (Taylor 2004). Following Derudder's (2006) typology, this chapter is an infrastructure-based attempt to analyze transnational urban networks by comparing the structure of these two infrastructural networks, on which this approach is usually based (Derudder and Witlox 2008).

On the other hand, transportation and communication networks are affected by the evolving world city system (Keeling 1995). Because of the private character of telecommunications and the aviation industry, the spatial distribution of their networks is mostly shaped by the spatially differentiated demand for such services. Considering that demand for communications is maximized among world cities and their "hinterworlds" (Taylor 2004), carriers primarily invest in locating their networks among such locations. This enables Graham and Marvin (1996, p. 3) to announce cities as the "power houses of communications". Despite their global reach, both networks are selective on which nodes of the urban network they interconnect with and on the intensity of the connections, following a cherry-picking pattern (ibid.).

Regardless of the plethora of aviation-related studies, rather limited research has been conducted on the spatiality of the Internet infrastructure (Bakis 1981; Hepworth 1989; Kellerman 1993). More importantly, with the exception of Choi et al. (2006) and Devriendt et al. (2010a), to my knowledge no other studies have attempted a comparison between these two networks from both a geographical and a topological standpoint.

For this comparative analysis a variety of methods are used: from simple statistical analysis to complex network analysis and quadratic assignment process (QAP). What is also important is that this comparison does not take place in an abstract topological space, but in real geographical space, using the European cities as the networks' nodes. For the needs of this analysis the Internet backbone capacity and air passengers have been aggregated at the city level.

The remainder of the chapter goes as follows: the next section uses economic argumentation to explain the topology of the two networks at a micro scale; the third section describes the data and the methods; after that, the derived urban geographies are examined; then the two networks' structures are analyzed and compared and the chapter ends with some conclusions.

5.2   ECONOMIC REALIZATION OF THE STRUCTURE OF THE TWO NETWORKS

Both networks are usually developed as privately owned networks by air carriers and Internet service providers (ISPs). Regardless of the fact that the focus of this chapter is the aggregated networks of numerous carriers, it is important to understand the nature of these infrastructures at the micro level. From the topological standpoint, both networks are rolled out as non-planar networks. The Internet function is based on the IP for data packet transport, which is characterized by multiple switch points between origin and destination. In contrast, aviation networks are designed to support less switching as the passengers' hassle increases dramatically with switching. While most air trips do not consist of more than three different legs, IP data packets usually go through ten different switching points (routers) before they reach their destinations.

At the level of individual aviation carriers, there are two main network structures nowadays: hub-and-spoke, which is the dominant structure for full service airlines (FSAs); and point-to-point, which is usually the preferred structure for low-cost carriers (LCCs). Hub-and-spoke networks appeared as a result of deregulation process in the United States (US) aviation industry in 1977 (Button and Stough 2000). The business model behind such topology is based on feed arrangements along spokes, with the traffic being diverted to the hub, which plays the role of a switching node (Alderighi et al. 2007; Gillena and Morrison 2003). Holloway (2003) indicates three types of externalities arising from such topology: economies of scope, which refer to the reduced cost because of channeling passengers through hub cities; economies of density, which are more important than economies of scale[19] (Williams and Baláž 2009; Dobruszkes 2006) as the increased passenger flows on specific spokes enable the carrier to use larger aircraft, which are characterized by lower cost per mile; and marketing economies of scale, which occur when the carriers take advantage of the information economies by choosing a hub airport and by marketing themselves as the dominant players in the region. Hub-and-spoke topology appears to be the most efficient structure for the FSAs due to the derived economies of density (Hendricks et al. 1995; Gillena and Morrison 2003). Indeed, Shy (2001) highlights that, when the carrier's operational fixed cost is high, hub-and-spoke is the preferred topology.

However, this is not the case for the LCCs, which base their function on point-to-point topologies (Dobruszkes 2006). Instead of feeding passenger traffic through hubs, LCCs tend to directly connect origin and destinations without interconnecting the overall network. Rather than establishing hub nodes, LCCs establish technical bases, which offer direct flights instead of switching facilities (Alderighi et al. 2007). The development of such carriers, with Ryanair being the pioneer for Europe in 1995, is an important factor for the development of the European aviation network. Dobruszkes (2006) identified four different types of LCC point-to-point networks: (1) small; and (2) broader networks with exclusivities; and (3) small; and (4) broader networks imitating charters. Such topologies fit better with the overall LCC business profile and result in higher returns: in accordance to Shy's (2001) argument, LCCs decrease fixed costs by using an array of policies including maximization of flying time per plane, pressure on the workforce, better occupation rates, less complex services to passengers, homogenous fleet type and use of secondary and cheaper airports (Gillena and Morrison 2003; Dobruszkes 2006). The resulting lower fixed costs make the diversification from hub-and-spoke topologies the most lucrative choice. Overall, two different types of networks currently coexist in Europe: the hub-and-spoke type developed around main airports for FSAs, and the point-to-point type for LCCs.

The economics behind the topology of the Internet backbone networks (IBNs) are more complicated. Contrary to what applies to the aviation networks, the main cost for the IP networks' roll-out is not the fixed cost of switching, but the high sunk cost of the fiber optic cables' installation, and consequently the main economic constraint is the number and the total length of network edges. Therefore a fully connected network, where the physical length and total number of the edges is maximized, is not the optimal choice for the Internet network designers. On the contrary, indirect links in the IP networks generate negative externalities as their extensive use is related with data transmission delays, known as latency, which degrade networks' efficiency (Obraczka and Silva 2000).

The complexity of the interpretation of the IBNs' structure is increased when other non-economic factors are considered. Resilience, which is defined as the "capability of a system to maintain its functions and structure in the face of internal and external change and to degrade gracefully when it must" (Allenby and Fink 2005, p. 1034), is among the main restrictions in the process of the network's design. The hub-and-spoke networks are the most vulnerable when the network is under attack, because such networks cannot function without the main hubs, which are usually the target of attacks by informed agents (Grubesic and Murray 2006). Even at the disaggregated level of the individual ISPs, their commercial success is related to their ability to provide security guarantees. Thus, clear hub-and-spoke networks are not the preferable choice for the IP networks. In addition, resilience is also enhanced by redundant links both at the aggregated but also at the micro level, as in the case of a link failure, redundant links can take over traffic.

Path dependency also affects networks' topology. ISPs, in order to achieve universal connectivity, interconnect with other ISPs and exchange data (peering) either in private points of presence (POPs) or in public Internet exchange points (IXPs). It is not surprising that the three IXPs with the highest Internet traffic in 2007 were among the first IXPs established in early 1990s in Europe and are located in Amsterdam, London and Frankfurt (Euro-IX 2008). Regardless of the ISPs' geographical scope, they connect to such points to exploit the emerging economies of scale (Greenstein 2004).

In summary, the following constraints for the Internet backbone carriers can be highlighted: (1) minimization of the length of the installed fiber optics and the number of network edges because of the fiber installation cost; (2) creation of hubs in order to achieve economies of scope and scale; (3) avoidance of clear hub-and-spoke structures because of the increased vulnerability; (4) reduction of the use of switching points in order to decrease latency; and (5) increase of presence in popular IXPs. Evidently, there is not a "universal" Internet network structure. It depends on the scope and priorities of each ISP. In reality, the IBNs combine different structures: minimally connected ring networks are usually enriched with redundant links and the result is partially connected mesh structures, which include both rings and hubs to meet the above constraints.

5.3   DATA DESCRIPTION

Two different datasets are utilized here: the international intercity Internet backbone (TeleGeography 2007) and aviation links in Europe for the period 2001–06 (ICAO 2008). For example, links between London and Paris as well as links between London and New York are included in the analysis, but links between London and Manchester, and New York and Tokyo, are excluded. For both networks, nodes are aggregated at the NUTS 3 level when multiple nodes exist in a region. Both binary and weighted links are considered: the former represent the existence of a connection between any two cities, while the latter represent the "lit" capacity of the intercity linkages in Mbps or the annual passenger flows. The above network weights are widely used in the field of Internet geography (Moss and Townsend 2000; Townsend 2001a, 2001b; Malecki and Gorman 2001; Malecki 2002a, 2004; Gorman and Kulkarni 2004; Rutherford et al. 2004), in world cities research (Choi et al. 2006; Derudder and Witlox 2005, 2008; Lee 2009) and in complex-network literature (Amaral et al. 2000; Gastner and Newman 2005; Guimera et al. 2005). The main difference is that while the bandwidth represents the capacity of the installed infrastructure (supply side), the passenger volume represents the usage of the service (demand side). As no data are available for intercity IP flows, it is assumed here that installed capacity reflects the demand for such communications.[20] Additionally, redundant connections are considered and multiple links between any two nodes are aggregated and the sum of all the weights is used.

Another difference is that the aviation network is directional whereas the IP one is not. In order to eliminate this, the directed aviation network was converted to a undirected one by symmetrizing its edges using the maximum value, following Choi et al.'s (2006) methodological choice.

To facilitate the analysis, initially the network attributes of the 62 European cities which participate in both networks are studied on the basis of all the links (including the extra-European ones). Then, a structural network comparison of the two subnets between these 62 cities takes place. An illustration of these networks can be found in Figures 4.2 and 5.1.

From a first glance it is obvious that there are structural differences between the two networks. While the most important IP edges (capacity greater than 2.5 standard deviations above the mean) form a ring with London, Paris, Amsterdam and Frankfurt, for the aviation network no such pattern emerges. On the contrary, the busiest links (passenger volumes greater than 2.5 standard deviations above the mean) are displayed in the form of star networks around nodal cities such as London and Paris (Figure 5.1). In total, the aviation network is denser as it consists of double the number of edges as the IBN (308 and 153 edges, respectively) because of the higher number of operators. However, no normalization process has been applied as the interest here is in the resultant aggregate network rather than a business view. Finally, in the six-year period the number of backbone edges increased by 15.7 percent while for the

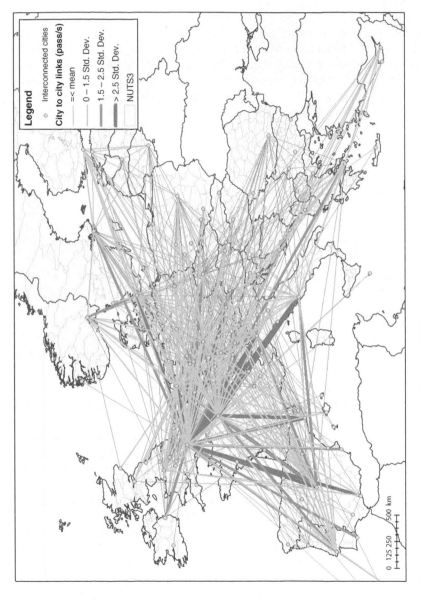

Figure 5.1 International aviation links in Europe, 2006

aviation network the increase reached only 8.8 percent, highlighting the still-evolving character of the former in terms of connecting more cities.

5.4 URBAN NETWORK GEOGRAPHIES

5.4.1 Urban Hierarchies and Roles

Firstly, the degree centrality for the binary and the weighted networks is presented. This is a measure of infrastructural capital as it represents the number of links through which a city is served as well as the installed capacity. Table 5.1 presents the degree centralities, which have been calculated by also considering the links with non-European cities. The observations are ranked according to the weighted degree centrality for the aviation network. The first observation is that the cluster of the four main cities performs similarly in the two networks: regardless the inclusion of weights, London, Paris, Frankfurt, and Amsterdam form a "golden diamond" of the most central nodes in both networks in Europe, with London being always the dominant city.

The main differences between the two networks are observed in the next tier of cities. Madrid is the fifth most central city with regard to passenger flows and the sixth based on the binary aviation links. However, it moves down to the twelfth position when the discussion moves to the Internet backbone binary degree centrality, but enjoys the seventh-highest international bandwidth accumulation in Europe, mostly due to the high-capacity link with London. Madrid is followed by Milan and Copenhagen. The Danish capital maintains almost the same position in both infrastructural networks. Milan is Italy's main hub for both networks, but is more central in the aviation network. Rome is Italy's second hub, but severe differences exist between the two networks: while it is the tenth most central city in Europe with regard to the aviation network in 2006, it is served by only one international IBN. In addition, cities such as Munich, which is part of Europe's "pentagon" (EC 1999), as well as some famous tourist destinations such as Barcelona, Prague, Lisbon and Athens, gain positions compared with their Internet bandwidth centrality ranking. On the other hand, cities outside Europe's pentagon such as Stockholm and Vienna as well as more core ones such as Hamburg, Brussels, Geneva and Zürich are more central in the IBN than in the international aviation one. In addition, some cities which are secondary according to traditional urban hierarchies, such as Manchester, Barcelona, Munich and Berlin, seem to have lower Internet degree centrality than aviation, presumably because much of the international Internet traffic passes through another major city. For

Table 5.1   *Centrality indicators for the most central cities in the Internet backbone and aviation network, 2006*

	Binary degree		Weighted degree		Betweenness		Eigenvector	
	Internet	Aviation	Internet	Aviation	Internet	Aviation	Internet	Aviation
London	100	100	100	100	100	100	100	100
Paris	49	72	66	57	35	50	70	67
Frankfurt	70	71	58	43	64	39	55	47
Amsterdam	32	54	50	38	13	33	52	54
Madrid	15	37	16	24	4	22	22	41
Milan	25	39	13	19	12	9	9	34
Copenhagen	17	26	18	15	8	3	10	25
Munich	6	31	3	14	0	14	1	24
Rome	1	21	0	14	0	1	0	31
Barcelona	7	20	2	11	1	4	3	30
Prague	9	30	5	9	3	9	3	18
Stockholm	19	17	20	9	2	0	5	19
Lisbon	16	17	2	9	9	11	3	21
Athens	16	15	3	8	5	5	2	19
Manchester	1	21	0	7	0	3	0	11
Oslo	7	12	5	6	0	0	3	13
Helsinki	5	12	5	5	0	0	1	11
Warsaw	10	17	6	5	6	1	5	11
Berlin	1	12	0	4	0	0	0	11
Düsseldorf	6	13	8	4	0	1	9	10
Geneva	10	6	8	4	0	0	7	15
Brussels	12	8	12	3	0	0	17	10
Cologne		14		3		2		6
Bucharest	7	12	1	3	0	2	1	6
Dublin	5	6	4	3	2	0	8	10
Vienna	28	6	14	3	14	0	4	7
Stuttgart	9	10	0	3	1	3	0	7
Hamburg	12	11	13	3	3	0	8	8
Zürich	14	9	7	2	2	0	5	5

Source: Tranos (2011).

the aviation network the cities' ranking based on the binary connections follows more or less the weighted ranking, but this is not the case for the IBN. This discontinuity reflects ISPs' ability to upgrade and rewire their networks, adjusting capacity to demand or reflecting different marketing policies (Gorman and Kulkarni 2004).

Table 5.1 also presents betweenness and eigenvector centrality, two measures which were defined in the previous chapter. As betweenness centrality includes only binary links, this measure has greater similarity with the binary degree centrality ranking. However, differences exist as Vienna is the fourth most central city, justifying its role as a gateway for Central and Eastern Europe (Rutherford et al. 2004). Lisbon also gains positions because of its role as a gateway city for Africa and Latin America as indicated by the existence of a vast number of low-capacity links between Lisbon and these continents (Tranos and Gillespie 2011). The opposite applies for Stockholm: despite the vast capacity which lands there, because of the end-track phenomenon (Grubesic and O'Kelly 2002; O'Kelly and Grubesic 2002; Wheeler and O'Kelly 1999) the Swedish capital does not appear to have a central role in the Internet function according to this measure.

With regard to the aviation network, differences also occur between binary degree and betweenness centrality. While Lisbon and Athens appear to gain positions in the ranking because of the relatively high number of links with cities outside Europe, most Northern European cities appeared to be less centralized because of the end-track phenomenon.

With reference to the IBN and eigenvector centrality, cities such as Madrid, Brussels, Dublin and Lisbon gain positions as they have more connections to central nodes. In contrast, cities such as Stockholm, Vienna, Helsinki, Munich and Rome appear to be less central due to the existence of fewer links with central nodes. With regard to the aviation network, Prague, Bucharest and Cologne gain some places in the relevant ranking, while Hamburg, Dublin and Geneva lose places.

In order to summarize the above, the methodological choice of Chapter 4 is adopted here again: cluster analysis is applied for all the different centrality measures. Cluster analysis, as mentioned before, is a suitable method for classifying data in an exploratory comparative analysis framework (Nijkamp et al. 1999). It is applied here in order to identify clusters of cities based on their performance on the above complementary centrality indicators. The resulting clusters will provide insights about the cities' network roles. In order to achieve this, the k means method is selected. This non-hierarchical method results in k new clusters, with k being defined a priori (Rogerson 2006).

After calibration tests, $k = 8$ is selected. As expected, London, Paris, Amsterdam and Frankfurt emerge as separate clusters (clusters 2, 4, 1 and 5, respectively). In addition, Madrid and Milan, which are characterized by similar patterns of relatively high centrality measures, but lower than the four cities listed above, are clustered together (cluster 6). The most interesting clusters are 3 and 8 and they are presented in detail in Table 5.2. Cluster 3 consists of cities which are more central in the aviation network, as is proved by the centralities of the derived clusters. While tourist destinations are an important part of cluster 3 (Barcelona, Prague, Rome,

Table 5.2   Clusters 3 and 8

Cluster	Cities	Cluster centers							
		I_b	A_b	I_w	A_w	I_Bet	A_Bet	I_Eig	A_Eig
3 (more central in aviation)	Athens, Barcelona, Copenhagen, Lisbon, Manchester, Munich, Prague, Rome	9	23	4	11	3	6	3	22
8 (more central in Internet)	Brussels, Budapest, Dublin, Düsseldorf, Geneva, Hamburg, Helsinki, Oslo, Stockholm, Warsaw, Wien, Zürich	12	10	9	4	3	0	6	10

Note: I: Internet backbone; A: aviation; b: binary degree centrality; w: weighted degree centrality; Bet: betweenness centrality; Eig: eigenvector centrality.

Source: Tranos (2011).

Athens and Lisbon) as well as Central European locations (Munich), important post-industrial nodes of the transnational urban system can be identified in cluster 8: Brussels as the location of the European Union (EU) headquarters, Geneva as the UN centre, Zürich as a financial and banking centre, but also the three Scandinavian capitals reflecting the knowledge-intensive character of the Nordic economies (Batowski and Pastuszak 2008; Benner 2003; Vence-Deza and González-López 2008). Finally, cluster 7 consists of cities which are not particularly central in any network.

5.4.2   Extroversive Cities

London's global character, which has been highlighted many times in this book, is reflected in the aviation network as well. As is shown in Table 5.3, in 2006 almost half of the passengers travelling through, from or to London (55 percent of all connections) had a non-European origin or destination. Table 5.4 gives a more detailed view for the most extroversive cities. The most popular origins (or destinations since the data is

Table 5.3 *Percentage of extra-European connections*

City	Internet 2006		Aviation 2006	
	Weighted (%)	Binary (%)	Weighted (%)	Binary (%)
Frankfurt	11	49	54	64
London	36	67	47	55
Paris	19	57	40	48
Manchester	0	0	34	29
Amsterdam	17	31	31	43
Madrid	4	47	29	39
Nice	0	0	26	50
Brussels	0	33	25	25
Munich	0	17	24	33
Milan	6	32	23	36
Zürich	3	14	20	31
Copenhagen	15	35	18	24
Lisbon	4	69	18	38
Rome	0	0	18	35
Marseille	0	0	13	25
Athens	21	25	13	32
Dublin	4	20	13	11
Düsseldorf	8	17	9	16
Berlin	0	0	9	18
Ljubljana	0	0	9	17
Oslo	9	29	8	18
Cologne	100	100	8	20
Helsinki	0	0	7	22
Hamburg	3	25	6	19
Bucharest	0	14	6	12
Stockholm	8	32	6	17
Barcelona	0	0	5	24
Riga	2	20	5	9
Warsaw	1	20	5	13
Prague	0	0	5	9

Note: Only the 30 most extroversive cities are appeared in this table.

symmetrized) for London are North American cities (24 percent of the passengers and 17 percent of connections) followed by Asian and Pacific cities (17 percent and 25 percent respectively). In addition, London's dominance for almost all the destinations is obvious. For instance, 38 percent of all the passengers travelling between Europe and the US and

Table 5.4 *Geographic allocation of the aviation edges of the most extroversive cities*

Regions	London		Paris		Amsterdam		Frankfurt		Brussels		Madrid		Munich		Lisbon	
Weighted:																
Africa	4	*39*	4	*25*	1	*3*	4	*16*			1	*2*			1	*1*
Asia & Pacific	17	*36*	14	*17*	14	*11*	23	*21*			0	*0*	13	*4*		
Europe	53	*16*	60	*10*	69	*8*	46	*6*	75	*1*	71	*5*	76	*3*	82	*2*
Latin America & Caribbean	1	*7*	3	*15*	1	*3*	2	*9*			22	*50*			13	*10*
Rest of Europe	1	*17*	1	*10*	2	*9*	2	*11*			0	*2*	1	*2*	1	*1*
US & Canada	24	*38*	18	*16*	14	*8*	23	*16*	25	*1*	5	*2*	10	*2*	4	*1*
Total	100		100		100		100		100		100		100		100	
Binary:																
Africa	6	*22*	7	*17*	3	*5*	5	*12*			4	*5*	4	*2*	4	*2*
Asia & Pacific	25	*24*	19	*13*	22	*11*	34	*23*			4	*1*	18	*5*		
Europe	45	*13*	52	*6*	57	*5*	36	*4*	75	*1*	61	*4*	67	*3*	63	*2*
Latin America & Caribbean	5	*13*	4	*10*	1	*3*	6	*15*			26	*35*			25	*15*
Rest of Europe	2	*7*	3	*7*	5	*9*	2	*4*			2	*2*	4	*4*	4	*2*
US & Canada	17	*20*	15	*13*	13	*8*	17	*15*	25	*2*	4	*2*	11	*4*	4	*1*
Total	99		100		100		100		100		100		100		100	

Canada travel through, from or to London. The same applies to the binary links. Nonetheless, just like the IBNs, London's dominance is smaller in comparison to the actual flows. In other words, the binary links are more widely distributed in Europe than the passenger flows. However, this inconsistency between binary and weighted connections is not that evident for the aviation network, for reasons explained above.

Yet, the most extroversive city is Frankfurt, since 54 percent of all its passengers and 64 percent of all its links are extra-European. Frankfurt seems to have a different role as a hub city for Asia since 34 percent of all its binary connections and 23 percent of all its passenger flows had an origin or a destination in the Asia and Pacific region. In terms of dominance, it is the second most important hub for this continent after London. Surprisingly enough, the financial capital of Germany seems to have a distinctive connection with the Asia and Pacific region in general: for both infrastructural networks Frankfurt is the second most important European hub for this region regarding the binary network, and also Asia and the Pacific is the region outside Europe which shares the most links.

In general, apart from the four most central cities, the rest appear to be more introversive. For all of them, the percentage of extra-European travel flows is less than 30 percent However, Lisbon and Madrid are again interesting cases since both of them have important links with Latin America and the Caribbean region. In 2006, 25 percent of Lisbon's binary connections and 13 percent of the passenger loads were with Latin America and 26 percent of Madrid's links and 22 percent of its passenger flows were with this region as well. In terms of dominance, Madrid is the main gateway city for this region in terms of both binary and weighted links. In comparison with the IBN, the importance of the ties between Madrid and Lisbon and Latin America and the Caribbean remains or even increases in terms of dominance as European hubs but also as a proportion of these cities' total links and flows. However, what is decreased in comparison to the IBN is the share of these cities' binary and weighted links with Africa. In the IBN London is the dominant city for communications with Africa. However, the share of Lisbon's and Madrid's binary links with this continent was high (56 percent and 20 percent respectively). Regarding the aviation network, though, London and Paris are the main hubs and also have the highest proportions of links with this continent, decreasing the role of Lisbon and Madrid in communications with Africa. All in all, Lisbon and Madrid have distinctive roles as gateway cities with Latin America in both infrastructural networks, but they only have such roles with Africa in the Internet backbone.

It should also be highlighted that the centrality of some cities such as Vienna, Geneva and Budapest for the aviation network has been

Table 5.5   Centrality correlations

Degree (w)	Degree (b)	Betweenness (b)	Eigenvector (w)
0.925	0.906	0.960	0.896
0.948	0.911	0.962	0.919
0.964	0.910	0.962	0.936
0.955	0.910	0.956	0.938
0.967	0.890	0.950	0.931
0.957	0.889	0.923	0.902

Note: All coefficients are significant at 0.01 level.

underestimated due to the exclusion of some airlines from the International Civil Aviation Organization (ICAO) dataset, such as Austrian Airlines. However, the spatial pattern of aviation centrality as presented here remains a good approximation of the reality.

5.4.3   Urban Role Similarities

In order to compare the similarities of the urban roles in these networks, correlation analysis is applied for the city centrality measures derived from the two networks. Table 5.5 presents Pearson's correlation coefficient for the Internet backbone and the aviation network based on all the different centrality measures which were discussed before. The centrality measures used here are based on the global extents of the two networks, but only the centralities for the 62 common cities are included in the correlation analysis. In general, correlation coefficients for all the different centralities measures are very high, indicating high associations between the two networks nodes' centralities and the consequent urban roles. Comparing the correlations of the different centralities there are some patterns that can be indicated. First, weighted degree centralities' correlation coefficients are higher than those for the binary networks, and eigenvector centralities' correlation coefficients are higher than those for the betweenness centralities. In other words the capacity and the flows that the cities create or attract are more associated between the aviation and the IBN than the number of the links that the cities are served by. This can be linked with the previous finding that the weights of the links are more related to economic geography than the structure of the binary links.

However, more interesting patterns emerge after focusing not on the entire sample of the 62 cities, but on the different clusters that are shaped. Going back to the cluster analysis results, the four most central cities were clearly distinguished from the remaining cities. This can also be seen in

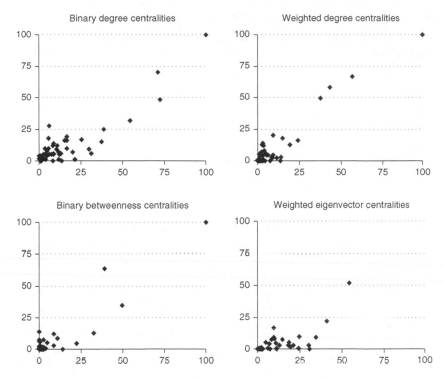

Figure 5.2   Scatter plots of the centrality measures for the two networks

Figure 5.2, where the scatter plots of the four different centralities measures for the two different networks are presented. In order to have a more accurate reflection of how associated the centrality measures for the two infrastructural networks are, Table 5.6 presents the correlation coefficients without the four most central cities, and only for the remaining 58 cities. What is interesting is that correlations based on these 58 cities are very low when comparing to those derived from the overall sample. So, it could be said that the high coefficients observed in Table 5.5 are highly affected by the similarities between the four main European hubs (London, Paris, Amsterdam and Frankfurt). Consequently, the similarities in the urban roles that the remaining cities perform in these two infrastructural networks are less intensive. Thus, correlation coefficients for the 58 cities vary from 0.39 to 0.603, indicating a mediocre association between the centralities of the two networks. In other words, apart from the four most central cities, the centralities of the rest of the 58 common cities vary significantly between the two networks.

Another interesting point is that the correlation coefficients for the

Table 5.6   Centrality correlations for the remaining 58 cities

Degree (W)	Degree (B)	Betweenness (B)	Eigenvector (W)
0.535**	0.527**	0.323*	
0.601**	0.572**	0.458**	0.496**
0.628**	0.567**	0.317*	0.593**
0.592**	0.534**		0.579**
0.604**	0.507**	0.390**	0.598**
0.606**	0.524**	0.603**	0.587**

Note: Coefficients significance: ** at 0.01 level, * at 0.05 level, blank for insignificant coefficient.

centralities of the 58 least central cities for the two networks are higher for the two degree centrality indicators than for betweenness and eigenvector. The correlation coefficients for the betweenness centrality are, for all six years but one, lower than the coefficients for the binary degree centrality, and accordingly the correlation coefficients for the eigenvector centrality are always lower than the coefficients for the weighted degree centrality. This means that when only the direct links are taken into consideration (degree centrality) the centrality measures of the 62 common cities are more associated between the two infrastructural networks. On the contrary, when the indirect links are taken into consideration (betweenness and eigenvector centrality) the centrality measures of the nodes of the two networks appear to be less associated. Despite the small differences, especially between degree and eigenvector centralities for the weighted network, the consistency of these differences indicates the dissimilar nature of these networks. The IBN structure enables and promotes communications through indirect links, while lengthy (that is, multiple hops) aviation indirect links usually result in more inconvenience and diminish the network's efficiency.

5.5   NETWORK TOPOLOGIES

5.5.1   Empirical and Theoretical Models

In this section, the topology and the overall network structures of the two infrastructural networks are under study. In order to approach these, complex network analysis is employed, which focuses on the connectivity patterns of the different actors ("who is connected to who") instead of the behavior of single actors (Latora et al. 2003, p. 2). The attributes of the two networks are compared with attributes of three widely used theoretical network models. Firstly, the random network (RN) model refers to large-scale networks with no obvious structure (Erdös and Rényi 1959). Because the nodes' degree distribution follows a Poisson distribution, the majority of nodes in an RN have the same number of links and they are located near the average degree k. Thus, vertices that deviate from this are rare (Reggiani and Vinciguerra 2007; Albert and Barabási 2002; Fosco 2004).

The second pillar is the small world (SW) networks, the basic feature of which is the coexistence of short average distance with high clustering coefficient,[21] a measure of a node's cliquishness (Fosco 2004; Latora and Marchiori 2001). Their degree distribution is quite similar with the RN networks with a peak value k which decays exponentially (Albert and Barabási 2002). However, a SW network can be approached as a set of clustered and highly connected at local level nodes, which coexist with links that span the entire network, linking furthest clusters.

The third pillar is the scale-free (SF) networks, which are characterized by the existence of a few highly connected super-hubs and a vast majority of less-connected vertices, a pattern which is reflected in a power law degree distribution (Barabási and Albert 1999). Such networks are formed based on growth and preferential attachment (Albert and Barabási 2002).

The main network elements in order to compare an empirical network with the above theoretical models are the average distance, the cluster coefficient, the vertex degree distribution and the s metric (Albert and Barabási 2002; Li et al. 2005). Regarding the latter, as illustrated in section 3.3.2, Li et al. (2005) proved that there is a variety of networks whose vertex degree distributions follow the same power law, but they are characterized by different quantitative and qualitative attributes. The s metric measures the hub structure of the network and the higher the value of the s is, the more common it is for highly connected nodes to be connected with similar highly connected ones. Thus, an empirical verification of an SF network cannot be based just on degree distributions and power laws, but needs to be accompanied by high s metric values.

Table 5.7 presents the above network statistics for the two networks. In general, average distances as well as diameter are always higher for the case of the IBN. As explained above, aviation networks are designed to facilitate shorter routes with fewer switching nodes in comparison to the Internet networks. In addition, the aviation network appears to be more clustered than the Internet backbone one. This difference in the coefficient reflects the higher importance of the direct links for the aviation network than for the Internet backbone one, as more links exist among a node's nearest neighbors in the former than in the latter.

Table 5.7   Network statistics

Networks		Average distance	Average distance RN	Diameter	Diameter RN	CC	CC RN
Internet	2001	2.337	2.670	5	6	0.598	0.107
backbone	2002	2.195	2.756	4	6	0.669	0.071
networks	2003	2.191	2.673	4	6	0.634	0.087
	2004	2.087	2.546	4	5	0.594	0.109
	2005	2.206	2.533	5	5	0.601	0.072
	2006	2.250	2.508	5	5	0.61	0.092
Aviation	2001	1.992	1.993	4	3	0.657	0.157
networks	2002	1.927	1.975	4	3	0.676	0.171
	2003	1.928	1.946	4	3	0.652	0.195
	2004	1.912	1.925	4	3	0.64	0.184
	2005	1.976	1.976	4	3	0.668	0.176
	2006	2.004	1.939	4	3	0.677	0.177

According to Table 5.7, both networks' average distances and diameters are shorter than or very close to the same measures for the same size RN networks. Moreover, clustering coefficients are always higher compared to the same-sized RN networks. This indicates the existence of SW characteristics for both networks.

Furthermore, the vertex degree distributions are empirically tested to explore whether the networks follow a power or an exponential law. For this exercise, cumulative distribution functions (CDFs) are utilized, which indicate the probability (or the frequency) that a node interacts with x or more other nodes. Contrary to the probability distribution function (PDF), CDFs have the ability to minimize the statistical noise usually present in the tail of the PDF (Newman 2005). CDF plots can be created by transposing the axis of a Zipf's rank–frequency plot (Adamic 2000; Newman 2005). Figure 5.3 illustrates the CDF for the two subnets of the 62 cities for the six-year period, for both the binary and weighted versions.

Overall, the plots for the weighted Internet networks are more differentiated over time in comparison to the aviation network. This occurs due to technological improvements such as the diachronic bandwidth upgrade and the still emerging character of the IBN. After applying ordinary least squares (OLS) for the CDF's curve estimation (Faloutsos et al. 1999; Gorman and Kulkarni 2004; Patuelli et al. 2007; Schintler et al. 2005) exponential laws fit better for both the weighted and the binary networks, indicating SW characteristics. The results can be seen in Table 5.8.

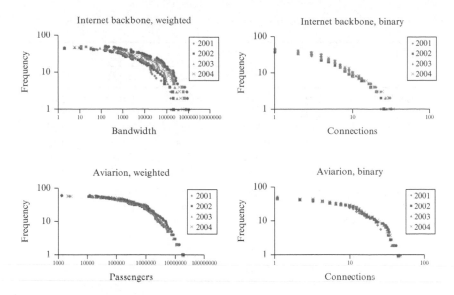

Source: Tranos (2011).

Figure 5.3   Internet backbone and aviation CDF

However, on closer observation, it seems that CDF plots for the weighted aviation networks consist of two different slopes: one almost parallel to the x-axis for the least-connected cities and a steeper one for the most-connected cities, forming a power-law tail. Indeed, if only the 20 most connected cities are plotted, the distributions of the weighted aviation network fit better with a power law as the R^2 is higher than 0.97. This indicates that an SF structure, which is related to a power-law degree distribution and to the existence of a small number of highly connected nodes and a bulk of poorly connected nodes, exists only for the first tier of the best-connected cities. By contrast, the second tier of cities seems to be more homogenous, as fits better with an exponential distribution, which is typical for SW networks. However, this is not the case for the IBN, the CDF of which is characterized by a rather homogenous exponential distribution, indicating clearer SW attributes.

The next step is the computation of the *s* metric using equation (3.3), which is relatively high for the aviation network during 2001–06 (0.687–0.712).[22] But even such values of the *s* metric are not enough for the emergence of SF hubs. If the five most connected cities for 2006 of both infrastructural networks were removed (8 percent of all networks' nodes), then the average distance among all reachable cities for the Internet

The geography of the Internet

Table 5.8   Power, exponential and Tanner functions – OLS results

Network		Weighted		Binary	
		Exp R^2	Power R^2	Exp R^2	Power R^2
Internet backbone	2001	0.800	0.736	0.967	0.83
network	2002	0.878	0.744	0.985	0.834
	2003	0.854	0.79	0.977	0.841
	2004	0.87	0.734	0.946	0.828
	2005	0.849	0.726	0.968	0.801
	2006	0.830	0.792	0.953	0.816
Aviation network	2001	0.833	0.77	0.990	0.71
	2002	0.864	0.793	0.977	0.69
	2003	0.867	0.783	0.969	0.691
	2004	0.866	0.789	0.981	0.724
	2005	0.878	0.701	0.978	0.729
	2006	0.899	0.729	0.973	0.718

backbone would be increased only by 10 percent, and for the aviation networks by 24 percent. The latter demonstrates a more vital role for the hubs in the aviation network than in the Internet backbone. However, for SF networks, the increase would be more than 100 percent (Albert et al., 2000).

To sum up, both networks do not fit with the SF model, verifying the results of previous studies such as Schintler et al. (2005) for the IBNs in the US and Europe, and Amaral et al. (2000) for the aviation network, among others. This can be justified by the physical constraints of both networks (Li et al. 2005; Amaral et al. 2000) illustrated in section 5.3. Both networks have some highly connected hubs, but they cannot hold the network together. The less homogenous distribution of technology and passenger loads in comparison to the binary links indicates the existence of SF properties when the weights are considered in the analysis, but at the same time the homogenous distribution of the actual connections clearly indicates SW characteristics. In addition, the aviation network's truncated CDF leads us to characterize it as a broad-scale network, which according to Amaral et al. (2000) is a subclass of SW networks just like SF networks. While physical constraints prevent the formation of a power-law degree distribution and result to truncated CDFs for the former, no such constraints are present in SF networks and this explains the formation of power-law degree distributions. However, this is not the case for the IBN, which appears to resemble SW networks.

Table 5.9   *QAP correlations between the Internet backbone and the aviation network*

Year	QAP
2001	0.126
2002	0.145
2003	0.145
2004	0.146
2005	0.153
2006	0.160

Note: All coefficients are significant at 0.01 level.

5.5.2   Network Structural Similarities

In order to compare the topologies of the two networks a quadratic assignment procedure (QAP) is employed. This is a non-parametric correlation test, which does not refer to actors, but to the whole network by correlating each pair of networks via permutations. The results can be interpreted as correlation coefficients (Choi et al. 2006; Chon 2004). For the case of the binary networks and for the subnets between the 62 cities, the structural similarities between the two infrastructural networks are low but significant with a steady increase for the whole six-year period (Table 5.9). Choi et al. (2006) compared the same networks for 82 world cities in 2002 and the result was an almost four times higher QAP coefficient (0.46). It seems that at a global scale there are similarities in these network topologies, but at a lower scale such similarities are weak. This is not surprising because of their nature as global networks designed to serve the distributed global centers of production and consumption. At such a scale, they are expected to share structural similarities since they serve the same cities. However, at a lower scale, when less important nodes of the transnational urban network are included in the analysis, the location decisions of the infrastructural networks' designers become less obvious, reflecting different scalar geographies.

5.6   CONCLUSIONS

The main aim of this chapter is to test empirically how the two components of the first layer of the space of flows facilitate the world city process by interconnecting European cities. Through this comparative analysis, the unique attributes of both networks and also the different roles that different cities perform in these networks emerge.

Both networks are characterized by the existence of some very well-connected cities, which play the role of hubs. While the aviation network is the result of the aggregation of numerous hub-and-spoke networks (individual carriers networks), the IBN is the result of the overlay of networks with more diverse structures. The results of the complex network analysis did not suggest any clear SF networks, but indicated structures closer to SF networks for the aviation network, which according to theory have a very few super-connected nodes and a bulk of low-connectivity nodes, as justified by the nature of these networks. Hubs are more vital for the aviation network than for the IBN, but in any case are not strong enough to keep the network together. This enables us to consider the aviation network as a broad-scale network, but this is not the case for the IBN, which resembles a SW.

The analysis indicates that the Internet backbone is more homogenous and less centralized than the aviation network in Europe. In addition, the Internet network appears to reinforce, but at the same time to challenge, the existing urban hierarchies as the different topologies result in different urban roles. London, Paris, Amsterdam and Frankfurt are the main hubs in Europe for both global infrastructural networks. Apart from these four, European cities have rather different centralities and distinctive roles with respect to the two networks. Both networks are articulations of the knowledge economy, but there are dissimilarities between them: both are influenced by the knowledge economy (Malecki 2004; Rimmer 1998; Tranos and Gillespie 2009), but only the aviation network's structure is much affected by the geography of the tourism industry (Keeling 1995). While the aviation network reflects more traditional urban hierarchies, the IBN results in an emerging contemporary urban geography in Europe, since it enables cities which are not part of the traditional core to become part of the first tier of the most connected cities and to perform more important roles in the European urban network than they usually do.

What is next on the research agenda is to understand the reasons behind the existing geographical distribution and to analyze whether and how cities can exploit these new roles to alter their development trajectories.

6. An explanatory analysis of the (unequal) distribution of the Internet backbone networks

6.1 INTRODUCTION

The discussion in Chapters 4 and 5 was focused on analyzing the unequal distribution of the Internet infrastructure among the European cities. After applying basic statistical and network analysis techniques, the elitist nature of the digital infrastructure became apparent as the Internet backbone networks (IBNs) tend to agglomerate in specific locations. This chapter drives the analysis a step further forward and focuses on explaining the factors that determine the spatial distribution of Europe's IBNs. As analyzed in Chapter 2, these backbone networks can be regarded as the infrastructural underpinning that enables the Internet to function, seamlessly and apparently placelessly from the viewpoint of the user. The aim of this chapter is then to identify, through the use of statistical modeling, the factors that influence the connectedness and the installed capacity between European cities. Firstly, connectedness refers to the probability of a city being connected to one or more backbone networks. Secondly, the installed Internet backbone capacity between any two cities refers to the weights of the network edges, which were initially analyzed in section 4.3. Two models are estimated here to identify the factors influencing the above: a probit model which predicts the probability of a region to be connected with at least one IBN, and a simple spatial interaction model (SIM) which predicts the installed capacity between two regions. While the former is expected to bring to light the socio-economic and geographic factors affecting the probability of a region being connected with the highest tier of the Internet infrastructure, the latter will utilize these findings in a geographic context and explore the role of physical distance in connecting two regions with such infrastructure.

Despite the interpretation of early commentators that the Internet has an anti-spatial nature (Mitchell 1995), we know that the Internet is not a homogenous system spread equally around places (Gorman and Malecki 2000). Indeed, the rapid Internet penetration led to deterministic views about the impact of information and communication technologies (ICTs) on spatial configuration, declaring the death of cities (Gilder 1995; Drucker 1998; Kolko 1999), the death of distance (Cairncross 2001), the emergence of tele-cottages (Toffler 1980) and, in general, the end of geography, because of the widespread penetration of ICTs. However, such narratives have not been accompanied by empirical research and hard evidence. Although we know that "cities are alive and well" (Malecki 2002a, p.419), and that ICTs did not generate such striking one-way impacts, there is not yet sufficient empirical knowledge about the relationship between the Internet and physical space, especially at the aggregated level of geographic analysis. Indeed, the complexity of cyber place (CP) prevents the a priori adoption of (over)simplistic approaches including the cartoonish "shrinking world" metaphor, which encompasses the complex interrelations between capital, space and technology and the subsequent recasting rather than shrinking impacts on space (Kirsch 1995).

A scalar issue needs also to be highlighted here. While in Chapter 4 and 5 the analysis focused on cities, now the scale of the analysis turns to regions. This can be justified by two reasons. From a theoretical standpoint, areas larger than the core urban areas can potentially benefit from or utilize such Internet infrastructure. In order to incorporate such spillover effects, the scale is extended to what is identified in Europe as NUTS 3 regions. This scale of analysis is also very close to the notion of the city-region, which was discussed earlier in Chapter 2. From an empirical standpoint, more statistical data is available at the regional level. Such data will be used to build the necessary explanatory variables for the above models. Technically, this scalar change is achieved by aggregating the urban Internet network measures to the NUTS 3 regions (that is, connectedness of a region and installed backbone capacity between any two regions).

The next section outlines the data and the methods used for the analysis. Then, section 6.3 presents the results of the analysis. Firstly, the probit model and the connectedness are discussed and then the analysis turns to the SIM and the role of distance in the formation of the IBN. The chapter finishes by presenting the main conclusions of this explanatory analysis.

6.2   MODELS, DATA AND METHODS

To answer the above research questions an empirical quantitative approach and modeling techniques have been adopted. The results of the network analysis of the Internet backbone infrastructure presented in Chapter 4 feed the econometric models, which explain the socio-economic factors behind the unequal distribution of the IBN. In order to achieve this, a panel data approach is implemented. As was briefly described in Chapter 3, panel data refers to a two-dimensional database where observations exist over time for a number of cross-section units. It is differentiated by simple cross-section datasets because it includes observations over time – contrary to a single point in time cross-sectional approach. It is also differentiated by time series because it contains observations for multiple cross-section units over time contrary to the one-unit approach of time series (Maddala 2001). Additionally, it is differentiated by the repeated cross-section or trend datasets, which contain data for the same variables but for different cross-section units over time (Finkel 1995).

The panel data approach is preferred to a simple cross-sectional approach for various reasons: (1) panel datasets provide a large number of data points, increasing the degrees of freedom and reducing the collinearity among explanatory variables, and as a result improve the efficiency of econometric estimates; (2) the longitudinal dimension of the panel data allows the analysis of a number of important economic questions which need sequential observations in order to be answered; and most importantly (3) panel data improves the researcher's ability to control for missing or unobserved variables (Hsiao 2003). Such omitted-variable bias as a result of unobserved heterogeneity is common in cross-section models (Rodríguez-Pose and Tselios 2008). The above methodological advantages, but also the structure of the existing data which has been derived by the network analysis, led to adopting a panel data approach.

In order to answer the research questions stated above, two econometric models are constructed. The first one is a probit model which predicts the probability that a European region is connected with at least one IBN, and can be represented as follows:

$$Pr(E_{it}^*) = \alpha_1 + \beta MACRO_{it} + \gamma URBAN_{it} + \delta WORLD_i + \zeta SPATIAL_i$$

$$+ Kt_t + u_{it} \tag{6.1}$$

$E_{i,t}^*$ is the probability for a region i in year t to be connected with at least one IBN, which is unobservable. Instead we observe a variable $connect_{i,t}$ defined as $\{ \begin{smallmatrix} connect_{it}=1 & if E_{it}^* > 0 \\ connect_{it}=0 & otherwise \end{smallmatrix}$. $MACRO$ is a vector including variables reflecting macroeconomic environment of region i in year t; $URBAN$ is a vector echoing the urban character of region i in year t; $WORLD$ is a vector reflecting the world city-ness of the region i; $SPATIAL$ contains variables reflecting spatial structure; and t is a time trend. u_{it} is the composite error, which can be further analyzed $u_{i,t} = v_i + \varepsilon_{it}$ with v_i denoting the time-invariant unobserved heterogeneity and ε_{it} the error term. Finally, α_1 is the constant term.

In order to estimate this model an extensive dataset has been constructed. The starting point is a binary variable which indicates whether a NUTS 3 region is connected or not to at least one IBN (variable *connect* in Table 6.1). In total, there are 8100 observations for 1350 regions over a six-year period (8100 observations = 1350 NUTS 3 × 6 years). This variable will be used to model the probability that a region has direct access to a backbone network.

This dataset is expanded with socio-economic data which will be used as explanatory variables (Table 6.1). The justification for the inclusion of these variables lies in the Internet geography literature. Firstly, the role of macroeconomic indicators of a region in attracting Internet backbone infrastructure is studied (vector *MACRO* in 6.1). Three such indicators are included in the analysis: (1) prosperity level depicted by gross domestic product (GDP) per capita *gdp_pc* (in Table 6.1) and measured in purchase power standards (PPS) per habitant; (2) market size represented by GDP (*gdp*) measured in PPS; and (3) the importance of the service economy measured as the share of the gross value added (GVA) of the tertiary sector in the regional GVA (*gva_srvc*). These three variables will be used to test the hypotheses that the probability of a region to be connected to at least one IBN is affected by market size, development level and the level of the service economy. These hypotheses can be justified by the argumentation developed in the relevant literature around the private nature of the ISP, their cherry-picking nature and the infrastructure allocation decisions based on the ISPs' expectations for demand (e.g. Graham and Marvin 2001).

In addition, one more variable indicating the lagging European regions during the period 2000–2006 is utilized. During that period, more than 35 percent of the European Union (EU)'s structural funds were transferred to the NUTS 2 regions which were characterized either by low development level in the pre-2000 period (less than 75 percent of the EU average), or by remoteness and/or by low population density (EU 2011). Based on this information, a binary variable was built indicating the location of a NUTS 3 region inside the borders of an Objective 1 NUTS 2 region (*obj1*).

Secondly, the urban character of a region as an attractor of the Internet infrastructure is tested. As was extensively discussed in Chapter 2, the Internet and accordingly the underpinning Internet infrastructure is mostly an urban phenomenon (Rutherford et al. 2004). In order to test this proposition, population density is used as a proxy for the urban character of a region (*pop_dens*).

Table 6.1 Descriptive statistics and explanatory variables for model 1

Variable	Description	Source	Obs.	Mean	Std. Dev.	Min	Max
connect (dep.)	IBN connectedness, binary variable	TeleGeography (2007)	8100	0.479	0.214	0.000	1.000
gdp_pc	GDP per capita	Eurostat (2011)	8043	20517.460	9368.793	2900.000	145100.000
gdp	GDP	Eurostat (2011)	8043	8046.906	13060.740	120.000	193540.000
gva_srvc	GVA of tertiary sector (share)	Eurostat (2011)	7412	0.664	0.105	0.215	0.950
pop_dens	Population density	Eurostat (2011)	7732	469.188	1058.573	1.100	20751.400
aviat_inter	Aviation passenger flows	ICAO (2008)	8100	103718.400	1169186.000	0.000	34500000.000
wc	World city-ness	GaWC (2008)	8100	0.051	0.220	0.000	1.000
obj1	Objective 1 regions	ESPON (2011)	8100	0.553	0.497	0.000	1.000
pentagon	Location in Europe's pentagon	ESPON (2011)	8100	0.417	0.493	0.000	1.000
coast	Coastal location	ESPON (2011)	8100	0.301	0.459	0.000	1.000
border	Border location	ESPON (2011)	8100	0.427	0.495	0.000	1.000
island	Insular location	ESPON (2011)	8100	0.053	0.223	0.000	1.000

Thirdly, as has been exposed by the discussion around the world and global city literature, the position of a city in the global hierarchy is related to and also relies upon its digital infrastructure (Sassen 2004; Taylor 2004). In order to test this proposition, the world city roster according to the Globalization and World Cities Research Network (GaWC) (2008; Taylor 2004) is utilized here. Based on this hierarchy, a binary variable is constructed which takes the value of 1 for these NUTS 3 regions which contain one of the cities included in GaWC's roster (*wc*).

In addition, the world city character also appears to be related to international aviation flows. As discussed in Chapter 2, aviation networks together with the IBN form the first layer of the space of flows (Castells 1996; Taylor 2004). In addition, such measures have been extensively utilized in understanding the world city network and the relevant transnational urban hierarchies (see also Chapter 5). Here, the weighted centrality measure for the international intercity aviation network, which was calculated in Chapter 5, is used as an explanatory variable for the distribution of the IBN (*aviat_inter*). The hypothesis which is tested with this variable is that digital infrastructure co-locates with intensive international aviation flows, mirroring either the attractiveness of world cities – to the extent that the latter is reflected in the international aviation flows, or path dependency patterns according to which cities which traditionally acted as transportation hubs retained their roles in the digital economy as well by attracting digital infrastructure.

Finally, a set of dummy variables are used to test the impact of spatial structure on the allocation of the IBNs. Firstly, the explanatory value of the location of a region inside Europe's pentagon[23] is tested (*pentagon*). The underlying hypothesis is that Europe's pentagon represents the core of Europe (EC 1999) and selective infrastructural networks will be attracted by this regional attribute. Then some physical characteristics of the European regions are also tested, such as the attractiveness of coastal (*coast*) and insular (*island*) regions. Coastal regions could be favored by submarine cables landing in port cities. On the contrary, insular regions might not attract digital infrastructure because of their remote character, but at the same time they might be favored by their location. The region of Palermo is an example of the latter case (see Chapter 4). Finally, the location of a region by national border as an attractor is also tested here (*border*). As discussed in Chapter 2, backbone networks are responsible for international and long-haul Internet connections (Malecki 2004). With the use of a dummy variable which takes the value of 1 for these regions located by national borders and 0 otherwise, the attractiveness of border regions is tested.

Table 6.1 presents the descriptive statistics of the dependent and independent variables. From a first observation it becomes apparent that the subset of regions which are connected with at least one IBN during the six-year study period are characterized by higher macroeconomic indicators, population density, aviation flows and world city-ness. However, these patterns will be further verified by the modeling analyses.

The second model utilized in this chapter is a simple SIM:

$$capacity_{ijt} = \frac{M_{it} M_{jt}}{d_{ij}^b} \tag{6.2}$$

Based on the Newtonian equation, the impact of physical distance d_{ij} between i and j on the Internet backbone capacity ($capacity_{ij,t}$) installed between i and j on year t will be estimated, given the geographic and socio-economic characteristics included in vectors M_{it} and M_{jt}.

A second dataset is build for the SIM. The spatial level of the second dataset changes from the regional i level to the interregional ij level. The dependent variable is the bandwidth capacity of the installed infrastructure between i and j (see variable *capacity* in Table 6.2). In total 304 unique ij links are included in the analysis. During the six-year study period from the potential 1824 links ($304 \times 6 = 1824$), only 1090 observations are present. This means that for 734 of all the potential links there was no active backbone connections during the study period. These 'births' and 'deaths' of links indicate the dynamic character of the IBN despite its nature as physical infrastructure. As explained in Chapter 2, rewiring is possible for the IBN due to the ease of activating (lighting) already installed fiber optic cables.

Having this variable as the starting point, the dataset is expanded with some of the explanatory variables used for the previous model. In more detail, GDP per capita, GDP and population density are included in the dataset both for regions i and j. These variables will represent the masses of the Newtonian equation. Table 6.2 presents the descriptive statistics of the dataset built for the estimation of the SIM.

6.3 EMPIRICAL ANALYSIS

6.3.1 Connectedness

The first model estimated in this section is the probit model predicting the probability that a region is served by at least one Internet backbone connection. The general model presented in the previous section (equation 6.1) can be represented in more detail:

Table 6.2 Descriptive statistics for the dependent and explanatory variables, model 2

Variable	Description	Source	Obs.	Mean	Std. Dev.	Min	MAX
capacity (dep.)	Installed backbone capacity between regions *i* and *j*	TeleGeography (2007)	1824	5063.258	18799.460	0.000	305169.000
gdp_pc_i	GDP per capita in region *i*	Eurostat (2011)	1803	44209.610	26977.090	6700.000	145100.000
gdp_pc_j	GDP per capita in region *j*	Eurostat (2011)	1797	35424.360	15654.700	4900.000	74800.000
gdp_i	GDP in region *i*	Eurostat (2011)	1803	57242.910	42293.260	3607.000	193540.000
gdp_j	GDP in region *j*	Eurostat (2011)	1797	53972.010	41363.890	2197.000	193540.000
pop_dens_i	Population density in regions *i*	Eurostat (2011)	1818	3175.146	4047.433	53.200	20751.400
pop_dens_j	Population density in regions *j*	Eurostat (2011)	1818	3661.351	5267.940	22.300	20751.400

$$\Pr (E_{it}^*) =$$

$$\alpha_1 + \beta_1 \ln(gdp\_pc_{it}) + \beta_2 \ln(gdp_{it}) +$$
$$\beta_3 gva\_srvc_{it} + \beta_4 obj1_i + \gamma_1 \ln(pop\_dens_{it}) + \delta_1 wc_i + \delta_2 \ln(aviat\_inter_{it})$$
$$+ \zeta_1 pentagon_i + \zeta_2 coast_i + \zeta_3 border_i + \zeta_4 island_i + kt_t + u_{it} \qquad (6.3)$$

Table 6.3 presents the results for the panel probit model using random effects estimators. This methodological choice will enable the inclusion of the time-invariant variables in the model. The underlying assumption is that the individual effects are uncorrelated with the regressors (Greene 2003). Based on the results of this model, conclusions about the role of regional characteristics in the connectedness of a region can be drawn. Firstly, the impact of the regional macroeconomic conditions is discussed (columns 1–3 in Table 6.3). The most consistent impact can be observed for the natural logarithm of the market size, which has a significant positive impact despite the different regression specifications. Similarly, the digital connectedness of a region appears to be negatively related to lagging – Objective 1 – regions. However, the other two macroeconomic variables do not have a consistent character. GDP per capita is positively related to the probability of a region being served by an IBN only in a univariate framework (column 1). To a certain extent, this is not surprising as the characterization of a lagging – Objective 1 – region includes the least prosperous regions according to the pre-2000 period. Regarding the service sector variable, it appears to be positively related with the probability of a region being connected with an IBN. Nonetheless, this relation stops being significant when the population density is incorporated in the regressions. In total, when the variables reflecting the urban and spatial regional characteristics are included in the models, GDP per capita and the share of service sector stop being significant predictors, while the market size and the lagging regions based on the pre-2000 period classification are significantly related, in a positive and negative way respectively, with regional connectedness.

Then, the natural logarithm of population density is used as a proxy for the urban character of the NUTS 3 regions (column 4). As discussed before, the Internet infrastructure is expected to favor highly urbanized regions, not only because the expectations for demand in these areas are higher, but also because the level of sophistication of the economy in urban areas could potentially enable the more efficient exploitation of the advantages that such digital infrastructure brings. The above argumentation is validated by the modeling exercise as the connectedness of a region with IBN appears to be positively related to population density. Interestingly enough, the magnitude of the coefficient only decreases slightly with the

Table 6.3 Probit model on the connectedness with IBN

	(1)	(2)	(3)	(4)	(5)	(6)	(7)	(8)
gdp_pc (ln)	4.036	−0.658	0.553	0.018		−0.236		−0.425
	(0.267)***	(0.675)	(0.719)	(0.02)		(0.3)		(0.53)
gdp (ln)		4.757	4.056	3.901		2.986		2.975
		(0.404)***	(0.406)***	(10.34)**		(7.34)**		(7.00)**
gva_srvc			5.395	1.882		−0.078		0.778
			(2.687)**	(0.62)		(0.02)		(0.27)
obj1			−3.616	−4.22		−3.464		−2.74
			(0.547)***	(6.88)**		(5.45)**		(3.77)**
pop_dens (ln)				0.885		0.671		0.782
				(3.81)**		(2.75)**		(2.81)**
avia1_inter (ln)					0.069	0.033		0.038
					(0.019)***	(1.19)		(1.38)
wc					7.704	3.801		3.525
					(0.530)***	(4.41)**		(3.69)**
pentagon							−0.215	−0.622
							(0.235)	(0.83)

	(1)	(2)	(3)	(4)	(5)	(6)	(7)	(8)
coast							0.131 (0.244)	-1.732 (2.51)*
border							0.155 (0.214)	2.614 (4.22)**
island							-0.156 (0.484)	1.695 (1.61)
t	-0.09 (0.040)**	-0.103 (0.048)**	-0.113 (0.053)**	-0.068 (1.2)	0.066 (0.040)*	-0.009 (0.17)	0.062 (0.036)*	-0.006 (0.11)
Constant	-47.135 (2.673)***	-44.694 (5.262)***	-59.301 (6.055)***	-47.039 (6.63)**	-7.59 (0.250)***	-34.535 (5.22)**	-7.488 (0.241)***	-33.893 (4.89)**
Observations	8043	8043	8043	7044	8100	7044	8100	7044
NUTS 3 regions	1348	1348	1348	1243	1350	1243	1350	1243

Note: Standard errors in parentheses; * significant at 10%; ** significant at 5%; *** significant at 1%.

inclusion of the other explanatory variables, which is an indication of the consistency of the urban character of this digital infrastructure.

The next element in the modeling exercise is to test whether the world city-ness is related to regional connectedness. The two variables used for this aim are the international aviation flows and a dummy variable indicating whether a region includes a city which is part of the GaWC (2008) world city roster. Both of them are positively related to regional connectedness when they are the only explanatory variables included in the regression (column 5). However, the impact of the aviation flows variable stops being significant when other explanatory variables are included in the model. On the contrary, the *wc* variable not only remains significant despite the different regression specifications, but its magnitude is higher than any other dummy variable, indicating the importance of the transnational urban interdependencies in the structure of the IBN (column 6).

Then, the spatial characteristics of the region are also tested. Firstly, it needs to be highlighted that spatial characteristics, as they are denoted by the dummy variables for the pentagon, coastal, border and insular location, are not significant predictors of the probability of regional connectedness when other repressors are not included in the model (column 7). In other words, only the combined impact of the spatial configuration variables with the other regressors is significant, and not their individual effect.

In more detail, the location of a region in Europe's pentagon does not play a significant role as an attractor of IBNs. In addition, coastal location is negatively related to regional connectedness. Thus, not only is the argument that coastal locations might be favored as landing points of submarine cables not valid, but an opposite phenomenon is observed: coastal regions are disadvantaged in attracting at least one Internet backbone connection. However, it needs to be highlighted here that the effect of this variable is marginally significant. Furthermore, border location is positively related with connectedness. This verifies the initial hypothesis that IBNs have a preference towards border locations as a means to empower their transnational character. Finally, insular location is not related to regional connectedness with at least one IBN. It seems that the peripherality of insular regions in European territory is not reflected in digital connectedness.

In order to test for potential endogeneity issues between regional connectedness and the explanatory variables, the poor man's exogeneity strategy is implemented (Hays et al. 2010). Endogeneity in this framework is related with simultaneity and is defined as the "simultaneous determination of response variables and regressors" (Baum 2006, p. 185). In this case, simultaneity might derive from the fact that connectedness is not related to the above described explanatory variables observed in year t, but instead to those observed in year $t - 1$. Such complications might arise because there is always an adoption period for an infrastructure or a new technology to be utilized (see for example the discussion about the productivity paradox in section 2.5.2). The modeling strategy to correct for potential simultaneity problems is the introduction of time lags between the dependent and independent variables (Maddala 2001; Banerjee and Duflo 2003). Because of the rather narrow time dimension of the panel dataset, only a one-year time lag is used for this analysis.

Table 6.4 presents the results of regression 8 from Table 6.3 using one-year lags of the time-variant right-hand-side variables from model (6.3) as the explanatory variables. The main difference between the regression in Table 6.4 and regression 8 from Table 6.3 is the magnitude of the effects, which is higher when the lagged regressors are introduced. Qualitatively speaking, though, the sign and the significance of the effects remained unchanged, validating the results presented in Table 6.3.

6.3.2 The Effect of Distance on Installed Capacity

The results of the previous model are utilized here to support the analysis of the effect of distance on the installed backbone capacity. Given the explanatory factors for regional connectedness, which were exposed in the previous section, the impact of physical distance on the installed capacity between two connected regions is estimated here. Although we know that spatial configuration and the importance of agglomeration for social and economic activities is valid in the frame of the digital economy, we still do not know whether and how the Internet is affected by the tyranny of distance. While it is established that the Internet is a friction-reducing technology (Cohen et al. 2002; Cohen-Blankshtain and Nijkamp 2004), the effect of physical distance on its structure is still uncertain. Put simply, we do not know whether costs related with physical distance can affect the structure of the IBN.

The novelty of this research lies on the fact that even though the geographic analysis of the Internet already has a short history of almost 15 years (Moss and Townsend 1997; Wheeler and O'Kelly 1999; Malecki and Gorman 2001; Malecki 2002a), the impact of distance on the formation of the Internet – and most specifically on the formation of CP, which is the most well-defined Internet element in a spatial context – has not yet been empirically tested. The above is not surprising, as it reflects the overall disregard of the Internet and the digital infrastructure by spatial scientists (Bakis 1981; Hepworth 1989; Kellerman 1993).

Table 6.4   Probit model on the connectedness with IBN, lagged regressors

Variable	
L.gdp_pc (ln)	−1.425
	(1.35)
L.gdp (ln)	6.239
	(8.98)**
L.gva_srvc	7.678
	(1.68)
obj1	−5.619
	(4.38)**
pop_dens (ln)	1.185
	(3.12)**
aviat_inter (ln)	0.012
	(0.32)
wc	7.95
	(5.21)**
pentagon	−2.091
	(1.14)
coast	−4.34
	(2.82)**
border	5.232
	(4.36)**
island	3.469
	(1.73)
t	−0.072
	(0.83)
Constant	−65.556
	(7.73)**
Observations	5803
NUTS 3 regions	1243

Notes: Standard errors in parentheses; * significant at 10%; ** significant at 5%; ***
significant at 1%. 'L.' denotes 2 one-year lag.

Distance is approached here as a measure of both cost and proximity.
Starting from the cost perspective, as explained above, IBN is a physical
infrastructural layer and of course the installation of this infrastructure
involves some cost. From the Internet service providers (ISPs)'s point of
view, the topology of their networks is the outcome of various factors.
They try to minimize installation cost, maximize network efficiency and
resilience, and adjust the above to the individual business models and the
geographic scope of each ISP. Summarizing the analysis from Chapter 5,

such constraints include: (1) minimization of the length of the installed fibre optics and the number of network edges because of the fibre installation cost; (2) creation of hubs in order to achieve economies of scope and scale; (3) avoidance of clear hub-and-spoke structures because of the increased vulnerability; (4) reduction of the use of switching points in order to increase network efficiency (minimize network latency); and (5) increase of presence in popular Internet exchange points (IXPs) in order to peer data with other ISPs. On the other hand, the IBN locations represent – to some extent – the ISPs' perspective for the demand for such services. Given the above constraints, ISPs will install more infrastructure between places that according to their market expectations will generate more demand for such digital infrastructure.

The generalized equation of the SIM (equation 6.2) can be written again in a more detailed form in order to reflect the explanatory variables. After the relevant logarithmic transformations the following linear model derives:

$$\ln(capacity_{ijt}) = \beta_1 \ln(M_{it}) + \beta_2 \ln(M_{jt}) + \beta_3 \ln(d_{ij}) + \beta_4 T_t + \beta_5 CNTR_{ij} + u_{ijt} \tag{6.4}$$

$capacity_{ijt}$ represents the installed capacity between region i and region j in year t; M_{it} and M_{jt} are vectors including the explanatory variables from the previous model (6.3) and depict the masses of the Newtonian equation; d_{ij} is the physical distance between i and j; T_t is a vector of yearly effects and $CNTR_{ij}$ is vector of country-to-country effects.[24]

According to the relevant literature, there are three main modeling approaches in estimating a linear panel data model (Johnston and Dinardo 1997; Maddala 2001): the pooled ordinary least squares (OLS), the fixed effects model (FE) and the random effects model (RE). The former is the simplest one and its main characteristic is that it ignores the panel structure of the data and uses simple OLS to estimate the model. Pooled OLS only differentiates from simple OLS in that the latter has information about N observations while the former includes information about N observations for T time periods resulting in $N \times T$ total number of observations. The assumptions that underlie this method reflect the assumptions of the classic linear model, namely that the composite error is uncorrelated with the dependent variables. Although pooled OLS is the simplest method, usually it is not appropriate for estimating panel data models (Johnston and Dinardo 1997).

The FE model can be approached as a derivative of the pooled OLS. In this estimation dummy variables are introduced to "account for the effects of those omitted variables that are specific to individual cross-sectional

units but stay constant over time, and the effects that are specific to each
time period but are the same for all cross-section units" (Hsiao 2003,
p. 30). More simply put, the FE estimation is not based on the variation
between different cross-section units, but instead on the variation within
cross-section units, removing the bias of the unobserved heterogeneity that might occur because of omitted variables. This is achieved by
utilizing the temporal dimension of panel datasets. By introducing first
differentiation, the error term is only based on the ε_{ijt} as the u_i and u_j time-
invariant factors are dropped because of the subtraction. Similarly, all the
time-invariant variables are dropped from the estimation. This process
results in unbiased coefficients estimation using OLS (Johnston and
Dinardo 1997). However, the main drawback of this estimation is that
the elimination of the cross-sectional variation might result in efficiency
reduction of the estimated regression parameters (Rodríguez-Pose and
Tselios 2008).

The third suggested model for estimating panel data is the RE. This
approach exploits the serial correlation in the composite error and the
model is estimated using a generalized least squares (GLS) framework
(Wooldridge 2003). Contrary to the FE approach where the effects of
the omitted cross-sectional variables are considered as fixed over time,
in this case the cross-sectional specific effects are considered as random
variables (Hsiao 2003). The υ_i are assumed to be independent of the u_{ijt} as
well as mutually independent (Maddala 2001). The main attribute of the
RE is that the cross-sectional variation is retained similarly to the pooled
OLS and contrary to the FE coefficients (Mairesse 1990). When no measurement errors occur, the pooled OLS and RE models result in similar
estimates when the variation across observations is mostly cross-sectional
(Partridge 2005).

The selection of the most appropriate estimation is based on how the
time-invariant interaction effect υ_{ij} is treated. As the main objective of this
model is to test the effect of distance, which is a time-invariant variable,
RE estimation needs to be chosen since the adoption of FE estimators
would have resulted in the elimination of distance from the SIM. Table 6.5
presents the relevant regressions. Regressions 1–4 include market sizes as
the Newtonian masses for i and j, regressions 5–8 GDP per capita, 9–12
population density and regressions 13–16 include all the above. For each
different block of regressions four different specifications are estimated.
Firstly, the simple SIM is presented (regressions 1, 5, 9 and 13). Then time
effects (regressions, 2, 6, 10 and 14), country-to-country effects (regressions 3, 7, 11 and 15) and the combined impact of time and country-to-
country effects are gradually added to the model.

The main observation that can be made from this table is the consistent

Table 6.5 *SIM on the installed capacity between two regions*

	(1)	(2)	(3)	(4)	(5)	(6)	(7)	(8)
d (ln)	-1.?59	-1.121	-0.913	-0.042	-0.754	-0.841	-0.695	-0.000
	(0.?64)***	(0.408)***	(0.135)***	(0.356)	(0.157)***	(0.369)**	(0.137)***	(0.354)
gdp_i (ln)	1.372	2.091	0.608	0.559				
	(0.?48)***	(0.211)***	(0.128)***	(0.203)***				
gdp_j (ln)	1.815	3.038	1.168	1.322				
	(0.?40)***	(0.228)***	(0.120)***	(0.221)***				
gdp_pc_i (ln)					2.204	3.42	0.946	1.243
					(0.215)***	(0.283)***	(0.202)***	(0.325)***
gdp_pc_j (ln)					3.427	5.09	1.935	2.349
					(0.229)***	(0.323)***	(0.219)***	(0.383)***
pop_dens_i (ln)								
pop_dens_j (ln)								
Constant	-25.313	-47.586	-9.774	-15.37	-51.129	-76.21	-21.523	-28.373
	(1.994)***	(3.718)***	(1.813)***	(3.723)***	(3.056)***	(4.374)***	(3.191)***	(5.799)***

Table 6.5 (continued)

	(1)	(2)	(3)	(4)	(5)	(6)	(7)	(8)
country-to-country effects	no	yes	no	yes	no	yes	no	yes
yearly effects	no	no	yes	yes	no	no	yes	yes
Observations	1060	1060	1060	1060	1060	1060	1060	1060
ij pairs	304	304	304	304	304	304	304	304

	(9)	(10)	(11)	(12)	(13)	(14)	(15)	(16)
d (*ln*)	−0.848	−0.048	−0.833	0.012	−0.83	−0.397	−0.841	−0.125
	(0.168)***	(0.451)	(0.149)***	(0.402)	(0.157)***	(0.416)	(0.138)***	(0.392)
gdp_i (*ln*)					0.841	1.027	0.407	0.304
					(0.176)***	(0.296)***	(0.157)***	(0.286)
gdp_j (*ln*)					1.061	1.284	0.931	0.858
					(0.199)***	(0.321)***	(0.175)***	(0.304)***
gdp_pc_i (*ln*)					1.917	3.202	0.731	1.168
					(0.273)***	(0.426)***	(0.251)***	(0.448)***
gdp_pc_j (*ln*)					2.56	3.625	0.965	1.41
					(0.334)***	(0.508)***	(0.311)***	(0.523)***
pop_dens_i (*ln*)	0.375	0.563	0.304	0.34	−0.546	−1.041	−0.082	−0.184
	(0.109)***	(0.172)***	(0.096)***	(0.153)**	(0.122)***	(0.211)***	(0.111)	(0.216)

pop_dens_j (ln)	0.36	0.58	0.336	0.457	-0.384	-0.385	-0.11	-0.014
	(0.086)***	(0.169)***	(0.076)***	(0.151)***	(0.099)***	(0.203)*	(0.088)	(0.194)
Constant	2.537	-5.181	1.955	-4.806	-52.293	-74.536	-23.556	
	(1.053)**	(3.083)*	(0.929)**	(2.711)*	(3.016)***	(4.408)***	(3.216)***	
country-to-country effects	no	yes	no	yes	no	yes	no	yes
yearly effects	no	no	yes	yes	no	no	yes	yes
ij pairs	302	302	302	302	302	302	302	302

Note: Standard errors in parentheses; * significant at 10%; ** significant at 5%; *** significant at 1%.

negative impact of distance. Indeed, the capacity between two connected regions is negatively related to the distance between these two regions. Distance has a significant negative impact for the simple version of the SIM (regressions 1, 5, 9 and 13): despite the different variables used to depict the Newtonian masses – that is, GDP, GDP per capita and population density – distance negatively affects the backbone capacity between i and j. Most importantly, even when all of the above variables are included in the regression, distance continues to have a significant negative impact. Going a step further in testing the robustness of the negative role of distance, yearly and country-to-country effects are gradually entered into the regressions. Even when these two effects are individually added in the models which use GDP and GDP per capita for the Newtonian masses (5, 6, 7 and 8), distance remains its negative and significant impact. The fact that distance maintains its significance even after the inclusion of the country-to-country effects signifies the robustness of the negative impact of physical distance on the Internet backbone capacity. However, the effect of distance stops being significant when country-to-country effects are included in the models which use population density (10) and the three explanatory variables together (14). In addition, distance is not a significant predictor of the installed capacity when both yearly and country-to-country effects are jointly inserted in regressions. Nonetheless, the latter does not diminish the robustness of the previous results, as when both yearly and country-to-country effects are included in the regressions, there is a rather large number of right-hand-side variables.

Apart from the distance effect, the coefficients for the variables depicting the Newtonian masses appear to have the same signs as in the previous model predicting regional connectedness. The only exemption is population density, which appears to be negatively related with the installed capacity and not always significant when the other explanatory variables are included in the regressions (13–16).

In addition, to further validate the above results of the analysis, alternative estimations are also presented in Table 6.6. Firstly, a two-way fixed-effects estimation is presented. This specification is differentiated by the usual FE because it addresses unobserved effects at two dimensions (Baltagi 1995). Thus, the error term u_{ijt} from equation (6.4) can be analyzed as follows: $u_{ijt} = \mu_{it} + \lambda_{jt} + v_{ij}$. In this case, μ_{it} and λ_{jt} are the i and j as well as time-specific effects (the masses of the Newtonian equation which are time-variant) and v_{ij} the remainder stochastic disturbance term. The two-way FE will result in omitting the i and j time-specific effects and enable us to estimate the effect of distance. Country-to-country and yearly effects are also included in this specification. The results in Table 6.6

Table 6.6 *SIM on the installed capacity between two regions, alternative specifications*

	2-way FE	Negative binomial	Poisson	Poisson
∂(ln)	−0.997	−0.141	−0.141	−0.144
	(3.00)**	(6.00)**	(6.00)**	(6.31)**
gdp_i (ln)	omitted	0.079	0.079	0.063
		(3.05)**	(3.05)**	(2.47)*
gdp_j (ln)	omitted	0.17	0.17	0.166
		(5.87)**	(5.87)**	(5.85)**
gdp_pc_i (ln)	omitted	0.133	0.133	0.097
		(3.15)**	(3.15)**	(2.36)*
gdp_pc_j (ln)	omitted	0.265	0.265	0.193
		(4.90)**	(4.90)**	(3.63)**
pop_dens_i (ln)	omitted	−0.016	−0.016	0.001
		(0.86)	(0.86)	(0.07)
pop_dens_j (ln)	omitted	−0.039	−0.039	−0.025
		(2.66)**	(2.66)**	(1.71)
Constant		11.624	−4.295	−3.314
		(0.1)	(7.45)**	(5.85)**
Country-to-country effects	yes	no	no	yes
Yearly effects	yes	no	no	yes
Observations	1057	1057	1057	1057
ij pairs	302	302	302	302

Note: Standard errors in parentheses. * significant at 10%; ** significant at 5%; *** significant at 1%.

confirm the negative impact of distance in the installed Internet backbone capacity.

Furthermore, following among others Fischer and Wang (2011), the count nature of the installed Internet backbone capacity is addressed using Poisson regressions, which is estimated by means of maximum likelihood estimation techniques. The latter addresses a potential drawback of OLS-based estimation, that the data might not meet the general assumption that counts of the dependent variable are log-normally distributed around their mean value with a constant variance (Hoekman et al. 2010). Therefore, Poisson and negative binomial estimations are presented in Table 6.6. Not surprisingly, the above different specifications validate the previous outcome since they result in a negative and equal-magnitude coefficient for the effect of distance on installed Internet backbone capacity between two regions.

6.4   CONCLUSIONS

The main objective of this chapter is to provide insights for the pull and push factors which shape the location of the highest tier of the Internet infrastructure. Using econometric techniques, firstly the impact of macro-economic conditions was estimated. From the factors tested here, market size and Objective 1 lagging regions have the strongest push and pull effects for a region to be connected to at least one IBN. What is interesting is that development level, reflected in GDP per capita, usually has no significant effects. This is in accordance with previous research (Tranos and Gillespie 2009), which also concluded that market size plays a more important role in regional connectedness than development level.

Furthermore, the analysis confirms the urban nature of the Internet infrastructure. IBNs are attracted by the level of urbanization in a region depicted by population density, and also by the position of region's urban agglomerations in the world city network. As discussed in Chapter 3, because of the private character of the telecommunications industry, the spatial distribution of such networks is shaped mostly by the spatially differentiated demand for such services. Considering that demand for communications is maximized among world cities and their hinterworlds (Taylor 2004), carriers invest primarily in locating the digital infrastructure among such locations. The above reflects the strong interrelation between digital infrastructure and global urban interdependencies, providing empirical justification for previous conceptual research on global cities (Sassen 2004) and the splintering urbanism (Graham and Marvin 2001, 1996) and the declaration of cities as the "power houses of communications" (Graham and Marvin 1996, p. 3). As Castells (1996) highlighted, such networks are global but not universal, as they are very selective about which nodes of the world urban network they include.

Next, the impact of spatial characteristics was tested. In regards to connectedness, physical attributes such as the location of a region in the geometric core of Europe or the coastal, insular and border character of a region are not important enough on their own to attract IBNs. However, given the previously described push and pull factors, coastal regions are disadvantaged in regards to connectedness. On the contrary, the probabilities for a region to be served by at least one IBN are higher in border locations, a finding which reflects the transnational character of this infrastructural network.

Finally, the analysis moved from a model explaining regional connectedness with IBNs to a SIM model exploring the impact of distance on the installed capacity between two connected regions. Despite the early discussions about the non-spatial nature of the Internet, the analysis revealed that even a system such as the Internet, the evolution of which was based on topological and not on geographical attributes, is affected by distance. Similarly to other interaction phenomena such as migration, communication, commuting, trade and so on, but also similarly to their underpinning infrastructural layers, such as transport infrastructure, the capacity of the highest tier of the Internet appears to be negatively related to distance. Put simply, the smaller the distance between two connected regions, the larger the installed capacity between them. Accordingly, this finding leads to the conclusion that Tobler's First Law of Geography, according to which "everything is related to everything else, but near things are more related than distant things" (Tobler 1970, p. 236), is valid in the digital economy. The above can be approached both as an indication for the role of distance as cost in physical connectivity (Waxman 1988) and also as an indication of higher demand for Internet backbone services between nearer destinations. This result is in agreement with previous studies which focus on the interlink between physical distance and the digital infrastructure (D'Ignazio and Giovannetti 2007).

In total, this chapter provided the bridge between Internet's topology and real-world geography. After understanding the topological attributes of the IBN and the derived urban hierarchies, the econometric analysis revealed the factors which shape the unequal spatial distribution of the highest tier of the Internet infrastructure. Despite the Internet's nature as a complex technical system, real-world geographies can explain much of the variability of the distribution of this element of the Internet infrastructure, which is responsible for its global character. Yet, the derived question is whether and how regions can take advantage of this infrastructure and use it as a development policy tool. This is the focus of the next chapter.

7. Internet infrastructure and regional economic development: a causality analysis

7.1 INTRODUCTION

This chapter explores the relationship between the Internet infrastructure and regional economic development at an aggregated pan-European level. Apart from identifying the significance of such a relationship, the main challenge here is to understand the direction of causality: do investments in digital infrastructure stimulate regional economies, or is economic development a pull factor for the Internet infrastructure?

As discussed in Chapter 2, technology has always been a component of growth models, but the assumptions behind this have varied over time. Solow's neo-classic model (1956) treats technology as an exogenous factor, independent of capital and labor (Pike et al. 2006; Aghion and Howitt 1998). Romer's (1986, 1990) endogenous growth theory emphasizes even more the impact of technology and technological change on growth process. New economic geography (Krugman 1991a, 1991b) identifies spatial structure as the result of simultaneous action of centripetal and centrifugal forces (Krugman 1998). Therefore, the information and communication technology (ICT)-related transport and communications cost reduction could lead to a disturbance of the current equilibrium between centrifugal and centripetal forces (Maignan et al. 2003).

In addition, productivity gains due to the extensive use of ICTs, which are integral elements of the digital economy (Antonelli 2003; Atkinson and McKay 2007), are well established in the literature, both at macro (national economies) and micro (firm) level. As analyzed in Chapter 2, such productivity gains emerge due to the general purpose technologies (GPT) nature of ICTs and mainly the Internet. However, these GPT productivity effects can only be materialized through investments in physical infrastructure (Lipsey et al. 2005). This role is played for the case of the Internet by the Internet infrastructure, which is defined as the hardware of the Internet. The Internet backbone network (IBN) is an essential element of this hardware. Consequently the emerging question, which will be explored in this chapter, is whether the spatially differentiated distribution of the digital infrastructure, as has been analyzed in the previous chapters, can result in localized developmental impacts. Despite the extensive discussion on productivity gains presented above and extensively discussed in Chapter 2, little research has yet taken place on the aggregate effect of this infrastructure at the meso-regional level.

From the technical point of view, we know that because of the unequal distribution of the Internet infrastructure as analyzed in Chapters 4 and 5, geographic location affects Internet connectivity and the speed at which data can be received and transmitted. Nonetheless, such differences in the quality of Internet connectivity are mostly visible to large users such as transnational corporations (TNCs), for the accommodation of which cities need to be served by the highest rank of the Internet's physical infrastructure. Thus, the agglomeration of digital infrastructure in specific locations may influence the economic development of these areas by advancing access to the digital economy and by affecting competitiveness at the micro-regional and consequently the meso-regional level. In practical terms, advancements in the highest tier of the Internet infrastructure can increase regional attractiveness for firms dependent on such infrastructure (financial firms, back-office activities, creative industries) and increase the productivity of existing firms as well as the quality of digital services for end-users (Cornford and Gillespie 1993).

On the other hand, communication networks can also be affected by the evolving world city system (Keeling 1995) and instead of the Internet infrastructure affecting regional economic development, regional economic development level could also be a pull factor for the distribution of the Internet infrastructure. As discussed in Chapter 6, regional connectedness with the IBN is affected by the position of regional urban centers in the world city network. Given the fact that the demand for the highest tier of the Internet infrastructure is probably maximized among cities which are intensively interconnected with the transnational urban network, a causality question can be raised: does the digital infrastructure stimulate or follow regional economic development?

Such a causality problem is not rare in regional science, and especially in the discussion about infrastructure and regional economic development. Banister and Berechman (2003) in their research on transport infrastructure noted that the empirical evidence is mixed. While some researchers conclude that increases in productivity may result in increases of infrastructural capital, others argue that the direction of causation is just the opposite. Interestingly both causal relations might also co-exist in specific locations.

As briefly presented above, arguments for both types of causal relationships can be found in the literature. Table 2.4 reviews a number of studies which have dealt with this problem. As discussed in section 2.5.6, the direction of causality between ICTs, and more specifically the Internet infrastructure, and regional economic development is an open burgeoning issue.

Revealing the direction of causality in such a relationship, apart from its academic importance, can provide valuable insights for the local and regional policy agenda. A significant causal relationship running from the Internet infrastructure to regional economic development could justify the inclusion of such infrastructure in local and regional development policy frameworks as a policy tool to stimulate economic activity. On the other hand, a unidirectional causal relation with causality running from economic development to ICTs will impair the efficiency of such policies, since economic development is just a pull factor for the location of the Internet infrastructure. A bidirectional causal relationship will result in a cyclical phenomenon: policies for ICT stimulation will also result in economic development, which in turn will result in further stimulation of the demand for and supply of ICT. In addition, the lack of a significant causal relationship between ICT and economic development prevents policy-makers from using one of them as a stimulating tool for the increase of the other (Wolde-Rufael 2007).

The structure of the chapter is as follows. Section 7.2 presents the data and the methodological framework of this chapter. Then, in section 7.3, the causality analysis takes place. In section 7.4, the results are discussed and the chapter ends with some concluding remarks.

7.2   DATA AND METHODOLOGICAL FRAMEWORK

In order to explore the relation between the IBN and regional economic development, the weighted degree centrality aggregated at NUTS 3 level will be utilized. Although other centrality measures, such as binary degree, betweenness and eigenvector centrality, have also been calculated in Chapter 4, weighted degree centrality is used here, as it reflects the digital infrastructural capital of the European NUTS 3 city regions instead of topological attributes of the network nodes.

In order to identify the causal relation between the Internet infrastructure and the level of economic development, Granger causality tests are employed. Such tests are based on a bivariate model where the dependent variable y is regressed against k lagged values of y and k lagged values of x. Using such a model, the null hypothesis can be tested according to which x does not cause y. If the test proves to be significant then the null hypothesis can be rejected, and then it can be concluded that x Granger-causes y (Hood III et al. 2008). This latter signifies that y is better predicted if all the information (both the lagged values of y and x) is included in the model than if the lagged values of x are excluded (Hurlin and Venet 2003). In order to evaluate both directions of causality between regional economic development and the Internet infrastructural capacity, this model is run twice, interchanging the dependent with the independent variable. For the purposes of the analysis, regional economic development is represented by gross domestic product per capita (GDP pc) at constant prices for the NUTS 3 city regions.

The Granger causality test appears to be the most widely used method for empirically assessing causal relationships between digital economy-related variables (infrastructure, teledensity, telecom investment) and economic development and growth, but also in general in econometrics, as all the studies presented in Table 2.4 are based on this method. Granger causality tests were initially introduced for time series (Granger 1969). However, recent developments on panel data analysis enable this application in models with such specifications (Hoffmann et al. 2005). Hood III et al. (2008) highlight three reasons why the Granger causality test works better with panel data: (1) panel data provides more flexibility in modeling the cross-section units than time-series analysis separately for each cross-section; (2) panel data allows more observations to be included in the analysis, and consequently more degrees of freedom than time-series data; (3) finally, and also because of (1) and (2) above, the Granger test is more efficient with panel than with time series data (Hurlin and Venet 2003).

7.3   EMPIRICAL GRANGER CAUSALITY ANALYSIS

In order to explore whether the Internet infrastructure Granger-causes regional economic development or the reverse, the following dynamic panel data model is applied:

$$ y_{i,t} = \alpha_i + \sum_{k=1}^{\rho} \gamma^{(k)} y_{i,t-k} + \sum_{k=1}^{\rho} \beta_i^{(k)} x_{i,t-k} + \varepsilon_{i,t} \qquad (7.1) $$

For each cross-section unit i, and for all t [1,T], the regressors are lagged values of the dependent variable ($y_{i,t-k}$) and lagged values of the independent variable ($x_{i,t-k}$), both of them for all cross-section units.[25] α_i represents the fixed effects, $\varepsilon_{i,t}$ the error term, k the lags, and ρ the time periods (Hood III et al. 2008). This model is run twice using both the natural logarithm of degree centrality and the GDP per capita as dependent variables.

With regard to the specifications of (7.1), in order to maintain sufficient degrees of freedom, it is assumed that γ^k are constant and β_i^k identical for all $k \in [1,\rho]$. While the former assumption prevents variation in the autoregressive coefficient among cross-section units from time period to time period, the latter only prevents variation in the regression coefficients from time period to time period[26] to address spatial heterogeneity (Hurlin and Venet 2003; Hood III et al. 2008).

An important distinction in the literature with regard to the different Granger causality applications for panel data is based on the treatment of the autoregressive and slope coefficients as being equal for all the cross-section units. Hurlin and Venet (2003) addressed the heterogeneity of the casual relations between the different cross-section units by not having such a restriction, and by testing the causality direction for each cross-section unit. Applications of this method include, among others, the work of Hood III et al. (2008) and Tervo (2009). Others (Shiu and Lam 2008; Hartwig 2010) assumed the equality of the coefficients across different-cross section units, and addressed the heterogeneity issue indirectly by splitting the panel into smaller and theoretically homogeneous groups. The latter can be approached as a special case of (7.1), where the loss of the ability to directly address the heterogeneity issue is offset by the use of estimators other than ordinary least squares (OLS), such as difference and system GMM (generalized method of moments), which address the endogeneity problem that might arise because of the simultaneity effect between the dependent and the independent variable.

In order to exploit the advantages of both methods (that is, consideration of the cross-section heterogeneity, and addressing the endogeneity problem) both of them are applied. Firstly, the Hurlin and Venet (2003) method is presented. This method provides causality insights at the level of the cross-section units. The first step is to examine whether both time series (degree centrality and gross domestic product per capita) are stationary. The stationarity condition is crucial for the consistency of the OLS coefficients. In order to do this, the Levin, Lin and Chu test is applied (Levin et al. 2002), according to which stationarity holds.[27]

This method tests for the existence of the following three possible causal scenarios (Hood III et al. 2008):

1. A homogeneous causal relationship between x and y for all cross-section units.
2. No causal relationship between x and y for any cross-section units.
3. A causal, but no constant across all cross-section units, relationship between x and y. Hurlin and Venet (2003) further distinguish two pos-

sible subcases: (a) different types of causal relationships across cross-sections; and (b) no evidence of any causal relationship for at least one cross-section unit.

In order to research the first scenario, first, the following hypothesis is tested:

H₁: For all i, x does not cause y (Hood III et al. 2008).

The testing of this hypothesis is based on the statistical test:

$$F_1 = \frac{(RSS_2 - RSS_1)/N\rho}{RSS_1/[NT - N(1 + \rho) - \rho]} \text{ (Hurlin and Venet 2003)} \quad (7.2)$$

This test examines whether or not the inclusion of the lagged independent variable increases the explanatory value of model (7.1) in predicting the dependent variable. In order to do so, the model described in (7.1) with N the number of the cross-section units, ρ the number of lags, and T the number of time periods is run twice: the first time, no restrictions are induced (unrestricted), but, the second time, a restriction is introduced referring to the nullity of the regression coefficients for all the lags. This restriction makes the prediction of the dependent variable dependent only on the fixed effects, and on the lagged version of the dependent variable (Hood III et al. 2008). Then the sum of the squared residuals for the unrestricted (RSS_1) and the restricted (RSS_2) model are calculated, and the F_1 test is estimated using (7.2). The significance of the test is based on the F distribution, with $N\rho$ and $NT - N(1 + \rho) - \rho$ degrees of freedom for the nominator and the denominator, respectively.

This hypothesis is tested for both directions: the lagged degree centrality impacts on GDP per capita, and vice versa for one- and two-year lags.[28] The results of these tests are shown in Table 7.1. Based on these test results, the first hypothesis (H_1) can be rejected only when the one-year lags of both variables are used as the explanatory variables. This means that the inclusion of the independent variable in both models increases the explanatory value of the models in predicting the dependent variable and, consequently, for the one-year lag periods there is a bidirectional causal relationship between the two variables.

The next step is to examine the nature of these causal relationships, as the F_1 test cannot conclude whether these exist for a subset or for all cross-section units. In order to examine this, a second hypothesis is tested:

H₂: x causes y for all i (Hood III et al. 2008).

Table 7.1 F_1 tests

	t−1	t−2
degree ➔ GDP pc	2.029***	0.593
GDP pc ➔ degree	1.964***	0.422

Note: ***p < 0.01.

This hypothesis is tested using the following *F* test:

$$F_2 = \frac{(RSS_3 - RSS_1)/\rho(N - 1)}{RSS_1/[NT - N(1 + \rho) - \rho]} \quad \text{(Hurlin and Venet 2003)} \quad (7.3)$$

Again RSS_1 refers to the sum of the square residuals of the unrestricted model, while RSS_3 is the sum of the square residuals of a new restricted model based on (7.1). The restriction here is that the regression coefficients are equal for each cross-section unit and over time[29] ($\beta_{i,t-1} = \beta_{i,t-k}$)(Hood III et al. 2008). This restriction will enable the examination of the homogeneity of the causal relationship. Similarly to the F_1 test, the significance of the F_2 test is based on the *F* distribution with $N\rho$ and $NT - N(1 + \rho) - \rho$ degrees of freedom for the nominator and the denominator, respectively. The F_2 test for the causal relationship from the one-year lagged degree centrality to GDP per capita is 1.940, and for the reverse relationship it is 1.870, and both of them are significant at $p < 0.01$. The latter result enables the rejection of the H_2 hypothesis, which means that the above causal relations are not homogeneous across the cross-section units. In other words, a causal relationship might only exist for a subset of the 48 city regions (weak heterogeneity) or might be invariant across city regions (strong heterogeneity).

To investigate for which city regions these causal relationships are true, a third hypothesis is tested:

H_3: For *i*, *x* does not cause *y* (Hood III et al. 2008).

In order to investigate this hypothesis, a test is calculated for each one of the 48 city regions included in the analysis.

$$F_3 = \frac{(RSS_{2,i} - RSS_1)/\rho(N - 1)}{RSS_1/[NT - N(1 + \rho) - \rho]} \text{(Hurlin and Venet 2003)} \quad (7.4)$$

For the restricted model, the nullity of the coefficient of the lagged explanatory variable for each cross-section unit is imposed ($\beta_i^k = 0$). In order to calculate the F_3 test, model (7.1) is calculated 96 times separately for each of the 48 cross-section units, and for both relationships. Then, the significance of these 96 F_3 tests is examined and, accordingly, the existence and the direction of the causal relationship for each cross-section unit is discussed. Table 7.2 presents the results of the F_3 test for all the city regions included in the analysis.

The first conclusion that can be drawn from the above tests is that for half of the 48 city regions included in the analysis, there is a causal relationship: for 18 regions the relationship runs from the degree centrality to GDP per capita; for six city regions causality runs from the GDP per capita to degree centrality; and for two city-regions the analysis identified a bidirectional relationship. This finding is important, as it is proves that for most of the city regions for which a significant causal relationship exists, the Internet infrastructure provision, as reflected in the accumulated bandwidth capacity (degree centrality) positively affects – in Granger causality terms – regional GDP per capita, rather than the GDP per capita being a pull factor for this infrastructure allocation.

Nonetheless, the main limitation of the Granger causality tests lies in the bivariate nature of the basic model, which does not account for spurious relationships. This can be partly addressed with the use of panel data, but also with the use of instrumental variables. Following Shiu and Lam (2008) and Hartwig (2010), (7.1) is estimated again for both directions using GMM: (1) for all the cross-section units, in order to confirm F_1; (2) for those cross-section units for which causality runs from degree centrality to GDP per capita (F_{3a}); (3) for those cross-section units for which causality runs from GDP per capita to degree centrality (F_{3b}); and finally, (4) for those cross-section units for which no causal relation was observed.[30] In order to address the endogeneity problem which might have arisen in the first estimation, the dynamic panel firstly introduces first differences of all variables in order to eliminate individual effects. In order to eliminate the correlation that might exist between the error terms and the differenced lagged dependent and the independent variables, Arellano and Bond (1991) introduced the use of lags of the dependent and independent variable as instruments in a GMM framework. Later, Arellano and Bover (1995) and Blundell and Bond (1998) suggested first differencing not on the regressors, but rather on the instruments, a choice which results in increasing the efficiency (Roodman 2006). The latter approach, known as system GMM, is used here.

After the model's estimation for both directions of causality, and for the different cross-section subsets identified from the first – fixed effects-based – causality tests, the Wald test is utilized in order to test the previously stated hypotheses. Table 7.3 presents the results of this analysis.

Table 7.2 F_3 test for all the NUTS 3 regions

Region of	Causality	F_{3a}	F_{3b}	Region	Causality	F_{3a}	F_{3b}
Budapest	degree → GDP pc	2.091***	0.166	Cologne	Bidirectional	2.23***	9.327***
Dublin	degree → GDP pc	9.059***	0.104	Gothenburg	Bidirectional	2.787***	5.09***
Düsseldorf	degree → GDP pc	4.599***	0.035	Amsterdam	No	0.697	0.102
Frankfurt	degree → GDP pc	1.951***	0.002	Athens	No	1.394	0.463
Hamburg	degree → GDP pc	2.648***	0.001	Barcelona	No	0.557	0.187
Hannover	degree → GDP pc	2.787***	0.137	Berlin	No	0	0.001
Helsinki	degree → GDP pc	5.853***	0.069	Bratislava	No	0.697	0.296
Ljubljana	degree → GDP pc	2.23***	0.402	Brussels	No	1.115	0.024
London	degree → GDP pc	29.407***	0.105	Bucharest	No	0.697	0.314
Luxembourg	degree → GDP pc	11.846***	0.126	Ehingen	No	0.279	0.36
Munich	degree → GDP pc	1.533**	0.018	Hilden	No	0.697	0.056
Paris	degree → GDP pc	2.23***	0.011	Lisbon	No	0	0.067
Prague	degree → GDP pc	2.509***	0.072	Madrid	No	0.557	0.101
Riga	degree → GDP pc	1.951***	0.46	Malmö	No	0.418	0.113
Stockholm	degree → GDP pc	5.296***	0.068	Maribor	No	0.139	0.118
Tallinn	degree → GDP pc	3.345***	0.408	Milan	No	0	0.047
Vilnius	degree → GDP pc	1.672**	0.606	Msida	No	0.139	0.17
Warsaw	degree → GDP pc	4.042***	0.331	Nice	No	0.697	0.002
Brno	GDP pc → degree	0.279	2.387***	Nicosia	No	0.139	0.119
Bielsko-Biala	GDP pc → degree	0.139	8.249***	Palermo	No	0	0.273
Graz	GDP pc → degree	1.394	11.74***	Rome	No	0	0.117
Nuremberg	GDP pc → degree	0.836	6.496***	Rotterdam	No	0.976	0.13
Portsmouth	GDP pc → degree	0	14.5***	Stuttgart	No	0	0.002
Turin	GDP pc → degree	0	5.877***	Vienna	No	0	0.001

Notes:
*** $p < 0.01$, ** $p < 0.05$.
F_{3a} tests the relation degree → GDP pc; F_{3b} test the relation GDP pc → degree.

Table 7.3 Estimation of (7.1) with system GMM and relevant Wald tests

	All		degree → GDP pc		GDP pc → degree		no causal relation	
	Dependent variable: GDP pc							
GDP pc (t−1)	1.049***	(0.027)	1.043***	(0.026)	0.989***	(0.036)	0.991***	(0.024)
degree (ln, t−1)	236.295***	(90.065)	521.812**	(218.544)	180.448	(302.774)	62.469	(72.213)
Constant	−2490.13***	(1166.596)	−5597.1**	(2338.441)	−242.75	(2046.386)	44.57	(408.456)
Hansen	23.79*		18.53		3.5		0.422	
Wald	6.88***		5.70**		0.36		0.387	
	Dependent variable: degree centrality (ln)							
degree (ln, t−1)	0.87***	(−0.093)	0.887***	(0.0867)	0.673**	(0.343)	0.915***	(0.132)
GDP pc (t−1)	0.00001	(0.00002)	0.00001	(0.00001)	−0.00003	(0.00009)	0.00004	(0.00005)
Constant	1.24*	(0.633)	0.941	(1.089)	2.653	(3.986)	0.094***	(0.757)
Hansen	15.62		14.62		6.23		15.87	
Wald	0.38		1.9		0.11		0.86	
obs.	240		100		40		110	

Note: * significance at the 10% level; ** significance at the 5% level; *** significance at the 1% level. Std. errors in parentheses.

GMM estimators validate only one direction of causality: when all the cross-section units are included in the analysis, GMM verifies that the direction of – the non-homogeneous – causality runs from the Internet backbone capacity to the GDP per capita. The same applies when the analysis only includes the cross-section units for which the first causality tests indicated a unidirectional relation from the degree centrality to the GDP per capita. However, this is not the case when the analysis is focused on those cross-section units for which there is evidence for reverse causality in the first stage of the analysis. For these cases, GMM did not confirm the initial results as, according to the GMM estimators, no causal relation can be identified for these cross-section units. It needs to be highlighted here that, for this case, only 40 observations were included in the regressions. However, even when all the cases are included in the analysis, the reverse relation with the causality running from economic development to the Internet infrastructure is not significant. Therefore, and also because of the robustness of GMM against endogeneity, the reverse causal relationship for these eight cases cannot be verified here. Finally, GMM confirms the previous results for those cross-section units for which no causal relationship was proved.

The geographical representation of the results (see Figure 7.1) is also interesting. Maybe the pattern is not clear-cut, but still there is a visibly higher concentration of city regions with a significant causal relationship running from the Internet infrastructure to the economic development level in the Northern part of Europe.[31] Conversely, for most of the city regions located in the Southern part of Europe (the Iberian Peninsula and the Mediterranean arc), and also for some of the Eastern and Central European city regions, there is no statistically significant causal relation between Internet infrastructure and the economic development level. Thus, an emerging North–South divide for the role of the Internet infrastructure as a significant – causal – predictor of regional economic development is the main outcome of the analysis.

7.4 DISCUSSION

The results of the above analysis are in accordance with previous studies dealing with ICT and (regional) economic development, which were presented in Table 2.4. Additionally, the heterogeneous nature of the causal relationship between the Internet infrastructure and regional economic development concurs with Capello and Nijkamp's empirical results (1996b, p. 26) that "mere accessibility to advanced telecommunications infrastructure and services does not necessarily lead to a better corporate

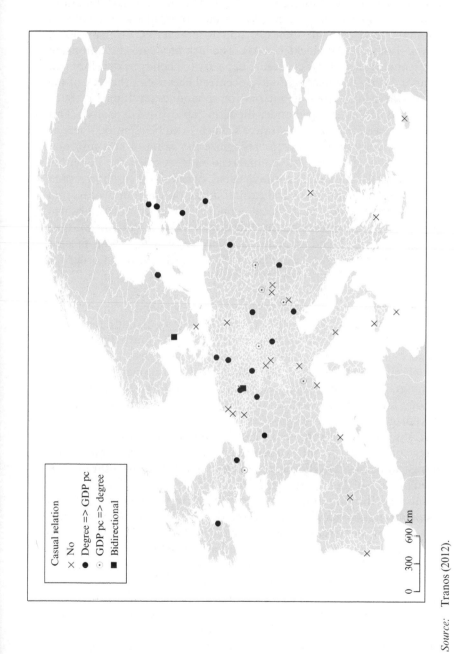

Legend (in image):

Casual relation
× No
● Degree => GDP pc
◉ GDP pc => degree
■ Bidirectional

0   300   600 km

Source: Tranos (2012).

Figure 7.1   Spatial heterogeneity of causal relations

191

and regional performance". Certainly, as happens with infrastructure in general (Banister and Berechman 2003; Huddleston and Pangotra 1990), digital infrastructure is a necessary, but not a sufficient, condition for economic development (Gillespie and Robins 1989; Graham 1999; Gibbs and Tanner 1997; Hackler 2003). The lack of a causal relationship running from the digital infrastructure capacity to economic development in 28 out of 48 city regions might have occurred because of the lack of the other necessary, but sufficient, factors for economic development. Such critical factors can be grouped under the term "absorptive capacity". This notion – borrowed from administrative science – can be identified here as the ability of a city or a region to "recognize the value of new information, assimilate it, and apply it to commercial ends" (Cohen and Levinthal 1990, p. 128). This "digital" absorptive capacity enables a city or a region to utilize the digital infrastructural capital in the production process and generate positive impacts in the local economy. In other words, absorptive capacity can be approached in this context as the "organizational, managerial, technical and strategic knowledge, which is not present everywhere, and is not at all a *public good*", but is necessary in order for the advantages of ICTs to be materialized (Capello and Nijkamp 1996a, p. 226).

From a geographical standpoint, the spatial heterogeneity in the existence of a causal relationship can be explained by the spatial differentiation of the regional capacity. Indeed, this emerging North–South divide in the significance of the causal relationship corresponds to the well-established socio-economic North–South divide in Europe which is related to, among other things, differences in economic development level and prosperity, technology adoption, innovation and human capital level (e.g. Cutrini 2010; Rodríguez-Pose and Tselios 2009; Paci and Usai 2000; EC 1999). In short, it seems that it is more difficult for the South of Europe to take advantage of the Internet infrastructure and use it as a development tool, in contrast to the higher efficiency in exploiting this infrastructure that is observed in the Northern part of Europe.

To illustrate this situation in a more formal way, Table 7.4 presents the results of an auxiliary regression, the dependent variable of which is a binary variable indicating the existence, or not, of a causal relationship from digital infrastructure to regional economic development. The regressors here are the three variables used as proxies for absorptive capacity at the city-region level: the gross value added (GVA) of the tertiary sector as a percentage of the total regional economy, reflecting the intensity of the service economy; the number of registered patents in high technology, which denote innovative regional environments; and the number of students as a percentage of the total number of student in each country,

Table 7.4   Auxiliary logit model

Dependent var.: significant or not causal relationship (degree ➔ gdp pc, binary)	
GVA in services	24.337
	(8.506)***
Beds	−0.00004
	(0.000)**
high tech	0.008
	(0.004)**
Students	0.04
	(0.015)***
Constant	−20.227
	(6.762)***
Observations	48
Pseudo R2	0.396

Note: Standard errors in parentheses. * significant at 10%; ** significant at 5%; *** significant at 1%.

which represents knowledge intensity. In addition, a control variable was also used to account for that part of the tertiary sector which is related to the tourism industry, and is not related to the digital economy.[32] For this reason the number of beds per region was used. It also needs to be mentioned that all variables used were the average of the period 2001–06.

The results of the logit model confirm the foregoing discussion. The Internet infrastructure appears to generate significant positive effects for regional economic development in places where: the (non-tourism) service industries represent a vital component of the regional economy; intensity of high-technology patents registration is observed; and there is a concentration of university students. These results are preliminary and further analysis needs to take place in order to understand in depth the factors behind the absorptive capacity in a digital economy framework. Nonetheless, the logit model provides a preliminary authentication of the critical framework factors which are necessary for a city region to take advantage of the digital infrastructure.

7.5   CONCLUDING REMARKS

The analysis has revealed in general that the Internet infrastructure does not follow, but precedes economic development. Indeed, it would have been an oversimplification to conclude that the topology of such a complex system as the Internet is merely based on the level of economic development. Although the Internet backbone providers incorporate expectations for demand in their location strategies, demand for such-high tier digital infrastructure is not based purely on the level of economic development. On the contrary, location strategies can be approached as an amalgamation of the expectations for demand and the topological constraints governing the efficiency of the IBNs (Tranos 2011).

This analysis does not come without limitations. Granger causality is an imperfect method for approaching causality issues, just like any other method (Hood III et al. 2008), with its bivariate nature being the main limitation. To increase the robustness of our analysis, a two-level approach was adopted here: a bivariate OLS, and a dynamic GMM framework for Granger causality tests. All of these indicate a causal relation running from the Internet infrastructure to regional economic development, and address the heterogeneity of regional space. Nonetheless, future research should elaborate on the present results and expand the Granger causality analysis to a multivariate framework in order to control for other factors, which affect regional economic development and the topology of cyberplace.

In total, the findings of the analysis are backed up by the literature and can be used as a justification for the inclusion of digital infrastructure in a local policy framework for stimulating the economy. This discussion takes place in the following and final chapter of this book.

8. Conclusions

The aim of this chapter is to summarize the key findings of this book, further discuss the results and link them with a policy framework. Firstly, based on the empirical results, the three research questions stated in the first chapter are briefly addressed here. Additionally, the contribution to the relevant literature is also highlighted. The next section focuses on policy recommendations based on the research's findings. This chapter ends with ideas for a future research framework.

8.1 RESEARCH QUESTIONS AND FURTHER CONTRIBUTION TO THE LITERATURE

As analyzed in the first chapter, there are three main research questions which initiated this book.

RQ1: How is the Internet infrastructure allocated across the European city-regions?

As explained in Chapter 3, in order to approach the Internet infrastructure, the international Internet backbone network (IBN) was studied. The geographical analysis firstly highlighted this infrastructural network's tendency to expand over time, including more links and also connecting more cities. Interestingly enough, the European part of the network appears to grow faster than the network of the extra-European links. Additionally, if the capacity of the backbone links is not taken into consideration, the IBN appears to be moderately centralized. However, when the capacity is included in the analysis, the network appears more centralized, indicating a higher concentration of the high-capacity links. From a geographic perspective, different roles were recognized for different cities, but one thing is for sure: over the six-year period, London was the main hub of the international IBN in Europe. Its importance is not limited only to the European part of the global network: London, along with New York, is one of the cities with the highest accumulation of bandwidth worldwide. Apart from London, Paris, Amsterdam and Frankfurt appear to be key locations for the topology of this network. Indeed, more than half of the total bandwidth accumulated in European city-regions is allocated across these four city-regions. Regardless of the importance of these hubs, analysis showed that they are not important enough to hold the network together, as no clear evidence of scale-free network (SF) attributes were found. However, the existence of small world network (SW) properties, such as low average distance and high clustering coefficient, highlight the efficiency of this network. The latter though appears to be quite different when technology (bandwidth) is excluded from the analysis and the focus turns on the topology of the IBN. Based on this analysis, the clear role of some cities as gateway locations for their hinterlands emerged. The important thing is that these hinterlands are not only independent of country borders, but sometimes overcome Europe's borders and reflect post-colonial relations. Additionally the binary links also reflect location and physical geography, contrary to the bandwidth distribution which seems to be more related with economic geography.

RQ2: Which are the socio-economic factors that shape the distribution of the Internet infrastructure across the European city-regions?

The analysis identified a set of components which appear to affect the regional connectedness with and the installed capacity between regions because of the IBN. In brief, the importance of macroeconomic conditions and especially market size, the influence of urbanization and world city-ness, as well as the negative effect of coastal and the positive effect of border regions, were highlighted as factors which significantly affect regional connectedness with IBN in Europe. In addition, the negative impact of distance in installed capacity was also identified with the use of a simple SIM. The latter highlighted the spatiality of the Internet despite the early discussions about ICTs and the death of distance.

RQ3: What are the impacts that the Internet infrastructure can generate on the development of city-regions in Europe?

The econometric modeling concluded that wherever a significant causal relationship between the Internet infrastructure and regional economic development exists, then the causality runs mostly from the Internet infrastructure to regional economic development. From the geography point of view, an interesting conclusion was the emergence of an almost North–South pattern of this causal relationship, with the Northern city-regions appearing to be more efficient in exploiting the installed Internet infrastructure. This geographic divide is related to the higher absorptive capacity and intensity of the knowledge economies, which enables

Northern regions to take advantage of the highest tier of the Internet infrastructure.

Apart from the above empirical results, which directly correspond to the three research questions, this research further contributes to the relevant literature. Firstly, as the Internet geography of Europe has not been explored in depth, this study is valuable in understanding how European cities and regions participate in this global infrastructural network and how they benefit by this network. Indeed, as highlighted in Chapter 2, the majority of empirical studies in the emerging field of the Internet geography are concerned with the United States (US) IBN, but also the quantitative data used in these papers only refers to the early 2000s. This study fills the gap of empirical research on the European Internet geography, but also presents and analyzes recent data after the telecoms crash of the early 2000s.

Furthermore, the explanatory analysis of connectedness and installed capacity of European regions is a contribution to the literature. As highlighted in section 2.3.2, apart from a very few exceptions, not many studies have attempted in the past to analyze the socio-economic reasons behind the distribution of the Internet infrastructure.

Additionally, this book contributes to the field of world cities research. The adoption of a relational approach – whenever this is possible – is a valid contribution due to the lack of such studies in this field (Taylor 2004; Short et al. 1996). In order to do so, this study contributes to the empirical justification of Castells's (1996) space of flows, bringing to light inter-urban relations to the extent that they are reflected in this infrastructural network. In short, this book contributes to bridging the gap between the theoretical work of Castells (1996), Sassen (2000a) and others, and the lack of empirical research about the emerging space of flows, as identified by Taylor (2004).

However, the Internet is not the only facilitator of the world city process and according to Taylor (2004) the first layer of the space of flows consists of both the Internet infrastructure and the aviation network: while the latter transports the main actors of the global city process – the managerial elites as they are identified by Castells (1996) – the former transports the ideas and the products of the digital economy. Additionally, a great discussion has taken place in the communications geography literature about the link between telecommunications and transportation. The burgeoning question is whether and to what extent there are complementarities between the two networks. This book draws upon these points by comparing the topology and the geography of these two networks as well as explaining the differences and the similarities in the way these two networks facilitate the world city process. The empirical results of this analysis, such as the illustration of the different roles that different cities perform in these two networks, contribute both to the world city literature, but also to the communications geography literature.

In addition, the present research also contributes to the field of regional science. It not only confirms that the Internet infrastructure is a significant predictor of the level of economic development of regions in Europe, but it also verifies the existence of a significant causal relationship running from the Internet infrastructure to regional economic development. These empirical results are a contribution to the relevant literature for two reasons. Firstly, it is the first time, to my knowledge at least, that empirical research has confirmed such a causal relationship. Regional scientists, economic geographers and urban planners have avoided including such networks in their research, because of their complex technical nature and the lack of relevant data. However, the radical expansion of the Internet and the digital economy increases the need to include this digital infrastructure in the research agenda. The robust results of this study can support this process. Secondly, there was always a debate about the direction of causality between infrastructural capital in general and more specifically within telecommunications – as was highlighted in section 2.5.6 – and (regional) economic development. This study contributes to this debate with the empirical results from the causality analysis.

To sum up, this study, apart from answering the three research questions by conducting empirical quantitative research tailored to the special needs of the study, also contributes to relevant but at the same time diverse fields of literature. Moreover, as will be illustrated in the next section, the empirical analysis of this book can also result in policy implications.

8.2   POLICY INSIGHTS

The same relatively limited interest that the research community has demonstrated for the link between ICT and (regional) economic development applies to policy domain as well (Cohen-Blankshtain and Nijkamp 2004; Graham and Marvin 1996). Hence, issues such as ICT, telecommunications, the Internet and the Internet infrastructure were neglected or misused by policymakers. A quite straightforward explanation for this relative lack of interest is the invisible and complex nature of this infrastructure (Batty 1990; Graham and Marvin 1996; Hackler 2003), contrary to the visible nature of other more traditional infrastructural capital such as the various transportation networks. As explained in Chapter 2, digital infrastructure only becomes visible when it stops working (Star 1999).

And apart from the lack of institutional data and knowledge about ICT (Cohen et al. 2002), it could also be assumed that policymakers are reluctant to invest in infrastructure that is not directly visible to their voters.

Apart from this book's academic ambition in supporting and promoting the inclusion of ICT and the Internet infrastructure in the field of regional science, this study also aspires to justify and promote the inclusion of these elements in the local and regional development agenda. Indeed, this study has demonstrated econometrically that for some of the interconnected (with international backbone networks) European regions, the accumulated bandwidth is a significant causal factor of economic development. The geographic analysis of the outcome of the econometric modeling and its interpretation using other relevant theoretical and empirical studies pointed out that the resulting North–South pattern is due to the spatial differentiation of the intensity of the knowledge economy and the regional absorptive capacity for exploiting this infrastructure.

The above findings can justify the inclusion of elements such as the Internet infrastructure in the local and regional development agenda. As literature suggests (Cieślik and Kaniewska 2004; Wolde-Rufael 2007), the existence of a causal relationship between ICT and economic development, where the causality runs from ICT to economic development, can justify the inclusion of digital infrastructure in a policy framework for stimulating the economy. However, the non-homogenous character of the impacts of ICT on (regional) economic development is the main reason for policymakers' misspecification about the investment on such infrastructure:

> The impact of telecommunications technologies on regional development is not a straightforward mechanism. One of the greatest mistakes would be to expect a direct linkage between the supply of new technologies and economic and regional development. The link between these two elements, technology on one side and economic and regional development on the other, is a rather complex phenomenon. Its successful results stem mainly from a collection of essential elements which have to be present and have to be exploited in the right way. (Capello and Nijkamp 1996a, p. 235)

ICT-related policies can be divided into three groups regarding their strategic approach (Cohen et al. 2002):

- Direct policies. Such policies aim at promoting the availability and the use of ICT. They target both the supply and demand of ICT infrastructure and services. They include a variety of policy tools from strategic city plans for ICT implementation to policies for bridging the digital gap.

- Indirect policies. This group of policies intends to achieve non-ICT goals with the use of ICT. For instance, the use of ICT as a tool for stimulating the (regional) economy is such an example. Again, both supply and demand-oriented policies are included here, such as the provision of ICT infrastructure – supply side – or e-governance-related services – demand side.
- By-the-way policies. These are policies of which the outcome only accidentally affects – directly or indirectly – the field of ICT. A well-known example in the literature is the US defense industry, which pushed ICT developments such as the Internet, but the policy goal was far from ICT-related (Markusen 1988).

However, the implementation of an indirect ICT policy for enhancing regional economic activity which only focuses on the supply side might not be enough. The investment in infrastructure appears to be a precondition for economic development, but it cannot automatically result in enhancing economic activity via the micro and the territorial effects described above (Gibbs and Tanner 1997; Gillespie 1991). Hence, as highlighted above, the supply-side policies should be accompanied by an existing regional capacity for exploiting this production input or/and by direct demand-side policies in order to advance this regional capacity.

However, unlike transport infrastructure, this precondition for development is mostly in the hands of the private sector (Priemus 2007). Telcos decide where and how they roll out their networks based on market assessments. The outcome of this process is usually the cumulative strengthening of the core regions and the resulting widening of the quality gap between core and peripheral regions in terms of connectivity, which in the long term might turn out to be a substantial burden for development (Camagni and Capello 2005). The question is whether and how could policymakers react in this process. Literature suggests the adoption of a moderate interventional approach in order to correct the outcome of the market forces (Cohen-Blankshtain et al. 2004) and the inclusion of ICT in urban policies (Horan and Jordan 1998; Couclelis 2000; Cohen et al. 2002). Indeed, recently cities have started being proactive in improving the level of ICT infrastructure in their territories (Hackler 2003). Examples include extension of the municipal Internet broadband networks, partnership with private telecom firms to extend their fiber networks, the building of networks and opening to Internet service providers (ISPs) (Cohen-Blankshtain and Nijkamp 2004; van Winden and Woets 2004), as well as a number of European Union (EU) initiatives (Capello and Spairani 2008; Camagni and Capello 2005).

To sum up, this research suggests that the level of the Internet infrastructure – at least as this is reflected in the accumulated international Internet backbone capacity – is a significant causal factor for economic development, and because of this attribute policymakers can use it as a means for stimulating the regional economy. However, two difficulties arise. Firstly, the effect of such infrastructure is not homogenous. Despite the importance of this infrastructure, not all places can benefit by this pre-condition for development. Regional capacity and related policies as well as other demand-side policies are necessary in order for a city or a region to exploit such endowment. Secondly, as this infrastructure is mostly a responsibility of the private sector and policymakers are not fully aware of its special (technical and non-technical) attributes, it is difficult to inte-grate such policy goals into urban and regional policies. Indeed, "ICT is a young concept, and ICT policy-making is still in its infancy" (Cohen et al. 2002, p. 34), but still, according to Martin (2003), investments in ICT are preferred to financing highways as it promotes technological convergence among regions with the use of public programs for telecommunications, the Internet and training of human capital.

8.3 EPILOGUE

The main aim in conducting this study was to explore the spatiality of the Internet, which is a technical system with strong topological attributes. Nonetheless, behind these characteristics there is an almost hidden spatial and territorial dimension, which has been largely neglected by both researchers in the spatial sciences and practitioners. In accordance with other studies located in this small, but still active and emerging research field of Internet Geography, the present book has attempted to reveal some of these hidden geographic attributes of the Internet.

Although spatiality is usually not an issue in the discussion around the Internet, this book aimed to address this viewpoint by approaching the Internet infrastructure from a spatial perspective, despite the concep-tual and technical difficulties. The novelty of this book lies not only in the spatial perspective, but mostly in the effort to quantify these issues through an evidence-based modeling approach. While research focusing on the Internet from a real-world geography perspective is not new in the literature, hard evidence deriving from modeling exercises has not yet been extensively utilized.

What this book has not touched upon is the inter-city Internet Protocol (IP) flows because of the lack of relevant data. Such a study could reveal the actual city-to-city interactions in a high spatial and temporal resolu-tion. Advances in network science would enable the study of the dynamics of IP (inter)urban interactions, revealing important information about the economic nature of these flows (Nagurney and Qiang 2009). However, it is difficult to gain access to such data. As mentioned above, although telcos collect such data for network calibration, access is usually restricted due to competition reasons. Additionally, there is no central authority with responsibility for collecting data on traffic flows (Kende 2000). Nonetheless, recent examples of partnerships between telcos and researchers from the fields of geography, planning and regional science raise confidence for the feasibility of such research projects. Examples include the MIT SENSEable City Laboratory NYTE project, which focused on mapping IP flows between New York City and the rest of the world (Ratti et al. 2008), but also advances in utilizing data from mobile phone operators (e.g. Ahas et al. 2007; Lambiotte et al. 2008; Reades et al. 2009).

To conclude, despite the inherent difficulty in approaching the Internet from a spatial perspective, the above analysis revealed not only the spatial dimension of the Internet, but also the interrelation between the so-called "placeless" Internet and spatial configuration. This overall finding leads to the final point of this book. Geography, planning, regional science and spatial sciences in general cannot afford to ignore the digital revolution and the intensification of the digital economy, for two reasons. Firstly, new digital phenomena, such as the Internet, have spatial reflections that need to be approached from a geographic standpoint. The spatial analysis of IP flows is such an example. Secondly, the profusion of new bottom-up data derived from digital sources, such as ISPs and mobile phone operators, enables the research community to study and quantify traditional geographic questions from a new perspective, achieving greater spatio-temporal resolution. From a policy perspective, such analytical efforts will enable researchers to inform policymakers and to include digital themes in the local policy agenda. For these two reasons, a focus on an e-regional science, which will address digital phenomena from a spatial perspective and utilize digital data to approach traditional geographical questions, appears as an exciting outlook.

Notes

1. Nevertheless, the above hypothesis has some limitations, which will be discussed in detail in Chapter 3, where this study's main data is presented.
2. According to Taylor (1997), the two different types of relational data that can be found in the literature are the flows between cities and the organizational links between them. For his seminal work presented here (Taylor 2004), the second type of relational data is used.
3. Other terms used to approach this phenomenon and not analyzed here are: "the weightless economy" (Quah 1996), "virtual economy", "e-economy" and so on.
4. It should be noted that the long cycle theory did not originated with him but rather with other earlier economists such as the Dutch Marxist Van Gelderen, who introduced this idea in 1913, 13 years before Kondratieff (Freeman and Soete 1997; Mumtaz 2003).
5. The part of knowledge which is not "codifiable" is identified as tacit knowledge and is embodied in practices, people and networks (Maignan et al. 2003).
6. It was developed by Ray Tomlinson in July 1970 (Castells 2001).
7. Apart from capital, classical economics identify land (or natural resources) and labor as the three basic resource categories. The appropriate combination of them leads to the production output and income (Biehl 1991).
8. Face-to-face communication can be divided into two components: the "conversation" and the "handshake", with the former being the "metaphor for simultaneous real-time interactive visual and oral messages", and the latter for the physical co-presence (Leamer and Storper 2001, p. 4). ICTs can only decrease the cost of the conversation component.
9. For simplification reasons, routing is excluded from this argument. In reality part of the installed capacity in a city is used for routing purposes and does not reflect direct city-to-city digital interactions.
10. NUTS stands for Nomenclature of Territorial Units for Statistics and represent the official territorial units for the provision of regional statistics (EC 2009). NUTS 2 regions have a more regional character, while NUTS 3 are closer to a metropolitan area or a city-region.
11. The Social Network Analysis software UCINET was utilized for this purpose (Borgatti et al. 2002).
12. In network analysis terminology "distance" does not refer to Euclidean distance, but to the number of nodes that separate any two nodes. And because usually there are plenty of different ways to connect any two given nodes (also known as a "walk"), we usually focus on the shortest distance, known as "geodesic distance" (Nooy et al. 2005). Some studies use the term "diameter" to name the above measure. For the needs of the present study, the term "diameter" is used to express the longest distance in the network.
13. Time series are differentiated by panel data because it lacks the cross-section dimension (Maddala 2001).
14. The "pentagon" is the core area of the European Union (EU) and is defined as "a geographical zone of global economic integration" (EC 1999). It is encompassed by London, Paris, Milan, Munich and Hamburg.
15. The points marked with the star symbol represent backbone links with capacity greater than 1.5 inter-quartile ranges.
16. These are: Frankfurt, Hamburg, Stuttgart, Karlsruhe, Düsseldorf, Munich, Nuremberg,

Berlin, Hameln, Hannover, Cologne, Saarbrucken, Krefeld, Dortmund, Dresden, Ehingen and Hilden.

17.   It should be highlighted here that the increase in the non-normalized centrality is not independent from the technology improvement and this is the reason why the normalized one is usually used.

18.   New York is the main exception to this. Even if only its backbone links with Europe are taken into consideration, its weighted degree centrality is equal to 46 percent of London centrality. This would enable New York to take the fifth position in the relevant rank for the European cities

19.   Economies of scale are related here with the extension of the network (Dobruszkes 2006).

20.   In reality, the installed "lit" capacity exceeds current average demand both due to infrastructure overbuild and because backbone capacity is designed to accommodate pick data packet flows which are much higher than the average. However, there is no evidence that this mismatch is spatially differentiated and existing lit capacity appears to be a fairly good proxy for the demand for intercity Internet communications.

21.   Clustering coefficient is the ratio between the existing numbers of edges among a node's nearest neighbors and the maximum number of these edges (Albert and Barabási 2002).

22.   For the Internet backbone network s metric was lower (0.596–0.651).

23.   The area enclosed by a pentagon with its corners being the cities of London, Hamburg, Munich, Milan and Paris, often used to denote the "core" area of Europe.

24.   In total, 153 unique country-to-country effects have been identified over the six-year period.

25.   Following Hood III et al. (2008), the instantaneous case (the current value of x is included as a regressor) is excluded from the model because of a potential simultaneity problem.

26.   Regressions coefficients are allowed to change from lag to lag.

27.   The values are -1.612 for degree centrality and -0.328 for GDP per capita, both significant at the 1 percent level.

28.   Owing to the limited time dimension of the panel data (T = 6), testing for $p > 2$ was not possible as it would lead to a major decrease of the observations.

29.   Because models with more than one lag have already been excluded from the analysis, this hypothesis in reality tests the equality across cross-section units in $t - 1$ ($\beta_i = \beta_j$).

30.   While Shiu and Lam (2008) and Hartwig (2010) divide regions into groups based on geographical or economical reasons, this chapter divides regions into groups based on the results following the method of Hurlin and Venet (2003).

31.   An attempt was made to perform the GMM-based causality analysis using a clear North–South division, following Shiu and Lam (2008) and Hartwig (2010). However, no significant results were produced based on such division, and therefore the division resulting from the first-stage causality analysis was used instead.

32.   Other service industries are also not related to the digital economy, but tourism industries tend to concentrate in specific locations, creating an extensive bias when the focus is to capture other non-tourism services.

References

Ache, P. (2000), 'Cities in old industrial regions between local innovative milieu and urban governance – reflections on city region governance'. *European Planning Studies* **8** (6): 693–709.

Adamic, L.A. (2000), 'Zipf, Power-laws, and Pareto – a ranking tutorial'. Information Dynamics Lab, HP Labs.

Aghion, P. and Howitt, P. (1998), *Endogenous Growth Theory*. Cambridge, MA: MIT Press.

Ahas, R., Aasa, A., Mark, Ü., Pae, T. and Kull, T. (2007), 'Seasonal tourism spaces in Estonia: case study with mobile positioning data'. *Tourism Management* **28** (3): 898–910.

Albert, R. and Barabási, A.-L. (2002), 'Statistical mechanics of complex networks'. *Reviews of Modern Physics* **74**: 47–97.

Albert, R., Jeong, H. and Barabási, A.-L. (2000), 'Error and attack tolerance of complex networks'. *Nature* **406**: 378–81.

Alderighi, M., Cento, A., Nijkamp, P. and Rietveld, P. (2007), 'Assessment of new hub-and-spoke and point-to-point airline network configurations'. *Transport Reviews* **27** (5): 529–49.

Allen, J. (1999), 'Cities of power and influence: settled formations'. In Allen, J., Massey, D., Pryke, M. (eds), *Unsettling Cities*. London: Routledge, pp 186–237.

Allenby, B. and Fink, J. (2005), 'Towards inherently secure and resilient societies'. *Science* **309** (5737): 1034–6.

Amaral, L.A.N., Scala, A., Barthelemy, M. and Stanley, H.E. (2000), 'Classes of small-world networks'. *PNAS* **97**: 11149–52.

Amin, A. and Graham, S. (1999), 'Cities of connections and disconnection'. In Allen, J., Massey, D. and Pryke, M. (eds), *Unsettling Cities*. London: Routledge, pp 7–48.

Amin, A. and Thrift, N. (1992), 'Neo-Marshallian nodes in global networks'. *International Journal of Urban and Regional Research* **16** (4): 571–87.

AMS-IX (2009), Amsterdam Internet Exchange. Accessed 28 July at www.ams-ix.net/about/Whatisix_Tier.pdf.

Antonelli, C. (2003), 'The digital divide: understanding the economics of new information and communication technology in the global economy'. *Information Economics and Policy* **15** (2): 173–99.

Arellano, M. and Bond, S.R. (1991), 'Some tests of specification for panel data: Monte Carlo evidence and an application to employment equations'. *Review of Economic Studies* **58**: 277.

Arellano, M. and Bover, O. (1995), 'Another look at the instrumental variables estimation of error-components models'. *Journal of Econometrics* **68**: 19–51.

Armstrong, H. and Taylor, J. (2000), *Regional Economics and Policy*. 3rd edn. Oxford: Blackwell.

Arnaud, B.S. (2009), 'Green IT/broadband and cyber-infrastructure'. Accessed 21 August at http://green-broadband.blogspot.com/.

Atkinson, R.D. and McKay, A. (2007), *Digital Prosperity*. Washington, DC: ITIF.

Audestad, J.A. (2007), 'Internet as a multiple graph structure: the role of the transport layer'. *Information Security Technical Report* **12** (1): 16–23.

Bakis, H. (1981), 'Elements for a geography of telecommunication'. *Geographic Research Forum* **4**: 31–45.

Baltagi, B.H. (1995), *Econometric Analysis of Panel Data*. 1st edn. Chichester: John Wiley & Sons.

Banerjee, A.V. and Duflo, E. (2003), 'Inequality and growth: what can the data say?'. *Journal of Economic Growth* **8** (3): 267–99.

Banister, D. and Berechman, J. (2003), *Transport Investment and Economic Development*. London: Routledge.

Banister, D. and Stead, D. (2004), 'Impact of information and communications technology on transport'. *Transport Reviews* **24** (5): 611–32.

Barabási, A.-L. and Albert, R. (1999), 'Emergence of scaling in random networks'. *Science* **286** (15 October): 509–12.

Baran, P. (1964), 'On distributed communications: I Introduction to distributed communications networks'. RAND series.

Batowski, M. and Pastuszak, Z. (2008), 'Sources of the success of Scandinavian knowledge economies'. *International Journal of Innovation and Learning* **5** (2): 109–18.

Batty, M. (1990), 'Invisible cities'. *Environment and Planning B* **17**: 127–30.

Batty, M. (1991), 'Urban information network: the evolution and planning of computer-communications infrastructure'. In Brotchies, J., Batty, M., Hall, P. and Newton, P. (eds), *Cities of the 21st Century*. New York: Wiley & Sons, pp 139–57.

Batty, M. (1997), 'Virtual geography'. *Futures* **29** (4–5): 337–52.

Batty, M. (2001), 'Cities as small worlds'. *Environment and Planning B* **28**: 637–8.

Baum, C.F. (2006), *An Introduction to Modern Econometrics Using Stata*. Boston, MA: STATA Press.

Beaverstock, J.V. (2002), 'Transnational elites in global cities: British expatriates in Singapore's financial district'. *Geoforum* **33** (4): 525–38.

Beckmann, M. (1967), 'On the theory of traffic flows in networks'. *Traffic Quarterly* **21**: 109–16.

Beckmann, M., McGuire, C.B. and Winsten, C.B. (1956), *Studies in the Economics of Transportation*. New Haven, CT: Yale University Press; also published (1955) as Rand-RM-1488-PR, Santa Monica, CA: Rand Corporation.

Beil, R., Ford, G. and Jackson, J. (2005), 'On the relationship between telecommunications investment and economic growth in the United States'. *International Economic Journal* **19** (1): 3–9.

Benner, M. (2003), 'The Scandinavian challenge: the future of advanced welfare states in the knowledge economy'. *Acta Sociologica* **46** (2): 132–49.

Biehl, D. (1991), 'The role of infrastructure in regional development'. In Vickerman, R.W. (ed.), *Infrastructure and Regional Development. European Research in Regional Science*. London: Pion Ltd, pp 9–35.

Black, W.R. and Nijkamp, P. (2006), 'Transportation, communication and sustainability: in search of a pathway to comparative research'. In Reggiani, A. and Schintler, L. (eds), *Methods and Models in Transport and Telecommunications Cross Atlantic Perspectives*. Berlin: Springer, pp 9–22.

Blum, B.S. and Goldfarb, A. (2006), 'Does the internet defy the law of gravity?'. *Journal of International Economics* **70**: 384–405.

Blundell, R. and Bond, S. (1998), 'Initial conditions and moment restrictions in dynamic panel data models'. *Journal of Econometrics* **87**: 115–43.

Bonarich, P. (2007), 'Some unique properties of eigenvector centrality'. *Social Networks* **29**: 555–64.

Borgatti, S.P., Everett, M.G. and Freeman, L.C. (2002), *Ucinet for Windows: Software for Social Network Analysis*. Cambridge, MA: Analytic Technologies.

Borland, J. and Hu, J. (2004), 'Why policies must change. Breaking the digital gridlock'. CNET News.com Digital Agenta Broadband.

Boyce, D.E., Mahmassani, H.S. and Nagurney, A. (2005), 'A retrospective on Beckmann, McGuire and Winsten's Studies in the Economics of Transportation'. *Papers in Regional Science* **84** (1): 85–103.

Braudel, F. (1984), *The Perspective of the World*. London: Collins.

Brenner, N. (1998a), 'Between fixity and motion: accumulation, territorial organization and the historical geography of spatial scales'. *Environment and Planning D* **16**: 459–81.

Brenner, N. (1998b), 'Global cities, glocal states: global city formation and state territorial restructuring in contemporary Europe'. *Review of International Political Economy* **5** (1): 1–37.

Bresnahan, T.F. and Trajtenberg, M. (1995), 'General purpose technologies "engines of growth"?'. *Journal of Econometrics* **65** (1): 83–108.

Bronzini, R. and Piselli, P. (2009), 'Determinants of long-run regional productivity with geographical spillovers: the role of R&D, human capital and public infrastructure'. *Regional Science and Urban Economics* **39**: 187–99.

Burton-Jones, A. (1999), *Knowledge Capitalism*. Oxford: Oxford University Press.

Button, K. (2000), 'New approaches to spatial economics'. *Growth and Change* **31**: 480–500.

Button, K. and Stough, R. (2000), *Air Transportation Networks: Theory and Policy Implications*. Cheltenham, UK and Northampton, MA, USA: Edward Elgar.

CAIDA (2009), The Cooperative Association for Internet Data Analysis. University of California. Accessed 28 May at www.caida.org.

Cairncross, F. (2001), *The Death of Distance 2.0*. London: Texere Publishing.

Camagni, R. and Capello, R. (2005), 'ICTs and territorial competitiveness in the era of internet'. *Annals of Regional Science* **39** (3): 421–38.

Capello, R., Nijkamp, P. (1996a), 'Regional variations in production network externalities'. *Regional Studies* **30** (3): 225–37.

Capello, R. and Nijkamp, P. (1996b), 'Telecommunications technologies and regional development: theoretical considerations and empirical evidence'. *Annals of Regional Science* **30** (1): 7–30.

Capello, R. and Spairani, A. (2008), 'Ex-ante evaluation of European ICT policies: efficiency vs. cohesion scenarios'. *International Journal of Public Policy* **3** (3–4): 261–80.

Castells, M. (1996), *The Rise of the Network Society*. Oxford: Blackwell.

Castells, M. (2001), *The Internet Galaxy*. Oxford: Oxford University Press.

Chakraborty, C. and Nandi, B. (2003), 'Privatization, telecommunications and growth in selected Asian countries: an econometric analysis'. *Communications and Strategies* **52** (3): 31–47.

Chamberlain, G. (1982), 'Multivariate regression models for panel data'. *Journal of Econometrics* **18** (1): 5–45.

Charles, D., Bradley, D., Chatterton, P., Coombes, M. and Gillespie, A. (1999), *Core Cities: Key Centres for Regeneration, Synthesis Report*. Newcastle upon Tyne: CURDS.

Cheshire, P. (1990), 'Explaining the recent performance of the European Community's major urban region'. *Urban Studies* **27** (3): 311–33.

Cheshire, P., Carbonaro, G. and Hay, D. (1986), 'Problems of urban decline and growth in EEC countries: or measuring degrees of elephant-ness'. *Urban Studies* **23** (2): 131–49.

Cho, S. and Mokhtarian, P.L. (2007), 'Telecommunications and travel demand and supply: aggregate structural equation models for the US'. *Transportation Research Part A* **41** (1): 4–18.

Choi, J.H., Barnett, G.A. and Chon, B.-S. (2006), 'Comparing world city networks: a network analysis of Internet backbone and air transport intercity linkages'. *Global Networks* **6** (1): 81–99.

Chon, B.-S. (2004), 'The dual structure of global networks in the enter-tainment industry: interorganizational linkage and geographical disper-sion'. *International Journal on Media Management* **6** (3): 194–206.

Chu, N., Oxley, L. and Carlaw, K. (2005), 'ICT and causality in the New Zealand economy'. Proceedings of the 2005 International Conference on Simulation and Modelling.

Cicślik, A. and Kaniewska, M. (2004), 'Telecommunications infrastruc-ture and regional economic development: the case of Poland'. *Regional Studies* **38** (6): 713–25.

Cohen, S.S., DeLong, J.B., Weber, S. and Zysman, J. (2001), *Tracking a Transformation: E-Commerce and the Terms of Competition in Industries*. BRIE-IGCC E-conomy Project Task Force, Washington, DC: Brookings Press.

Cohen, S.S., DeLong, J.B. and Zysman, J. (2000), 'Tools for thought: what is new and important about the "e-conomy"'. Berkeley Roundtable on International Economics working paper no. 138, Berkeley, CA.

Cohen, W.M. and Levinthal, D.A. (1990), 'Absorptive capacity: a new per-spective on learning and innovation'. *Administrative Science Quarterly* **35** (1): 128–52.

Cohen-Blankshtain, G. and Nijkamp, P. (2004), 'The appreciative system of urban ICT policies: an analysis of perceptions of urban policy makers'. *Growth and Change* **35** (2): 166–97.

Cohen-Blankshtain, G., Nijkamp, P. and Montfort, Kv. (2004), 'Modelling ICT perceptions and views of urban front-liners'. *Urban Studies* **41** (13): 2647–67.

Cohen, G., Salomon, I. and Nijkamp, P. (2002), 'Information-communications technologies (ICT) and transport: does knowledge underpin policy?', *Telecommunication Policy* **26** (1–2): 31–52.

Cohendet, P. and Steinmueller, W.E. (2000), 'The codification of knowl-edge: a conceptual and empirical exploration'. *Industrial and Corporate Change* **9** (2): 195–209.

Corey, K.E. (1982), 'Transactional forces and the metropolis'. *Ekistics* **297**: 416–23.

Cornford, G. and Gillespie, A. (1993), 'Cable systems, telephony and local economic development in the UK'. *Telecommunication Policy* **17** (8): 589–603.

Couclelis, H. (2000), 'From sustainable transportation to sustainable accessibility: can we avoid a new tragedy of the commons?'. In Janelle, D. and Hodge, D. (eds), *Information, Place and Cyberspace: Issues in Accessibility*. Berlin: Springer, pp 341–56.

Cronin, F.J., Colleran, E.K., Herbert, P.L. and Lewitzky, S. (1993a), 'Telecommunications and growth: the contribution of telecommunications infrastructure investment to aggregate and sectoral productivity'. *Telecommunications Policy* **17** (9): 677–90.

Cronin, F.J., Parker, E.B., Colleran, E.K. and Gold, M.A. (1991), 'Telecommunications infrastructure and economic growth: an analysis of causality'. *Telecommunications Policy* **15** (6): 529–35.

Cronin, F.J., Parker, E.B., Colleran, E.K. and Gold, M.A. (1993b), 'Telecommunications infrastructure investment and economic development'. *Telecommunications Policy* **17** (6): 415–30.

Crucitti, P., Latorab, V., Marchioric, M. and Rapisarda, A. (2004), 'Error and attack tolerance of complex networks'. *Physica A* **340**: 388–94.

Cushman & Wakefield (2008), 'European cities monitor'. Cushman & Wakefield Global Real Estate Solutions, accessed 2 March 2009 at www.europeancitiesmonitor.eu/.

Cutrini, E. (2010), 'Specialization and concentration from a twofold geographical perspective: evidence from Europe'. *Regional Studies* **44** (3): 315–36.

D'Ignazio, A. and Giovannetti, E. (2007), 'Spatial dispersion of interconnection clusters in the European Internet'. *Spatial Economic Analysis* **2** (3): 219–36.

Dasgupta, P. and David, P.A. (1994), 'Toward a new economics of science'. *Policy Research* **23**: 487–521.

Davoudi, S. (2003), 'Polycentricity in European spatial planning: from an analytical tool to a normative agenda'. *European Planning Studies* **11** (8): 979–99.

Derudder, B. (2006), 'On conceptual confusion in empirical analyses of a transnational urban network'. *Urban Studies* **43** (11): 2027–46.

Derudder, B., Devriendt, L. and Witlox, F. (2007), 'Flying where you don't walk to go: an empirical analysis of hubs in the global airline network'. *Tijdschrift voor Economische en Sociale Geografie* **98** (3): 307–24.

Derudder, B. and Witlox, F. (2005), 'An appraisal of the use of airline data in assessing the world city network: a research note on data'. *Urban Studies* **42** (13): 2371–88.

Derudder, B. and Witlox, F. (2008), 'Mapping world city networks through airline flows: context, relevance, and problems'. *Journal of Transport Geography* **16** (5): 305–12.

Devriendt, L., Derudder, B. and Witlox, F. (2008), 'Cyberplace and cyberspace: two approaches to analyzing digital intercity linkages'. *Journal of Urban Technology* **15** (2): 5–32.

Devriendt, L., Derudder, B. and Witlox, F. (2010a), 'Conceptualizing digital and physical connectivity: the position of European cities in Internet backbone and air traffic flows'. *Telecommunications Policy* **34** (8): 417–29.

Devriendt, L., Derudder, B. and Witlox, F. (2010b), 'Conceptualizing digital and physical connectivity: the position of European cities in Internet backbone and air traffic flows'. *Telecommunications Policy* **34** (8): 417–29.

Dickinson, R.E. (1947), *City, Region and Regionalism*. London: Routledge.

Dixon, R.J. and Thirlwall, A.P. (1975), 'A model of regional growth rate differentials along Kaldorian lines'. *Oxford Economic Press* **27**: 201–14.

Dobruszkes, F. (2006), 'An analysis of European low-cost airlines and their networks'. *Journal of Transport Geography* **14** (4): 249–64.

Dodge, M. (2008), *Understanding Cyberspace Cartographies: A Critical Analysis of Internet Infrastructure Mapping*. London: UCL.

Dodge, M. and Kitchin, R. (2000), *Mapping Cyberspace*. London and New York: Routledge.

Dodge, M. and Shiode, N. (2000), 'Where on Earth is the Internet? An empirical investigation of the geography of Internet real estate'. In Wheeler, J.O., Aoyama, Y. and Warf, B. (eds), *Cities in the Telecommunications Age: The Fracturing of Geographies*. New York: Routledge, pp 42–53.

Dodge, M. and Zook, M.A. (2009), 'Internet based measurement'. In Kitchin, R. and Thrift, N. (eds), *The International Encyclopedia of Human Geography*. Oxford: Elsevier, pp 569–79.

Drucker, P.F. (1998), 'From capitalism to knowledge society'. In Neef, D. (ed.), *The Knowledge Economy*. Woburn, MA: Butterworth-Heinemann, pp 15–34.

Dutta, A. (2001), 'Telecommunications and economic activity: an analysis of Granger causality'. *Journal of Management Information Systems* **17** (4): 71–95.

EC (1999), *ESDP – European Spatial Development Perspective*. Luxembourg: Office for Official Publications of the European Communities.

EC (2004), *Strengthening Competitiveness through Co-operation*: Brussels: European research in information and communication technologies.

EC (2009), NUTS Regions. Accessed 6 August at http://ec.europa.eu/ eurostat/ramon/nuts/splash_regions.html.

The Economist (2002), 'The great telecoms crash'. 18 July.

Erdil, E. and Yetkiner, I.H. (2009), 'The Granger-causality between health care expenditure and output: a panel data approach'. *Applied Economics* **41**: 511–18.

Erdös, P. and Rényi, A. (1959), *On Random Graphs*. Debrecen, Hungary: Publicationes Mathematicae, pp 290–97.

ESPON (2005a), *Potentials for Polycentric Development in Europe*. Luxemburg: ESPON.

ESPON (2005b), *Project 1.2.2 Telecommunication Services and Networks: Territorial Trends and Basic Supply of Infrastructure for Territorial Cohesion*. Luxemburg: ESPON.

ESPON (2011), 'Database public files'. Accessed 28 December at www. espon.eu/.

EU (2011), 'Summaries of EU legislation'. Accessed 28 December at http:// europa.eu/legislation_summaries/regional_policy/provisions_and_ instruments/g24203_en.htm.

Euro-IX (2006), *2006 Report on European IXPs*. European Internet Exchange Association.

Euro-IX (2008), 'The European IXP scene'. European Internet Exchange Association. Accessed 10 December at www.euro-ix.net/news/meet event/gpf3_euro-ix.pdf.

Eurostat (2011), 'Regional data'. Accessed 28 November 2010 at http:// epp.eurostat.ec.europa.eu/portal/page/portal/eurostat/home/.

Evans-Cowley, J., Malecki, E.J. and McIntee, A. (2002), 'Planning responses to telecom hotels: what accounts for increased regulation of co-location facilities?'. *Journal of Urban Technology* **9** (3): 1–18.

Faloutsos, M., Faloutsos, P. and Faloutsos, C. (1999), 'On power-law relationships of the Internet topology'. *Computer Communication Review* **29**: 251–62.

Finkel, S.E. (1995), *Causal Analysis with Panel Data*. Thousand Oaks, CA: SAGE Publications.

Fischer, M.M. and Wang, J. (2011), *Spatial Data Analysis: Models, Methods and Techniques*. Heidelberg, Dordrecht, London and New York: Springer.

Florens, J.-P. and Mouchart, M. (1982), 'Note on noncausality'. *Econometrica* **50** (3): 583–91.

Fosco, C. (2004), 'Local preferential attachment'. Accessed 16 May 2008 at http://merlin.fae.ua.es/constanza/.

Freeman, C. (1978–79), 'Centrality in social networks conceptual clarification'. *Social Networks* **1** (3): 215–39.

Freeman, C. (1987), *Technology Policy and Economic Performance: Lessons from Japan*. London: Pinter Publishers.

Freeman, C. and Perez, C. (1988), 'Structural crisies of adjustment: business cycles and investment behaviour'. In Dosi, G., Freeman, C., Nelson, R., Silverberg, G. and Soete, L. (eds), *Technical Change and Economic Theory*. London: Pinter Publishers, pp 38–66.

Freeman, C. and Soete, L. (1997), *The Economics of Industrial Innovation*. 3rd edn. London and New York: Continuum.

Friedmann, J. (1986), 'The world city hypothesis'. *Development and Change* **17** (1): 69–84.

Friedmann, J. (1995), 'Where we stand: a decade of world city research'. In Knox, P.L. and Taylor, P.J. (eds), *World Cities in a World-System*. Cambridge: Cambridge University Press, pp 21–47.

Fujita, M. and Krugman, P. (2004), 'The new economic geography: past, present and the future'. *Papers in Regional Science* **83** (1): 139–64.

Garcia, B.E. (2000), 'Global crossing to build facility'. Accessed 3 December 2008 at www.internetcoast.org/index.php?src=news&refno=370.

Gastner, M.T. and Newman, M.E.J. (2005), 'The spatial structure of networks'. *European Physical Journal B – Condensed Matter and Complex Systems* **49** (2): 247–52.

GaWC (2008), 'The world according to GaWC 2008'. Accessed 29 June 2011 at www.lboro.ac.uk/gawc/world2008t.html.

Geddes, P. (1915), *Cities in Evolution*. London: Williams.

Geels, F.W. and Smit, W.A. (2000), 'Failed technology futures: pitfalls and lessons from a historical survey'. *Futures* **32** (9–10): 867–85.

Gibbs, D. and Tanner, K. (1997), 'Information and communication technologies and local economic development policies: the British case'. *Regional Studies* **31** (8): 765–74.

Gibson, W. (1984), Neuromancer. New York: Ace Books.

Gilder, G. (1995), *Forbes*, 27 February, p 56.

Gilder, G. (2000), *Telecosm*. New York: Free Press.

Gillena, D. and Morrison, W.G. (2003), 'Regulation, competition and network evolution in aviation'. *Journal of Air Transport Management* **11** (3). 161–74.

Gillespie, A. (1991), 'Advanced communications networks, territorial integration and local development'. In Camagni, R. (ed.), *Innovation Networks: Spatial Perspectives*. London: Belhaven, pp 214–29.

Gillespie, A., Richardson, R. and Cornford, J. (2001), 'Regional development and the new economy'. *European Investment Bank Papers* **6** (1): 109–31.

Gillespie, A. and Robins, K. (1989), 'Geographical inequalities: the spatial bias of the new communications technology'. *Journal of Communication* **39** (3): 7–18.

Goldberger, A.S. (1964), *Econometric Theory*. New York: John Wiley & Sons.

Gore, A. (1993), Remarks by Vice President Al Gore at National Press Club, December 21. Accessed 31 January 2009 at www.ibiblio.org/nii/goremarks.html.

Gorman, S.P. and Kulkarni, R. (2004), 'Spatial small worlds: new geographic patterns for an information economy'. *Environment and Planning B* **31** (2): 273–96.

Gorman, S.P. and Malecki, E.J. (2000), 'The networks of the Internet: an analysis of provider networks in the USA'. *Telecommunications Policy* **24** (2): 113–34.

Gorman, S.P. and Malecki, E.J. (2002), 'Fixed and fluid: stability and change in the geography of the Internet'. *Telecommunications Policy* **26** (7–8): 389–413.

Gorman, S.P. and McIntee, A. (2003), 'Tethered connectivity? The spatial distribution of wireless infrastructure'. *Environment and Planning A* **35** (7): 1157–71.

Gottmann, J. (1961), *Megalopolis: The Urbanized Northeastern Seaboard of the United States*. New York: MIT Press.

Gottmann, J. (1983), *The Coming of the Transactional City*. College Park, MD: University of Maryland, Institute for Urban Studies.

Graham, B. (1998), 'Liberalization, regional economic development and the geography of demand for air transport in the European Union'. *Journal of Transport Geography* **6** (2): 87–104.

Graham, S. (1999), 'Global grids of glass: on global cities, telecommunications and planetary urban networks'. *Urban Studies* **36** (5–6): 929–49.

Graham, S. (2004), 'Excavating the material geographies of cybercities'. In Graham, S. (ed.), *The Cybercities Reader*. London: Routledge, pp 138–42.

Graham, S. and Marvin, S. (1996), *Telecommunications and the City*. London and New York: Routledge.

Graham, S. and Marvin, S. (2001), *Splintering Urbanism*. London and New York: Routledge.

Granger, C.W.J. (1969), 'Investigating causal relations by econometric and cross-spectral methods'. *Econometrica* **37** (3): 424–38.

Greene, W.H. (2003), *Econometric Analysis*. 5th edn. Upper Saddle River, NJ: Pearson Education.

Greenstein, S.M. (2004), 'The economic geography of Internet infrastructure in the United States'. In Cave, M., Majumdar, S. and Vogelsang,

I. (eds), *Handbook of Telecommunications Economics*, Volume II. Amsterdam: Elsevier, pp 289–372.

Grubesic, T.H. and Murray, A.T. (2006), 'Vital nodes, interconnected infrastructures, and the geographies of network survivability'. *Annals of the Association of American Geographers* **96** (1): 64–83.

Grubesic, T.H. and O'Kelly, M.E. (2002), 'Using points of presence to measure accessibility to the commercial Internet'. *Professional Geographer* **54** (2): 259–78.

Guimera, R., Mossa, S., Turtschi, A. and Amaral, L.A.N. (2005), 'The worldwide air transportation network: anomalous centrality, community structure and cities' global roles'. *Proceedings of the National Academy of Sciences of the United States of America* **102** (22): 7794–9.

Hackler, D. (2003), 'Invisible infrastructure and the city: the role of telecommunications in economic development'. *American Behavioral Scientist* **46** (8): 1034–55.

Hall, P. (1966), *The World Cities*. London: Weidenfeld & Nicolson.

Hall, P. (1998), 'Globalization and the world cities'. In Lo, F.-C., Yeung, Y.-m. (eds), *Globalization and the World of Large Cities*. Tokyo: United Nations University Press, pp 17–36.

Hall, P. (2009), 'Looking backward, looking forward: the city region of the mid-21st century'. *Regional Studies* **43** (6): 803–17.

Hall, P. and Pain, K. (2006), *The Polycentric Metropolis: Learning from Mega-city Regions in Europe*. London: Earthscan.

Hanneman, R.A. and Riddle, M. (2005), *Introduction to Social Network Methods*. Riverside, CA: University of California, Riverside, published in digital form at http://faculty.ucr.edu/~hanneman/.

Hardy, A. (1980), 'The role of the telephone in economic development'. *Telecommunication Policy* **4** (4): 278–86.

Harris, G.R. (1998), 'The Internet as a GTP: factor market implications'. In Helpman, E. (ed.), *General Purpose Technologies and Economic Growth*. Cambridge, MA: MIT Press, pp 145–66.

Hartwig, J. (2010), 'Is health capital formation good for long-term economic growth? Panel Granger-causality evidence for OECD countries'. *Journal of Macroeconomics* **23**: 314–25.

Harvey, D. (1982), *The Limits to Capital*. Chicago, IL: University of Chicago Press.

Hays, J.C., Kachi, A., Jr, R.J.F. (2010), 'A spatial model incorporating dynamic, endogenous network interdependence: a political science application'. *Statistical Methodology* **7**: 406–28.

Headrick, D.R. (1991), *The Invisible Weapon: Telecommunications and International Politics 1851–1945*. New York: Oxford University Press.

Helpman, E. (1998), 'General purpose technologies and economic growth:

introduction'. In Helpman, E. (ed.), *General Purpose Technologies and Economic Growth*. Cambridge, MA: MIT Press, pp 1–13.

Hendricks, K., Piccione, M. and Tan, G. (1995), 'The economics of hubs: the case of monopoly'. *Review of Economic Studies* **62** (1): 83–99.

Hepworth, M. (1989), *Geography of the Information Economy*. London: Belhaven Press.

Hirschman, A. (1958), *The Strategy of Economic Development*. New York: Yale University Press.

Hoekman, J., Frenken, K. and Tijssenc, R.J.W. (2010), 'Research collaboration at a distance: changing spatial patterns of scientific collaboration within Europe'. *Research Policy* **39** (5): 662–73.

Hoffmann, R., Lee, C.-G., Ramasamy, B. and Yeung, M. (2005), 'FDI and pollution: a granger causality test using panel data'. *Journal of International Development* **17** (3): 311–17.

Holloway, S. (2003), *Straight and Level: Practical Airline Economics*. 2nd edn. Aldershot: Ashgate.

Hood, M.V. III, Kidd, Q. and Morris, I.L. (2008), 'Two sides of the same coin? Employing Granger causality tests in a time series cross-section framework'. *Political Analysis* **16** (3): 324–44.

Hoover, K.D. (2001), *Causality in Macroeconomics*. Cambridge: Cambridge University Press.

Horan, T.A. and Jordan, D.R. (1998), 'Integrating transportation and telecommunications planning in Santa Monica'. *Journal of Urban Technology* **5** (2): 1–20.

Hsiao, C. (2003), *Analysis of Panel Data*. 2nd edn. Cambridge: Cambridge University Press.

Huddleston, J.R. and Pangotra, P.P. (1990), 'Regional and local economic impacts of transportation investment'. *Transportation Quartely* **44** (4): 579–94.

Hurlin, C., Venet, B. (2003), 'Granger causality test in panel data models with fixed coefficients'. University of Orleans working paper.

ICAO (2008), Data from the International Civil Aviation Organization. Accessed 3 February at www.icaodata.com/.

IHDP (2005), *Science Plan. Urbanization and Global Environment Change*. Bonn, Germany: IHDP.

ITU (2004), *Via Africa. Creating Local and Regional IXPs to save Money and Bandwidth*. Geneva: ITU.

Jochimsen, R. (1966), *Theories der Infrastructur, Grundlagen der Marktwirtschaftlichen Entwicklung*. Tubingen, Germany: J.C.B. Mohr.

Johnston, J., Dinardo, J. (1997), *Econometric Methods*. 4th edn. New York: McGraw-Hill.

Kaldor, N. (1970), 'The case for regional policies'. *Scottish Journal of Political Economy* **18**: 337–48.

Kam, J. (2006), 'No pain, no gain: rethinking the telecoms crash'. *Technology Analysis and Strategic Management* **18** (5): 497–514.

Kay, J. (1993), 'Efficiency and private capital in the provision of infrastructure'. In OECD (ed.), *Infrastructure Policies for the 1990s*. Paris: OECD, pp 55–74.

Keeling, D.J. (1995), 'Transport and the world city paradigm'. In Knox, P.L. and Taylor, P.J. (eds), *World Cities in a World System*. Cambridge: Cambridge University Press, pp 115–131.

Kellerman, A. (1993), *Telecommunications Geography*. London: Belhaven Press.

Kellerman, A. (2002), *The Internet on Earth*. Chichester: Wiley.

Kende, M. (2000), 'The digital handshake: connecting Internet backbones'. OPP working paper no 32.

Kirsch, S. (1995), 'The incredible shrinking world? Technology and the production of space'. *Environment and Planning D: Society and Space* **13** (5): 529–55.

Kitchin, R. (1998a), *Cyberspace*. New York: Wiley.

Kitchin, R. (1998b), 'Towards geographies of cyberspace'. *Progress in Human Geography* **22** (3): 385–406.

KMI Research Group (2001), PAN European fiberoptic network routes planned or in place. http://www.kmiresearch.com/, No longer available.

Kolko, J. (1999), 'The death of cities? The death of distance? Evidence from the geography of commercial Internet usage'. In *Selected Papers from the Telecommunications Policy Research Conference 1999*, Newcastle.

Kondratieff, N. (1926), 'The long waves in economic life'. *Archiv für Sozialwissenschaft und Sozialpolitik* **56** (3): 573–609; reproduced and translated (1935) in *Review of Economic Statistics* **17** (576): 1105–15.

Korilis, Y.A., Lazar, A.A. and Orda, A. (1999), 'Avoiding the Braess paradox in non-cooperative networks'. *Journal of Applied Probability* **36** (1): 211–22.

Krugman, P. (1991a), *Geography and Trade*. Cambridge, MA: MIT Press.

Krugman, P. (1991b), 'Increasing returns and economic-geography'. *Journal of Political Economy* **99** (3): 483–99.

Krugman, P. (1998), 'What's new about the new economic geography?'. *Oxford Review of Economic Policy* **14** (2): 7–17.

Kunzmann, K.R. (1998), 'World city regions in Europe: structural change and future challenges'. In Lo, F.-C. and Yeung, Y.-m. (eds), *Globalization and the World of Large Cities*. Tokyo: United Nations University Press, pp 37–75.

Lambiotte, R., Blondel, V.D., Kerchove, Cd., Huens, E., Prieur,

C., Smoreda, Z. and Dooren, P.V. (2008), 'Geographical dispersal of mobile communication networks'. *Physica A* **387**: 5317–532.

Lambooy, J.G. (2002), 'Knowledge and urban economic development: an evolutionary perspective'. *Urban Studies* **39** (5–6): 1019–35.

Lambooy, J., Nagengast, E., Raat, N. and Veldkamp, L. (2000), *De ruimtelijke effecten van ICT in Nederland. Een essay* [*The Spatial Effects of ICT in the Netherlands. An Essay*]. Amsterdam: Regioplan Stad en Land BV.

Landes, D. (1998), *The Wealth and Poverty of Nations*. New York: WW Norton.

Latora, V., Crucitti, P., Marchiori, M. and Rapisarda, A. (2003), 'Complex systems: analysis and models of real-world networks'. In Musumeci, F., Brizhik, L.S. and Ho, M.-W. (eds), *Energy and Information Transfer in Biological Systems: How Physics Could Enrich Biological Understanding*, Singapore: World Scientific Publishing, pp 188–204.

Latora, V. and Marchiori, M. (2001), 'Efficient behavior of small-world networks'. *Physical Review Letters* **5** (87): 1987011–14.

Latora, V. and Marchiori, M. (2002), 'Is the Boston subway a small-world network?'. *Physica A* **314**: 109–13.

Leamer, E.E. and Storper, M. (2001), 'The economic geography of the Internet age'. *Journal of International Business Studies* **32** (4): 641–65.

Lee, H.-S. (2009), 'The networkability of cities in the international air passenger flows 1992–2004'. *Journal of Transport Geography* **17** (3): 165–77.

Levin, A., Lin, C.-F. and Chu, C.-S.J. (2002), 'Unit root tests in panel data: asymptotic and finite sample properties'. *Journal of Econometrics* **108** (1): 1–24.

Leydesdorff, L. (2006), *The Knowledge-based Economy: Modeled, Measured, Simulated*. Boca Raton, FL: Universal Publishers.

Li, L., Alderson, D., Tanaka, R., Doyle, J.C. and Willinger, W. (2005), 'Towards a theory of scale-free graphs: definition, properties, and implications (extended version)'. *Internet Mathematics* **2** (4): 431–523.

Liebenau, J., Atkinson, R., Karrberg, P., Catro, D. and Ezell, S. (2009), *The UK's Digital Road to Recovery*. London: LSE Enterprise LTD and the Information Technology and Innovation Foundation.

Lipsey, R.G., Carlaw, K.I. and Bekar, C. (2005), *Economic Transformations: General Purpose Technologies, and Long Term Economic Growth*. Oxford: Oxford University Press.

Louter, P. (2001), *Ruimte voor de digitale economie. Verkenning van de relaties tussen ICT en uimtelijkeconomische ontwikkeling* [*Space for the Digital Economy. Survey of the Relationships between ICT and Spatial-economic Development*]. Delft, Netherlands: TNO Inro.

Lundvall, B.-Å. (ed.) (1992), *National Innovation Systems: Towards a Theory of Innovation and Interactive Learning*. London: Pinter.

Maddala, G.S. (2001), *Introduction to Econometrics*. Chichester: John Wiley & Sons Ltd.

Maignan, C., Pinelli, D. and Ottaviano, G.I.P. (2003), 'ICT, clusters and regional cohesion: a summary of theoretical and empirical research'. Accessed 13 July 2011 at www.ssrn.com/abstract=438507.

Mairesse, J. (1990), 'Time-series and cross-sectional estimates on panel data: why are they different and why they should be equal'. In Hartog, J., Ridder, G. and Theeuwes, J. (eds), *Panel Data and Labor Market Studies*. New York: North-Holland, pp 81–95.

Malecki, E.J. (2002a), 'The economic geography of the Internet's infrastructure'. *Economic Geography* **78** (4): 399–424.

Malecki, E.J. (2002b), 'Hard and soft networks for urban competitiveness'. *Urban Studies* **39** (5–6): 929–45.

Malecki, E.J. (2004), 'Fibre tracks: explaining investment in fibre optic backbones'. *Entrepreneurship and Regional Development* **16** (1): 21–39.

Malecki, E.J. and Gorman, S.P. (2001), 'Maybe the death of distance, but not the end of geography: the Internet as a network'. In Leinbach, T.R. and Brunn, S.D. (eds), *Worlds of E-Commerce: Economic, Geographical and Social Dimensions*. Chichester: Wiley, pp 87–105.

Malecki, E.J. and Moriset, B. (2008), *The Digital Economy*. New York: Routledge.

Malecki, E.J. and Wei, H. (2009), 'A wired world: the evolving geography of submarine cables and the shift to Asia'. *AAA Geographers* **99** (2): 360–82.

Markusen, A. (1988), *Regions: The Economics and Politics of Territory*. Totawa, NJ: Rowman & Littlefield.

Martin, P. (2003), 'Public policies and economic geography'. In Funck, B. and Pizzatti, L. (eds), *European Integration, Regional Policy and Growth*. Washington, DC: World Bank, pp 19–32.

Martin, R. (1999), 'Critical survey. The new "geographical turn" in economics: some critical reflections'. *Cambridge Journal of Economics* **23** (1). 65–91.

Matsumoto, H. (2007), 'International air network structures and air traffic density of world cities'. *Transportation Research Part E* **43**: 269–82.

McCann, P. and Acs, Z.J. (2011), 'Globalisation: countries, cities and multinationals'. *Regional Studies* **45**: 17–32.

Miles, I. and Matthews, M. (1992), 'Information technology and the information economy'. In Robins, K. (ed), *Understanding Information*. London: Belhaven Press, pp 91–112.

Milgram, S. (1967), 'The small world problem'. *Psychology Today* **1** (1): 61–7.

Mitchell, W.J. (1995), *City of Bits: Space, Place and the Infobahn.* Cambridge, MA: MIT Press.

Mokhtarian, P.L. (1990), 'A typology of relationships between telecommunications and transportation'. *Transportation Research* **24A** (3): 231–42.

Mokhtarian, P.L. (2002), 'Telecommunications and travel: the case for complementarity'. *Journal of Industrial Ecology* **6** (2): 43–57.

Moriset, B. (2003), 'The new economy in the city: emergence and location factors of internet-based companies in the metropolitan area of Lyon, France'. *Urban Studies* **40** (11): 2165–86.

Moss, M.L. (1987), 'Telecommunications: world cities and urban policy'. *Urban Studies* **24**: 534–46.

Moss, M.L. and Townsend, A.M. (1997), 'Tracking the net: using domain names to measure the growth of the Internet in US cities'. *Journal of Urban Technology* **4** (3): 47–60.

Moss, M.L. and Townsend, A.M. (2000), 'The Internet backbone and the American metropolis'. *Information Society* **16** (1): 35–47.

Mumtaz, K. (2003), *Schumpeter Innovation and Growth.* Kathmandu: Ashgate Publishing Group.

Musgrave, R.A. and Musgrave, P.B. (1984), *Public Finance in Theory and Practise*, vol 4. New York: McGraw-Hill.

Myrdal, G. (1957), *Economic Theory and Underdeveloped Regions.* London: Duckworth.

Nagurney, A. and Qiang, Q. (2009), *Fragile Networks.* Hoboken, NJ: Wiley.

National Research Council (1998), *Fostering Research on the Economic and Social Impacts of Information Technology.* Washington, DC: National Academy Press.

Neef, D. (1998), 'The knowledge economy: an introduction'. In Neef, D. (ed.), *The Knowledge Economy.* Woburn, MA: Butterworth-Heinemann, pp 1–14.

Newman, M.E.J. (2005), 'Power laws, Pareto distributions and Zipf's law'. arXiv:cond-mat/0412004v3.

Newman, M.E.J. (2008), 'Mathematics of networks'. In Blume, L.E. and Durlauf, S.N. (eds), *The New Palgrave Encyclopedia of Economics.* 2nd edn. Basingstoke: Palgrave Macmillan.

Nijkamp, P. and Jonkhoff, W. (2001), 'The city in the information and communication technology age: a comparative study on path dependency'. *International Journal of Technology, Policy and Management* **1** (1): 78–99.

Nijkamp, P., Rietveld, P. and Spierdijk, L. (1999), 'Classification techniques in quantitative comparative research: a meta-comparison'. Serie research memoranda, Free University, Amsterdam, pp 1999–56.

Nooy, W.d., Mrvar, A. and Batagelj, V. (2005), *Exploratory Social Network Analysis with Pajek*. Cambridge: Cambridge University Press.

Nordlun, C. (2004), 'A critical comment on the Taylor approach for measuring world city interlock linkages'. *Geographic Analysis* 36 (3): 290–96.

O'Kelly, M.E. and Grubesic, T.H. (2002), 'Backbone topology, access, and the commercial Internet, 1997–2000'. *Environment and Planning B* 29 (4): 533–2.

Obraczka, K. and Silva, F. (2000), 'Network latency metrics for server proximity'. paper presented at the Global Telecommunications Conference 2000, IEEE, pp 421–7.

OECD (1996), *The Knowledge-Based Economy*. Paris: OECD.

OECD (2003), *The Sources of Economic Growth in OECD Countries*. Paris: OECD.

OECD (2006), 'OECD broadband statistics to June 2006'. Accessed 21 July 2009 at www.oecd.org/document/9/0,3343,en_2649_34225_37529673_1_1_1_37441,00.html.

Paci, R. and Usai, S. (2000), 'Technological enclaves and industrial districts: an analysis of the regional distribution of innovative activity in Europe'. *Regional Studies* 34 (2): 97–114.

Paltridge, S. (2002), *Internet Traffic Exchange and the Development of End-to-End International Competition*. Paris: OECD.

Parr, J.B. (2005), 'Pespectives on the city-region'. *Regional Studies* 39 (5): 555–66.

Partridge, M.D. (2005), 'Does income distribution affect US state economic growth?'. *Journal of Regional Science* 45 (2): 363–94.

Patuelli, R. and Reggiani, A., Gorman, S.P., Nijkamp, P. and Bade, F.-J. (2007), 'Network analysis of commuting flows: a comparative static approach to German data'. *Networks and Spatial Economics* 7: 315–31.

Pelletiere, D., Rodrigo, C.G. (2001), 'Economic geography and policy in the network age'. In Feldman, M.P. and Link, A.N. (eds), *Innovation Policy in the Knowledge-Based Economy*. Boston, MA: Kluwer Academic Publishers, pp 231–57.

Perez, C. (1983), 'Structural change and the assimilation of new technologies in the economic system'. *Futures* 15 (4): 357–75.

Peterson, L.L. and Davie, B.S. (2003), *Computer Networks*. San Francisco, CA: Morgan Kaufmann Publishers.

Pike, A., Rodríguez-Pose, A. and Tomaney, J. (2006), *Local and Regional Development*. London and New York: Routledge.

Porat, M. (1977), *The Information Economy: Definition and Management*.

Vol 1. Special Publication 77-12, Office of Telecommunications, Washington, DC: US Department of Commerce.

Priemus, H. (2007), 'The network approach: Dutch spatial planning between substratum and infrastructure networks'. *European Planning Studies* **15** (5): 667–86.

Prufer, J., Jahn, E. (2007), 'Dark clouds over the Internet?'. *Telecommunications Policy* **31** (3–4): 144–54.

Quah, D.T. (1996), 'The invisible hand and the weightless economy'. Centre for Economic Performance, London School of Economics and Political Science occasional paper no. 12.

Quah, D.T. (1998), 'A weightless economy'. *UNESCO Courier*, December.

Ratti, C., Sassen, S., Mitchell, W.J., Townsend, A.M., Moss, M., Research ATL and Calabrese, F. (2008), *NYTE*. Cambridge, MA: SA+P Press.

Reades, J., Calabrese, F. and Ratti, C. (2009), 'Eigenplaces: analyzing cities using the space-time structure of the mobile phone network'. *Environment and Planning B* **36** (5): 824–36.

Reggiani, A. and Vinciguerra, S. (2007), 'Network connectivity models: an overview and applications to the space-economy'. In Friesz, T. (ed.), *Network Science, Nonlinear Science and Infrastructure Systems*. New York: Springer-Verlag, pp 147–65.

Richardson, R. and Gillespie, A. (2000), 'The economic development of peripheral rural areas in the information age'. In Wilson, M.I. and Corey, K.E. (eds), *Information Tectonics*. Chichester and New York: Wiley, pp 199–217.

Rimmer, P.J. (1998), 'Transport and telecommunications among world cities'. In Lo, F.-C. and Yeung, Y.-M. (eds), *Globalization and the World of Large Cities*. Tokyo: United Nations University Press, pp 433–70.

Roberts, D. (2006), 'Broadband gluttons'. *Financial Times*, 15 April.

Rodríguez-Pose, A. (2008), 'The rise of the city-region concept and its development policy implications'. *European Planning Studies* **16** (8): 1025–46.

Rodríguez-Pose, A. and Tselios, V. (2008), 'Inequalities in income and education and regional economic growth in western Europe'. *Annals of Regional Science* **44** (2): 349–75.

Rodríguez-Pose, A. and Tselios, V. (2009), 'Mapping regional personal income distribution in Western Europe: income per capita and inequality'. *Czech Journal of Economics and Finance* **5** (1): 41–70.

Rogerson, P.A. (2006), *Statistical Methods for Geography*. London: SAGE.

Romer, P.M. (1986), 'Increasing returns and long-run growth'. *Journal of Political Economy* **94**: 1002–37.

Romer, P.M. (1990), 'Endogenous technological change'. *Journal of Political Economy* **98** (5): 71–102.

Roodman, D. (2006), 'How to do xtabond2: an introduction to "difference" and "system" GMM in Stata'. Center for Global Development working paper no. 103.

Roughgarden, T. (2005), *Selfish Routing and the Price of Anarchy*. Cambridge, MA: MIT Press.

Rutherford, J. (2004), *A Tale of Two Global Cities*. Aldershot, UK and Burlington, VT: Ashgate.

Rutherford, J., Gillespie, A. and Richardson, R. (2004), 'The territoriality of Pan-European telecommunications backbone networks'. *Journal of Urban Technology* **11** (3): 1–34.

Rutherford, J., Gillespie, A. and Richardson, R. (2005), 'Technological connectivities of European cities? The potentials and pitfalls of the use of telecommunications data in measurements of world city network formation'. Accessed 8 February 2009 at www.lboro.ac.uk/gawc/rb/rb181.html.

Salomon, I. (1986), 'Telecommunications and travel relationships: a review'. *Transportation Research* **20A** (3): 223–38.

Sassen, S. (1991), *The Global City. New York, London and Tokyo*. Princeton, NJ: Princeton University Press.

Sassen, S. (2000a), *Cities in a World Economy*. 2nd edn. Thousand Oaks, CA: Pine Forge Press.

Sassen, S. (2000b), 'Digital networks and the state: some governance questions'. *Theory, Culture and Society* **17** (4): 19–33.

Sassen, S. (2004), *The Global City. New York, London and Tokyo*. 2nd edn. Princeton, NJ: Princeton University Press.

Sassen, S. (2008), 'New York City's two global geographies of talk'. In: C. Ratti (ed), *MIT, Senseable Lab*. New York: NYTE, pp 10–15.

Schintler, L., Gorman, S.P., Reggiani, A., Patuelli, R., Gillespie, A., Nijkamp, P. and Rutherford, J. (2005), 'Complex network phenomena in telecommunication systems'. *Networks and Spatial Economics* **5** (4): 351–70.

Scott, A.J. (1998), *Regions and the World Economy: The Coming Shape of Global Production, Competition and Political Order*. Oxford: Oxford University Press.

Scott, A.J. (2001), 'Globalization and the rise of city-regions'. *European Planning Studies* **9** (7): 813–26.

Scott, A.J. and Storper, M. (2003), 'Regions, globalization, development'. *Regional Studies* **37** (6–7): 579–93.

Sen, P., Dasgupta, S., Chatterjee, A., Sreeram, P.A., Mukherjee, G. and Manna, S.S. (2003), 'Small-world properties of the Indian railway network'. *Physical Review E* **67** (3): 03–06.

Shiller, D. (1999), *Digital Capitalism: Networking the Global Market System*. Cambridge, MA: MIT Press.

Shinjo, K. and Zhang, X. (2004), 'ICT capital investment and productivity growth: Granger causality in Japanese and the USA industries'. Working paper.

Shiu, A. and Lam, P.-L. (2008), 'Causal relationship between telecommunications and economic growth in China and its regions'. *Regional Studies* **42** (5): 705–18.

Short, J., Kim, Y., Kuus, M. and Wells, H. (1996), 'The dirty little secret of world cities research: data problems in comparative analysis'. *International Journal of Urban and Regional Research* **20** (4): 697–719.

Shy, O. (2001), *The Economics of Network Industries*. Cambridge: Cambridge University Press.

Smith, D. and Timberlake, M. (2002), 'Hierarchies of dominance among world cities: a network approach'. In Sassen, S. (ed), *Global Networks; Linked Cities*. New York and London: Routledge, pp 117–41.

Solow, R.M. (1956), 'A contribution to the theory of economic growth'. *Quarterly Journal of Economics* **70**: 65–94.

Star, S.L. (1999), 'The ethnography of infrastructure'. *American Behavioral Scientists* **43** (3): 377–91.

Stephenson, N. (1996), 'Mother earth mother board'. *Wired Magazine* **4** (12).

Stevens, S. (1998), 'The knowledge-driven economy'. In Neef, D. (ed.), *The Knowledge Economy*. Woburn, MA: Butterworth-Heinemann, pp 87–94.

Taaffe, E.J., Gauthier, E.L. and O'Kelly, M.E. (1996), *Geography of Transportation, vol 2*. Upper Saddle River, NJ: Prentice-Hall.

Tanenbaum, A.S. (2003), *Computer Networks*. 4th edn. Upper Saddle River, NJ: Pearson Education, Prentice Hall.

Tassey, G. (1992), *Technology Infrastructure and Competitive Position*. Boston, MA: Kluwer Academic Press.

Tassey, G. (2008), 'Modeling and measuring the economic roles of the technology infrastructure'. *Economics of Innovation and New Technology* **17** (7–8): 615–29.

Taylor, P.J. (1997), 'Hierarchical tendencies amongst world cities: a global research proposal'. *Cities* **14** (6): 323–32

Taylor, P.J. (1999), 'So-called "world cities": the evidential structure within a literature'. *Environment and Planning A* **31** (11): 1901–4.

Taylor, P.J. (2001), 'Urban hinterworlds: geographies of corporate service provision under conditions of contemporary globalization'. *Geography* **86** (1): 51–60.

Taylor, P.J. (2004), *World City Network*. London and New York: Routledge.

Taylor, P.J., Ni, P., Derudder, B., Hoyler, M., Huang, J. and Witlox, F. (eds) (2010), *Global Urban Analysis: A Survey of Cities in Globalization*. London: Earthscan.

Telegeography (2007), *Global Internet Geography*. Washington, DC: PriMetrica.

TeleGeography (2011), TeleGeography's home page. Accessed 8 January at www.telegeography.com.

Tervo, H. (2009), 'Centres and peripheries in Finland: Granger causality tests using panel data'. *Spatial Economic Analysis* **4** (4): 377–90.

Tobler, W. (1970), 'A computer movie simulating urban growth in the Detroit region'. *Journal of Economic Geography* **46** (2): 234–40.

Toffler, A. (1980), *The Third Wave*. New York: William Morrow.

Townsend, A.M. (2001a), 'The Internet and the rise of the new network cities, 1969–1999'. *Environment and Planning B* **28** (1): 39–58.

Townsend, A.M. (2001b), 'Network cities and the global structure of the Internet'. *American Behavioral Scientist* **44** (10): 1697–716.

Townsend, A.M. (2003), *Wired/Unwired: The Urban Geography of Digital Networks*. Boston, MA: MIT Press.

Tranos, E. (2011), 'The topology and the emerging urban geographies of the Internet backbone and aviation networks in Europe: a comparative study'. *Environment and Planning A* **43** (2): 378–92.

Tranos, E. (2012), 'The causal effect of the Internet infrastructure on the economic development of the European city-regions'. *Spatial Economic Analysis* **7** (3): 319–37.

Tranos, E. and Gillespie, A. (2009), 'The spatial distribution of Internet backbone networks in Europe: a metropolitan knowledge economy perspective'. *European Urban and Regional Studies* **16** (4): 423–37.

Tranos, E. and Gillespie, A. (2011), 'The urban geography of Internet backbone networks in Europe: roles and relations'. *Journal of Urban Technology* **18** (1): 35–49.

Tranos, E., Reggiani, A. and Nijkamp, P. (2013), 'The accessibility of cities in the digital economy'. *Cities* **30**: 59–67.

Triplett, J.E. (1998), *The Solow Productivity Paradox: What Computers Do to Productivity?* Washington, DC: Brookings Institution.

UN (2006), *Information Economy Report*. New York and Geneva: UN.

van Oort, F., Raspe, O. and Snellen, D. (2003), *De ruimtelijke effecten van ICT* [*The spatial impacts of ICT*]. Rotterdam: NAi Uitgevers.

van Winden, W. and Woets, P. (2004), 'Urban broadband Internet policies in Europe: a critical review'. *Urban Studies* **41** (10): 2043–59.

Venables, A.J. (2001), 'Geography and international inequalities: the impact of new technologies'. *Journal of Industry, Competition and Trade* **1** (2): 1566–79.

Vence-Deza, X. and González-López, M. (2008), 'Regional concentration of the knowledge-based economy in the EU: towards a renewed oligo-centric model?'. *European Planning Studies* **16** (4): 557–78.

Wallerstein, I. (2004), *World-Systems Analysis*. Durham, NC: Duke University Press.

Walsh, J.A. (2007), *People and Place: A Census of the Republic of Ireland*. Maynooth, Ireland: National Institute for Regional and Spatial Analysis.

Watts, D.J. and Strogatz, S.H. (1998), 'Collective dynamics of small-world networks'. *Nature* **393**: 440–42.

Waxman, B.M. (1988), 'Routing of multipoint connections'. *IEEE Journal on Selected Areas in Communications* **6** (9): 1617–22.

Wheeler, D.C. and O'Kelly, M.E. (1999), 'Network topology and city accessibility of the commercial Internet'. *Professional Geographer* **51** (3): 327–39.

Williams, A.M. and Baláž, V. (2009), 'Low-cost carriers, economies of flows and regional externalities'. *Regional Studies* **43** (5): 677–91.

Wolde-Rufael, Y. (2007), 'Another look at the relationship between telecommunications investment and economic activity in the United States'. *International Economic Journal* **21** (2): 199–205.

Wooldridge, J.M. (2003), *Introductory Econometrics: A Modern Approach*. 2nd edn. Mason, OH: South-Western.

Yoo, S.H. and Kwak, S.J. (2004), 'Information technology and economic development in Korea: a causality study'. *International Journal of Technology Management* **27** (1): 57–67.

Youtie, J. (2000), 'Field of dreams revisited: economic development and telecommunications in LaGrange, Georgia'. *Economic Development Quarterly* **14**: 146–53.

Zook, M.A. (2000), 'The web of production: the economic geography of commercial Internet content production in the United States'. *Environment and Planning A* **32**: 411–26.

Zook, M.A. (2001), 'Old hierarchies or new networks of centrality? The global geography of the Internet content market'. *American Behavioral Scientist* **44** (10): 1679–96.

Zook, M.A. (2006), 'The geographies of the Internet'. *Annual Review of Information Science and Technology* **40**: 53–78.

Index